The TRUE COST
of LOW PRICES

The TRUE COST
of LOW PRICES

The Violence of Globalization

Second Edition

JEFFRY ODELL KORGEN
AND
VINCENT A. GALLAGHER

ORBIS BOOKS
Maryknoll, New York 10545

Founded in 1970, Orbis Books endeavors to publish works that enlighten the mind, nourish the spirit, and challenge the conscience. The publishing arm of the Maryknoll Fathers and Brothers, Orbis seeks to explore the global dimensions of the Christian faith and mission, to invite dialogue with diverse cultures and religious traditions, and to serve the cause of reconciliation and peace. The books published reflect the views of their authors and do not represent the official position of the Maryknoll Society. To learn more about Maryknoll and Orbis Books, please visit our website at www.maryknollsociety.org.

Library of Congress Cataloging-in-Publication Data
Korgen, Jeffry Odell.
    The true cost of low prices : the violence of globalization / Jeffry Odell Korgen and Vincent A. Gallagher. – 2nd ed.
       p.   cm.
    Rev. ed. of: The true cost of low prices / Vincent A. Gallagher.
    Includes bibliographical references and index.
    ISBN 978-1-62698-002-0 (pbk.)
    1. International trade – Social aspects. 2. Poverty – Developing – countries.
3. Labor – Social aspects – Developing countries. I. Gallagher, Vincent A.
II. Gallagher, Vincent A. True cost of low prices. III. Title.
HF1413.G25 2013
306.3 – dc23   2012030387

To Julie and Jessica Korgen,
global Christian disciples
of the twenty-first century

Contents

Acknowledgments

Like movements for peace and justice, social ministry books emerge from a community of Christian disciples surrounding the authors. We would like to thank a few of these people who helped us in special ways. Joan Rosenhauer of Catholic Relief Services pointed the way toward several essential sources. Dan Misleh of Catholic Coalition on Climate Change provided essential background for chapter 6. Bill Purcell at Notre Dame also offered key direction at early stages of writing. Charles Kernaghan and Barbara Briggs at the Institute for Global Labour and Human Rights provided helpful background and their own compelling reports.

Mary DeLorey at Catholic Relief Services offered essential insights on human trafficking. Rev. David Schilling and Susana McDermott at the Interfaith Center on Corporate Responsibility were exceedingly generous with their time. Rev. Fletcher Harper of Greenfaith provided background and sources for the environment chapter. Kim Bobo of Interfaith Worker Justice gave not only her own insights, but also pointed the way to Rebecca Fuentes at the Tri-State Workers Center, who was very generous with her time.

Sr. Pat Daly, OP, at the Tri-State Coalition for Responsible Investment provided key insights on investor responses to human trafficking. Mary Wright of JustFaith Ministries surfaced "Following Jesus, Our Tortured Brother." Marie Dennis of Pax Christi International helped decode the role of international finance organizations. Stehanie Sheerin of the Fair Trade Resource Network provided invaluable background on Fair Trade chocolate as well as delicious guacamole. Roger Karapin at CUNY provided valuable sources.

Patricia Odell reviewed early manuscripts with great tact and commitment. My dear wife, Kathleen Odell Korgen, generously provided hugs, encouragement, insight, sources, and editing, always willing to offer her gifts, even when it meant stepping away from her own projects. Susan Sullivan of the U.S. Conference of Catholic Bishops (USCCB) also offered prescient insights on the manuscript. And the JustFaith group at St. John Vianney Parish in Colonia, N.J., provided a reader's perspective on the later drafts. Each person who reviewed the manuscript had an important impact on what you now read. Thank you to all!

The Hameem Factory fire in Bangladesh claimed the lives of 29 garment workers, locked inside by company security guards. The fire bore many similarities to New York City's Triangle Shirtwaist Factory fire in 1911, which claimed the lives of 146 garment workers and led to antisweatshop legislation in the United States.

Abbreviations

ATS	Alien Tort Statute
AUC	United Self-Defense Forces of Colombia
CEO	Chief Executive Officer
CIW	Coalition of Immokalee Workers
CDC	Centers for Disease Control
CIA	Central Intelligence Agency
CRS	Catholic Relief Services
DDT	An insecticide
DSC	Dynamic Social Compliance
ECPAT	End Child Prostitution, Child Pornography, and Trafficking of Children for Sexual Purposes
FARC	Revolutionary Armed Forces of Colombia
FGM	Female Genital Mutilation
FTGE	Florida Tomato Growers Exchange
GAO	Government Accountability Office
GMO	Genetically Modified Organism
ICCR	Interfaith Center on Corporate Responsibility
IJM	International Justice Mission
ILO	International Labour Organization
IMF	International Monetary Fund
IPCC	Intergovernmental Panel on Climate Change
IWJ	Interfaith Worker Justice
LDC	Less Developed Country
MDG	Millennium Development Goals
NAE	National Association of Evangelicals
NAFTA	North American Free Trade Agreement
NFL	National Football League
NGO	Nongovernmental Organization
NRCAT	National Religious Campaign Against Torture
OSHA	Occupational Safety and Health Administration

PCB	A toxic fluid used in motors, capacitors, and transformers
PEPFAR	President's Emergency Plan for AIDS Relief
PRI	Panchayat Raj Institution
PRSP	Poverty Reduction Strategy Paper
SAP	Structural Adjustment Program
SBD	Small Business Development
SOA	School of the Americas
TASSC	Torture Abolition and Survivors Support Coalition International
UNEP	United Nations Environment Programme
UNICEF	United Nations Children's Fund
USCCB	United States Conference of Catholic Bishops
WHD	Wage and Hour Division, U.S. Department of Labor
WHISC	Western Hemisphere Institute for Security and Cooperation
WHO	World Health Organization
WFP	World Food Programme
WRC	Worker Rights Consortium

1

The Violence of Globalization

Listen; your brother's blood is crying out . . . from the ground!
—Gen. 4:10

A Bangladeshi garment worker trapped in a sweatshop fire. A fifteen-year-old Malian gold miner, exposed to toxic chemicals and dangerous working conditions. A six-year-old Chinese girl poisoned by lead exposure from a nearby factory. An entire family in India living as modern-day slaves. An undocumented immigrant dishwasher in San Francisco denied thousands of dollars in overtime pay. All are victims of the violence of globalization—violence structured into the global economy.

The violence of globalization is "social sin," to use the words of Blessed Pope John Paul II, referring to "every sin against justice . . . every sin against the dignity and honor of one's neighbor . . . and every sin against the common good and its exigencies in relation to the whole spectrum of the rights and duties of citizens."[1] Social sins are woven into the fabric of our global system. They are the true cost of the low prices we pay for food, apparel, electronics, and many other goods and services.

Globalization itself is not the problem. Globalization has been occurring for centuries in fits and starts since God scattered the people of Babel. The story of globalization recalls the Silk Road, connecting the empires of Europe, Asia, and Africa; the Apostle Thomas evangelizing in India; and, most of all, the Columbian Exchange of people, crops, livestock, weapons, insects, grasses, bacteria, and viruses between the Eurasian landmass, Africa, and the Americas beginning in 1492.[2] Frequently brutal, sometimes liberating, always advancing, globalization has produced, in the twenty-first century, an integrated world economy, characterized by institutionalized violence, the sum of a million choices privileging profit over people.

Let's be clear—globalization itself is neither inherently good nor inherently evil. The term refers to the integration of markets, cultures, and peoples, part of life on Earth for centuries, but vastly accelerated since the 1970s. In today's globalized world, life in one location is influenced by events thousands of miles away. Companies might be headquartered in one country, produce goods in another (sometimes with migrant labor), and sell those goods in still another nation. Nonprofit organizations might draw membership from many nations and take action in others.

When we refer to the violence of globalization, we do so with the understanding and hope that globalization does not have to be this way. The reality of globalization does not necessarily mean that workers will be locked in burning factories or that slavery will endure. We make choices every day that produce these effects—the violence of globalization is not inevitable. As consumers, as workers, as citizens, as business leaders, we all make decisions that affect the direction globalization will take. These choices seem small at times, but their sum has great power—to produce peace and social justice or institutionalized violence and social injustice.

INSTITUTIONALIZED VIOLENCE

Why do we use the term "institutionalized violence"? In my[3] professional work, I have investigated hundreds of cases of worker injury and death in the United States and Latin America. Over time, I came to realize that most were caused by decisions to risk workers' safety for economic gain. For example, workers lose fingers and hands when protective shields are taken off machines to increase productivity. Buildings can be constructed more quickly if managers do not provide fall protection. And hundreds of thousands of workers have suffered asbestosis and death from lung disease and cancers caused by exposure to asbestos, because managers refused to install ventilation systems and required workers to follow unsafe practices that violate safety laws.

We often think of violence as a sudden act that results in injury. But isn't it also violent to produce goods with unguarded machines that amputate just as surely and brutally as machetes? Shouldn't we call it violence when children in a developing country develop brain damage from exposure to lead brought home from work on their parents' clothing—and this work was moved from the United States because it is cheaper to run a factory in a nation that does not enforce environmental laws? Isn't it violence when "free trade agreements" like NAFTA (North American Free Trade Agreement) drive farmers throughout Mexico out of business, pushing them toward illegal migration into the United States? Isn't it violence to produce goods and offer services manufactured or provided by child laborers, slaves, sweatshop workers, or victims of wage theft?

Violence snuffs out the lives of children—born and unborn—through abortion, war, and the drug trade, but when the International Monetary Fund (IMF), through its structural adjustment programs (now called Poverty Reduction Strategy Papers), requires the Ministry of Health in a developing country to cut funding for antibiotics, which results in children dying needlessly, isn't this also violence? When wealthy nations purchase land to grow food for themselves in a developing country where millions of children go hungry and suffer diseases related to malnutrition, could we not term this violence as well? If your child worked at a dump scavenging for electronics carrying small amounts of precious metals, and was exposed to the hazards of biological, industrial, and human waste to help feed your hungry family, would you see that as a form of violence?

In Genesis, Cain slew Abel out of jealousy over the Lord's tepid reaction to his own ritual sacrifice. The episode is the first act of violence in the Bible. The aftermath is described in chapter 4: "Then the Lord said to Cain, 'Where is your brother Abel?' He said, 'I do not know; am I my brother's keeper?' And the Lord said, 'What have you done? Listen; your brother's blood is crying out to me from the ground!'" (Gen. 4:9–10)

Today, the victims of the violence of globalization cry out like Abel's blood from the earth, and some consumers echo Cain, asking, "Am I my brother's and sister's keeper?" But many others are simply unaware of the institutionalized violence permeating the global economy. Evidence of the violence of globalization surrounds us, but one must wander far from the front page of the newspaper or Google the right keywords to discover the story. The violence of globalization is occasionally reported by the mainstream media, but usually as instances of individual sin, of "bad people" or "bad choices," or simply "bad luck," and rarely as part of a broader system of institutionalized violence. For many of us, the institutionalized violence of globalization comes as a shock. Why wasn't this on the news?

But why should we expect structural sin to be closely examined by the mainstream media, when it is almost exclusively owned by corporations whose primary interest is to make profits and return dividends to stockholders? Let's take a moment to look at the newspaper business. In 1945, about 80 percent of U.S. newspapers were family owned. Many of these families went into journalism to make a difference in their communities, and profit was a secondary consideration. Today, over 80 percent of newspapers and their derivative websites are run by publicly traded, for-profit corporations.[4] Many of these corporations are merely subsidiaries of still-larger global conglomerates. In addition, the boards of directors of these large media corporations are almost entirely composed of board members from the largest corporations in America.[5] Are these directors vetting every story, ordering compliant editors to cover some stories but not others? Are corporations that purchase advertising controlling every word uttered or printed? Probably not, but independent studies indicate that, whether through the self-censorship of editors and journalists, or by the intervention of top management, advertisers, and board members, rarely does a true critic of institutionalized violence emerge as a spokesperson on an issue addressed by the mainstream media.[6] This lack of diversity of perspectives is one reason most Americans know about the 2010 earthquake in Haiti but not the decimation of Haiti's rice industry by U.S. farm subsidies. Because their access to diverse points of view is limited, many people never get the opportunity to begin to develop a critical perspective on the violence of globalization.

Among those unaware of the violence of globalization are large numbers of Catholics. Perhaps they contribute to service organizations and even volunteer from time to time. But far too many see their responsibility beginning and ending with a charitable donation or a Saturday of volunteer work.

Perhaps a story can illustrate. I once gave a presentation on Catholic social teaching to the Wall Street Catholic Young Adults, a loose association of up-and-comers in the world of New York finance.[7] I shared with the group the seven themes of Catholic social teaching, as articulated by the U.S. Conference of Catholic Bishops, and Pope John Paul II's call for forgiveness of the debts of the world's poorest countries. The presentation went better than I expected, perhaps because of the open bar. Afterward, five women approached me together. "This is great!" one of them exclaimed. "And we're doing it already! We're building a Habitat for Humanity house in Newark!"

A house in Newark?

That's what over a century of authoritative Catholic teaching on the economy and the rights and responsibilities of employers amounted to. Here we had young Catholic leaders, well on their way to piloting the economy, conversing about Catholic social teaching, and the best they could come up with was a service project in a nearby city. Don't get me wrong, I think Habitat is a great organization, and these young women were sincere in their desire to live the faith, but couldn't they have thought bigger? Couldn't they apply questions raised by authoritative Catholic doctrine on the economy to their role in the economy? Consider this question: If all of the Catholics working on mortgage-backed securities had applied their faith to the workplace, could the Great Recession have been averted?

Perhaps Pope Benedict XVI had these questions in mind when he wrote his third encyclical, *Charity in Truth (Caritas in Veritate)* in 2009. This book-length teaching document described true "integral human development," that is, the full flourishing of the human person, as the product of love purified by the search for truth. Addressing the global economy, the pope stressed that the search for profit is useful only if it serves development in this larger sense.[8] Benedict called for economic activity "directed toward the pursuit of the common good," such as the creation of profit-making businesses that pursue social ends,[9] for example, the sale of Fair Trade products. The pontiff also noted, with deep concern, growing global inequality and governmental retreat from social safety-net programs, even as the world's wealth has grown.[10]

In *Charity in Truth*, Benedict asserted a number of rights previously affirmed in Catholic social teaching and urgently needed in an era of accelerated globalization, including rights to food and clean water,[11] life,[12] and religious freedom.[13] Above all, he called for an economic development based on "gratuitousness" or gratefulness to God (a different use of the word than Americans may be accustomed to), and a world where "the poor are not to be considered a 'burden,' but a resource."[14] Benedict stressed that this vision applied not simply to economic development sponsored by church organizations, but also, "Justice must be applied to every phase of economic activity."[15]

This idea of human gratefulness inspiring the entire global economy carried into a doctrinal note from the Pontifical Council for Justice and Peace in 2011. This teaching document, issued by the Vatican department responsible for writing the *Compendium of the Social Doctrine of the Church*, recommended the creation of a "world political authority" to protect human dignity from what we call, in these pages, the violence of globalization. Unlike the World Bank and the IMF, this worldwide body would defend not the national interests of donor countries and corporations headquartered in these nations, but rather integral human development.

Whether this specific policy prescription will come to pass, the church's guiding principles, rooted in scripture and tradition, are clear—we must reject the diffidence of Cain and transform the structures of sin into a globalization characterized by supreme gratefulness to God, what Blessed John Paul II called "a globalization without marginalization."[16] The church is not "against" globalization in and of itself—we are in fact the oldest global nongovernmental organization. But we stand in prophetic outrage at the locked fire exits in the sweatshops of Bangladesh, the epidemic of wage theft in the United States, the poisoning of God's creation worldwide, and the murderous global expansion of slavery. Our response begins with exposing the hidden violence of globalization.

READING THE SIGNS OF THE TIMES,
LEARNING WHAT THE CHURCH TEACHES,
TAKING ACTION

We often view poignant appeals on behalf of charities providing emergency aid to hungry people, but learn little about the causes of hunger. We occasionally hear about "human trafficking," especially for sexual purposes, but few people realize how many of the goods and services they consume are connected to slavery worldwide and in the United States. We don't connect the beautiful rain-forest timber used to construct a new deck with the assassination of an Ohio nun in Brazil. We put money into our retirement plans, but can we say we know whether we own (and profit from) shares in companies that exploit the most vulnerable workers in the world? We often hear that Americans are the most generous people in the world when it comes to private giving, but how often do we discuss our miserly approach to government foreign aid—which stands at about 1.6 percent of federal discretionary spending (while a majority of Americans believe foreign aid is 20 percent of the federal budget) and a mere 0.16 percent of our gross domestic product? The United Nations Millennium Development Goals, which the United States helped to develop (and approved), request 0.7 percent of our gross domestic product.[17]

The untold—or undertold—story of the violence of globalization is what you will find in this book: the true cost of low prices. Each of the next seven chapters focuses on a different dimension of social sin within globalization: sweatshops, exploitation of immigrant workers, slavery, torture and assassination, abuse of God's creation, hunger, child labor, and violence against women. In each chapter you will first meet a person injured by the violence of globalization. You will then learn more of the "signs of the times" (a phrase from the Second Vatican Council referring to social analysis of our times) related to their story, the causes and consequences connected to that particular issue, and what the church teaches about it. Finally, you will encounter emerging signs of hope—how the church and people of goodwill are working with the victims of the violence of globalization to chart a new course, toward a globalization characterized by justice and charity.

Two principles of the social doctrine of the church will provide light on this journey. Like St. Augustine's two daughters of hope—anger and courage—solidarity and subsidiarity guide our response to the social sin we will encounter in these chapters. *Solidarity* is the very basic idea that people are interdependent. The concept begins to answer the question posed of Jesus in Luke's Gospel: "Who is my neighbor?" (Luke 10:25–37). Explanations of and references to solidarity can be found throughout Catholic social teaching documents. The word appears twenty-seven times in the *Catechism of the Catholic Church,* which describes solidarity as "a direct demand of human and Christian brotherhood."[18] The concept of solidarity is the Catholic Christian's rejoinder to Cain's question, "Am I my brother's keeper?"

Complementing this vision of solidarity is the principle of *subsidiarity*. Subsidiarity, the notion that the smallest *possible* social unit should take on the challenges of social life, is like a two-sided coin. Referencing Catholic social teaching, some pundits and politicians speak only of one side—that we need to first look to the smallest possible social grouping to solve social problems. But subsidiarity does not end there. What if that social group is unable to solve the problem? A larger social unit must step in (the other side of the coin), still respecting the rights and responsibilities of the first group, but intervening, nevertheless. Examples of the application of the principles of solidarity and subsidiarity abound in the book's seven Signs of Hope sections.

Discussion questions conclude each chapter. These questions are meant to draw people together to sort out the challenges presented in this book. The structures of sin have never and will never be dismantled in isolation. Discussion brings us together, refines truth, and builds community. Our faith then compels us to act together on that truth. The suggestions offered in the "Go Make a Difference" sections are intended for readers who would like to take the next step in responding to the violence of globalization.

There is much in the following chapters that will horrify, challenge, and inspire you. If you ever find yourself overwhelmed by what you read, just take a moment and set the book down to pray or talk to others who share your concerns. Our aim in writing this book is not to elicit cries of "Ain't it awful!" or to simply condemn globalization, but to provoke Christians to encounter the realities of the global economy, consider the teachings of the church, and act in solidarity with others. The end in view is a globalization that will match Pope Benedict's vision of a global economy built on the unity of the human family rather than the fratricide of Cain. As disciples of Jesus Christ, nothing less is expected of us.

2

The Search for
the Most Desperate Workers

Tania Munsura crawled to the window ledge on the ninth floor of the burning Hameem apparel factory in Savar, Bangladesh. She felt no ill feeling toward Mr. Azad (the factory owner) or any of the security guards who had locked the fire exits. She could only think of her family. "If I stay, my body will be burned beyond recognition," she reasoned, "but if I jump, my father can claim my body and give me a proper burial."[1]

Tania migrated from the Pabna district of Bangladesh to the city of Savar in 2008, seeking a better life. The prospect of grinding dollar-a-day poverty, illiteracy, and arranged marriages in Pabna could not compare to the promise of good factory jobs in Savar. What she found was another story, a story of the most desperate workers in the world, an illustration of the violence of globalization.[2]

Financially, Tania's life was better in Savar. She earned 26 cents an hour as a sewing operator, stitching together toddler denim shorts for Gap and other clothing for J. C. Penney and Phillips-Van Heusen (now PVH), along with occasional work for Target, VF Corporation, and Abercrombie & Fitch. It was enough to provide a meager existence for herself and allow her to save a small amount for the future.

But the leering bosses, forced overtime, repetitive work, and lack of almost any time off were serious problems, not to mention the threats workers received if they discussed forming a union. Tania spent up to ninety hours per week in the factory, working as much as thirty-two hours of mandatory overtime. On average, she received one day off per month. She was not the only one from her village to make the calculation that this form of backbreaking poverty was preferable to the one left behind. Her own brother had migrated to Jordan, where he worked at a similar factory in the American Free Trade Zone until he was deported, along with every other Bangladeshi male, for organizing workers to demand better pay and working conditions. Now, the companies based in Jordan recruited only women, believing them to be more compliant.

The Hameem factory in Savar was no different, employing 80 percent women, aged twenty to twenty-five. Like Tania, they hoped to save a little money, get married, and raise their own families. In all, almost 7,500 hundredpeople worked in the eleven-story building. When they tried to organize a union, Hameem management had the union leader imprisoned and fired nineteen of the workers most involved in the organizing. Management illegally continues to forbid unions at the factory.

When the fire broke out on December 14, 2010, workers smelled smoke ten minutes before any alarms rang. They made their way to the exits and found them locked by company security guards concerned about employee theft. Firefighters' ladders could not reach above the eighth floor, and the fire continued to spread throughout the upper floors. Some workers escaped, using a long cord of fabric as a rope ladder to reach the lower floors, but twenty-nine others, like Tania, died in the fire, cornered by flames into an unspeakable quandary—jump or burn?

In the United States, a fire like the one at Hameem changed American labor history forever. Almost a hundred years earlier, on March 25, 1911, 146 young women garment workers making 14 cents per hour ($3.18 today) perished in the Triangle Shirtwaist Factory fire in New York City. Like Tania, these women typically worked fourteen-hour shifts with few days off. They were also locked inside the factory ("How else could you control so many young girls?" asked a Triangle floor manager) and could not escape the fire. Many died when they jumped from the ninth floor (firefighters' ladders could only reach the seventh floor) so their parents would have bodies to bury.[3]

Public outrage over the Triangle fire helped bring about serious reforms in American labor laws, such as requirements for sprinkler systems, exit doors that opened outward and could not be locked, the minimum wage, time-and-a-half for overtime, and the right to organize a union.[4] These changes gave some semblance of meaning to these young women's deaths, and the reforms were duly noted at centennial memorials in 2011.

In Bangladesh, no such change has been forthcoming. The factory owner, A. K. Azad, who is also president of the influential Federation of Bangladesh Chambers of Commerce and Industries, insisted the fire "was the work of sabotage,"[5] and publicized this explanation through his television station and newspaper, despite the absence of any evidence supporting his claim. Mr. Azad provided only $2,083.33 in compensation to each family of the twenty-nine dead workers and just $347.22 each to the thirty-six workers hospitalized.

No major public outcry has emerged in Bangladesh since the fire, no serious investigation, and no changes in worker safety and compensation laws. Ironically, it was one of the big apparel companies, PVH, that brought together the companies whose products were produced in the Hameem factory to meet with the government to discuss factory safety, though little came of this meeting. Millions of Bangladeshis continue to work under these conditions in the apparel industry with their own government demonstrating very little concern for their well-being. While this sector of Bangladesh's economy is still its strongest, there is increased pressure on Bangladeshi apparel factories to cut costs, as some production has already relocated to still poorer (and more desperate) countries like Lesotho in southern Africa. On the other hand, rising wages in China are driving other factories to relocate to Bangladesh.[6]

SIGNS OF THE TIMES

Neocolonialism and the Race to the Bottom

One way of looking at the search for the most desperate workers is through the lens of neocolonialism. During the period of European colonialism (1492–1948), Great Britain, France, Italy, Spain, and other European powers sent soldiers to Asia, Africa, and the Americas to dominate and exploit natural resources, food, and labor. Japan established a similar relationship with Korea and parts of China from the early twentieth century until World War II. By use of guns and slavery, these empires established political, economic, and military control over countries that became their colonies.

When many colonies received their independence in the years following World War I and World War II, a period of "neocolonialism" followed, whereby the same European powers, the United States, and a resurgent Japan found new ways to dominate the political and economic affairs of weaker nations. Neocolonialism accomplishes through economic entanglements and the policies of international finance organizations what colonialism accomplished through force. Instead of sending troops, the former colonial powers support the less developed countries' (LDC's) military and government, offering the conditional leverage of global financial institutions, such as the World Bank and the IMF, while the corporations based in these more developed countries extract natural resources and outsource jobs to workers in the LDCs. Outsourcing involves setting up subsidiary companies or contracting with businesses in LDCs to supply particular goods and services to corporations in more developed countries.

The World Bank and the IMF play important roles in maintaining neocolonial relationships. Founded in 1945, the IMF is headquartered in Washington, D.C., and governed by 188 member countries. The IMF is the central institution of the International Monetary System, that is, the system of international payments and exchange rates among national currencies that enables business to take place between countries. It was established to promote international monetary cooperation, exchange stability, and orderly exchange arrangements: to foster economic growth and high levels of employment; and to provide temporary financial assistance to countries to help ease balance-of-payment adjustments. While the IMF is concerned mainly with short-term financial stabilization, the World Bank's focus is mainly on long-term development, poverty reduction, project funding, and structural adjustment.

The World Bank is an association of five institutions owned by 188 member countries. It is run like a cooperative with its member countries as shareholders. The United States is the largest, with Japan, Germany, the United Kingdom, and France rounding out the five biggest shareholders. The World Bank makes loans at low or market interest rates based on a country's ability to repay. The bank also provides grants, interest-free loans, and technical assistance. It currently distributes $25 billion in aid to LDCs, with the goal of fighting poverty while promoting long-range balanced growth of international trade. In the early 1980s, it began to go beyond simply lending for projects like roads and dams to providing broad-based support in the form of structural adjustment loans. These loans had to be approved by the IMF, which imposed new conditions on the loans—the structural adjustment policies.

Borrowing nations had to make certain "adjustments" to their political and economic structures in order to remain eligible for further loans and grants. These adjustments usually included:

- Deregulating prices and devaluing currency
- Cutting spending in health, education, sanitation, agriculture, and other services
- Privatizing state-owned industries
- Eliminating trade barriers
- Modernizing the export of crops like coffee, cocoa, bananas, sugar, and peanuts.
- Deregulating the labor market, making it easier for employers to hire and fire and control labor.

If the indebted country complied with the structural adjustment requirements, the World Bank and the IMF gave the green light to foreign investors, commercial banking institutions, and nations donating foreign aid. If the indebted country refused to implement the structural adjustment policies, it would be refused loans and funding from outside sources. Nations that refuse to go along with the structural adjustment policies or refuse to repay their loans face disaster as a result of economic isolation.

But even if a country goes along with the structural adjustment policies, the results could—and often are—disastrous for the poor and vulnerable. For example, currency devaluation helps a country sell its goods, but 30–50 percent increases in prices resulting from these changes in the value of local currencies make poor people poorer. In addition, cuts in government spending help governments pay their loans back more quickly, but they reduce health and education services and cause spikes in unemployment rates. Finally, the privatization of state-owned industries can bring about abrupt changes like massive increases in prices and waves of layoffs.

These challenges would be bad enough if elected representatives of the people in the LDCs had made the decisions. But these are not the decisions of democratically elected governments; they are the conditions imposed by former colonial powers through international finance organizations as the condition for financial aid and investment. Today, the former colonial powers retain a great deal of control over developing countries through these economic weapons. The structural adjustment policies have become the occupying force of neocolonialism.

The New Global Elites

But the neocolonial paradigm alone does not provide the complete picture. Increasingly in former colonies, economic elites are emerging who have earned substantial fortunes and become major players in the global economy, making common cause with elites from the more developed countries.[7] The rich from both wealthy countries and developing nations stay in the same hotels, attend the same conferences, hold memberships in the same clubs, and send their children to the same universities. This phenomenon occurred in earlier decades, but uneven economic growth in developing nations has taken it to new extremes. We now live in a world in which inequality among nations is decreasing,[8] but inequality within nations is increasing,[9] and the richest person in the world is from Mexico.[10]

As global economic elites purchase shares in multinational corporations, and the companies they establish go multinational, the leadership of these businesses becomes increasingly international, drawing from both colonizer and colonized nations. Not tied to any one country and its singular history, global corporations now bounce operations from nation to nation, seeking the most desperate workers. If a better deal can be found one year in Mexico, the factory moves to Mexico. If El Salvador can provide workers willing to work for lower wages and harsher working conditions, the factory folds and moves there. If China can provide a still more desperate workforce, the factory moves again, always with the threat of further relocation.

China's role complicates matters further. Once one of the poorest countries in the world, China now boasts the earth's second-largest economy and its second-largest military, despite an extreme poverty rate (people living on $1.25 per day or less) of about 15 percent: 200 million people![11] The rapid increase in low-wage factories in China is government policy, an attempt to lift its people out of the worst of its Maoist-era poverty (when the extreme poverty rate was about 83 percent, using the World Bank's $1.25/day standard, adjusted for inflation[12]) through rapid economic development. While this strategy has been partially successful, some of the worst environmental and human rights abuses in the global economy occur in China, as we will see throughout this book.

Going South—The Race to the Bottom

In the 1980s and 1990s, a major shift in the global economy occurred when growing numbers of manufacturers began to relocate from the more developed northern countries to the LDCs of the global south in search of the most vulnerable and desperate workers, a key ingredient in keeping prices low and profits high. Labor costs are a significant part of production expenses. In order to stay competitive, many companies look for workers willing to work for the lowest wages. The most desperate will work for the lowest rate.

In the United States, during the 1960s and 1970s, corporations relocated many unionized manufacturing jobs from northern states to southern states to avoid unions and to pay lower wages. As transportation costs declined and trade agreements removed tariffs, these jobs were relocated farther south to Mexico and Central America in the 1980s and 1990s. Now they are increasingly moving from Latin America to Asia. Recently, some factories have moved from Asia to Africa. In order to keep prices low and stay competitive, companies constantly work to lower their costs. If they don't, their profits will go down, and with them, their stock values. The executives and managers who are under constant pressure to increase profits and stock prices won't keep their positions unless they join the search for the most desperate workers.

The CEOs and the chairs of corporate boards of directors know that the relatively high cost of labor in the United States is related to the justice of the workers' rights laws and regulations that are now part of our political and economic systems. These laws and regulations (those passed and adopted in the wake of the Triangle Shirtwaist Factory fire are marked with an asterisk) include:

*Child labor laws

*Minimum-wage laws

Occupational safety and health laws

Environmental protection laws

*The right to organize labor unions

Equal pay for men and women

*Time-and-a-half pay for overtime (over forty hours a week)

Age discrimination laws

Americans with Disabilities Act

Civil rights protections for race and creed

Workers' compensation laws

Unemployment benefits

Social Security disability benefits

Business leaders are also keenly aware of the costs associated with compliance with both labor and environmental protection laws. So in order to keep prices low, remain competitive, and increase profits, many businesses lay off American workers and relocate to countries where they can legally avoid paying living wages, use child labor, require long working hours, ignore hazards, fire older workers without cause, pay women less than men, pass over women for promotions, repress unions, and dodge environmental protections.

It is just good business, the reasoning goes, to squeeze and exploit the poorest, most desperate workers to the greatest degree. In fact, it is an imperative for survival if you want to earn as much as your competitors. These are the perverse incentives within our economic system, the root of the violence of globalization. Thousands of American and multinational corporations have abandoned millions of American workers so they do not have to bother with the cost of justice in our system. The notion of what kinds of jobs can be outsourced has expanded dramatically in the past decade, as seen in Oakland, California, when American workers began assembling a prefabricated San Francisco–Oakland Bay Bridge, made in China, in 2011. Turning to China saved the state of California hundreds of millions of dollars, but cost Californians jobs. Three thousand Chinese workers have been employed by this project.[13] Outsourcing might make sense for a private corporation—its mission is to generate profits—but the mission of a state government is to promote the common good, a mission hardly served by exporting jobs overseas to the nation's closest competitor.

The latter decades of the twentieth century and the first years of the twenty-first witnessed a steady stream of companies firing U.S. workers and moving production south and east. Most of the products we use every day are now produced outside the country by very poor people. For example, 98 percent of all clothing purchased in the United States is made by poor people in developing nations,[14] and 80 percent of toys are made in China.[15]

Take a moment and look around your house. Open your closet and examine your clothing. You will see labels from Latin America and Asia and almost nothing from the United States and Europe. Look around your local mall or shopping center. You will see that almost every product available comes from the labor of poor people living in developing countries.

Are Sweatshops Good for the Poor?

It is true that manufacturing provides employment for people living in poverty in developing countries. In many countries, these jobs have indeed lowered rates of extreme ($1.25 a day or less) poverty. Jeffrey Sachs and other economists have described this as a positive development, writing that sweatshop jobs are "the first rung on the ladder out of extreme poverty"[16] and the first stages of what every highly developed country experienced in its own industrialization. Sachs points to Bangladesh itself as a sign of hope, noting that infant mortality has dropped from 145/1,000 in 1970 to 48/1,000 in 2002, and overall life expectancy has risen from forty-four years to sixty-two years. The World Bank has also reported a drop in extreme poverty in Bangladesh, from 34.3 percent of the population to 25.1 percent from 2000 to 2005.[17]

Sachs also points out a phenomenon often seen among sweatshop workers in the developing world—they are grateful for the job. They have escaped the extreme poverty of the countryside and now "save for some small purpose from their meager pay, manage their own income, have their own rooms, choose when and whom to date and marry, choose to have children when they feel ready, and use their savings to enhance their literacy and job-market skills."[18] These workers are subjected to low pay, abysmal working conditions, forced overtime, and pressure not to form a union, but that doesn't mean they want to lose these jobs. The key question is—is it just?

Given the sharply different responses to the two factory fires, a full century apart, can we expect today's sweatshops to naturally evolve into tomorrow's clean, safe factories staffed by middle-class, organized workers (a best-case scenario)? Considering the mobility of production, reforming the sweatshop economy may be more difficult than Sachs and others will admit. At the time of the Triangle fire, there was nowhere for American sweatshops to go. The apparel factory owners had to deal with the concerns of an enraged public. Today, a company facing pressure to reform in one country can just pack up and move to a country of still more desperate workers. Or, in some cases, they might stay right where they are and simply import "guest workers" more desperate than the host country's citizens.

The mobility of production and labor is a feature of globalization that is here to stay. But just as companies are now global, responses to the violence of globalization can be too. As a global institution (and we've been part of globalization for two thousand years), the church is uniquely qualified to respond effectively to the violence of globalization. For us, the essential question is not whether factories in developing countries should or should not exist, but how to ensure that these jobs promote human dignity and honor the rights of workers. The Institute for Global Labour and Human Rights provides a disturbing orientation to the challenges we face in aiding the world's most desperate workers.

Documenting the True Cost of Low Prices

The Institute for Global Labour and Human Rights (formerly the National Labor Committee) is a Pittsburgh-based nonprofit organization devoted to defending the rights of workers, helping them organize for justice, and educating consumers about how they can help. The following summaries of the institute's research illustrate how the violence of postcolonial globalization undermines human dignity:

It's a Small World after All. The next time you buy Disney toys, note how affordable they are, but also consider the price the workers have paid to bring you this product. Young Chinese workers producing items such as the Disney Princess Fancy Fashion kit toil in temperatures that often reach 95 degrees—they understand the meaning of the word "sweatshop"! These workers at the Daewi factory in Dongguan, China, work thirteen-and-a-half-hour days with forced overtime for about $50.00 per week, significantly lower than the Chinese legal minimum of $71.34 for this length of workweek. According to local law, factory management must sign a contract for each worker that delineates hours, wages, benefits, holidays, insurance, maternity leave, health and safety, and other details. At the Daewi factory, workers sign blank sheets of paper upon commencing employment, and factory owners then fill in the details of these "contracts" later.[19]

The degree of forced overtime demanded in the Daewi factory exceeds China's legal limit by 400 percent. Exhausted workers who arrive to a shift ten minutes late are docked a day and a half's worth of wages. If they arrive thirty minutes late they are docked three days' wages. Singing on the job results in a fine of seven hours wages ("Hi ho, hi ho, it's off to work we go"). Eight workers share a dorm room, using beds infested with bed bugs. They pay for their own room, board, and uniforms through salary deductions. Disney auditors (brought on board after National Labor Committee exposés in the 1990s revealed horrific factory conditions among Disney suppliers in Haiti) view doctored wage slips and have not intervened.

Guest Sweatshop Welcomes Poor Asians to Jordan. In Jordan, successive Free Trade Agreements have produced "Qualifying Industrial Zones," where workers manufacture apparel that can enter the United States duty free. These treaties have created clusters of sweatshops in the Middle East like the Rich Pine Factory in Jordan, which sews clothing for Liz Claiborne, Macy's, Kohl's, Ralph Lauren,

Hudson Bay, and others, according to labels smuggled out of the factory.[20] Workers, mainly temporary migrants from countries like China, Bangladesh, and Sri Lanka, earn 86.5 cents per hour, which usually adds up to a little over $2,000 per year. Most work obligatory overtime, which typically adds up to an eighty-hour work week. Six to eight workers each share a 10-by-10-foot to 12-by-12-foot dorm room, sleeping on metal bunk beds. There is no heat (a misery in the winter), no electrical outlets, and each worker gets two buckets of lukewarm water per week to wash with. Sick days are not allowed.

Antisweatshop activity has yielded both government and apparel company monitoring, but this auditing has not been as effective as it could be, according to the Institute for Global Labour and Human Rights. The Arab inspectors who work for U.S. companies spend most of their time meeting with management in their offices and very little time with workers. *Businessweek* magazine notes that this is a problem not limited to Jordan; it is also rampant in China.[21] Jordanian government inspectors meet with factory owners, but the Institute for Global Labour and Human Rights reports no workers have ever known an auditor to interview a fellow worker. The Jordanian government has even awarded Rich Pine its "Golden List" status, naming it as one of the best garment factories for workers in Jordan, adding a bitter irony to this story.

The True Cost of "American" Cars. My uncle used to chasten Mom about owning a Japanese car.[22] "You should buy American," he would say. I wonder what he would think about the Yuwei Plastics and Hardware Product Company Ltd. in Dongguan, China,[23] which supplies automobile parts to Ford. Workers earn a base wage of 80 cents per hour and work fourteen-hour shifts, seven days a week. Serious injuries have become a problem at the plant, with four cases of maimed hands or fingers occurring in the last several years. New hires are instructed that they must "work hard and endure hardship."

Chin Woo (pseudonym) understands this expression. On March 13, 2009, the twenty-one-year-old man was told by his supervisor to turn off the infrared safety monitor on his "punch press," a sixty-ton machine that stamps out 3,600 "RT Tubes" (a metal gear shift) daily for Ford, one every twelve seconds. Without the safety monitor, the machine's productive capacity could be increased, but so too the risk of amputation. Three fingers and several knuckles were torn from his left hand when it later became trapped in the press, leaving the hand inoperative. He received a total compensation payment for the loss of three fingers of $7,430. According to the Institute for Global Labour and Human Rights, a similar injury in the United States would result in a $144,292 payment.[24] Chin was fired and was not given the severance pay due him. Now he worries that he will never work again and, worse, that no woman will marry him because of his new deformity.

Fans of a Free Trade Zone. National Football League apparel is as popular as ever with sports fans who keep their team close to their hearts. But when you purchase a woman's T-shirt with a Pittsburgh Steelers, Dallas Cowboys, Indianapolis Colts, Cincinnati Bengals, or Denver Broncos logo, think not only of your team, but also of the fifteen hundred mostly women workers locked into a Salvadoran Free Trade Zone, surrounded by barbed wire and patrolled by guards armed with shotguns.[25]

Workers sew women's NFL T-shirts for the Ocean Sky Apparel Factory in afternoon temperatures reaching 98 degrees, soaked in their own sweat. According to the Institute for Global Labour and Human Rights, the drinking water is contaminated with fecal E. coli, which causes a number of intestinal illnesses. Six workers who shared this information with fellow workers were fired in 2011. In order to meet production goals, many of the workers arrive early and work through lunch—all unpaid overtime labor.

Workers earn a base wage of 72 cents per hour, bumped to 92 cents if they earn the attendance bonus. The Salvadoran Ministry of the Economy has determined that these wages are one-fourth of what is needed to provide the basic needs of a family. The wages work out to 8 cents per $25 T-shirt. If the NFL demanded that the women's wages double to 16 cents per shirt and added the additional 8 cents to the price of the shirt, would consumers stop buying the product? Would you?

Exhausted "Work Study" Students Don't Use Computers, They Build Them. The KYE Factory in Dongguan, China, produces computer mice for Microsoft with a workforce of close to a thousand "work-study" students, their high school studies interrupted for several months of factory work. These young people are typically sixteen or seventeen years old but some have been found who are as young as fourteen or fifteen.[26] They spend 83 hours per week at the factory, working 68 hours per week. This total is down from a prerecession high of 80.5 hours a week of work. A typical shift lasts from 7:45 a.m. to 10:55 p.m. daily.

The young workers make 65 cents per hour, reduced to 52 cents per hour after deductions for food in the dismal cafeteria. Fourteen workers share each dormitory room and receive only a bucket of lukewarm water for a daily sponge bath. Hours are long, but the pace is also frenetic, as workers try to reach production goals of two thousand mice per twelve-hour shift. Some of the teens have fallen asleep on their shift from sheer exhaustion. During the summer, factory temperatures reach 86 degrees, and workers are quickly covered in sweat. Microsoft has a published code of conduct, but workers are unaware of it, and management does not appear to be following the code.

The most disturbing element of this reality is that these sweatshops are not the exception. Microsoft's closest competitor, Apple Computer, for example, came under renewed scrutiny in 2012 because of forced overtime and unsafe conditions at its main supplier, Foxconn, in China. The electronics giant had been under fire since 2006 because of such violations of the law and international standards, but it was a rash of worker suicides that brought Foxconn to the attention of the general public.[27]

In many cases, these stories are representative of the local manufacturing sector. A quick visit to other antisweatshop websites like walmartwatch.org or laborrights.org would yield many more equally harrowing stories of the violence of globalization. The "signs of the times" point to the sweatshop remaining a persistent element of the global economy without significant intervention.

As described above, the ethical dilemmas that globalization presents are not easy. Extreme poverty has decreased in most countries with a large sweatshop sector. But must workers like Tania perish in factory fires behind locked doors? Must foreign workers turn off safety devices for U.S. companies to stay competitive? Do wages need to be a fraction of what it takes to raise a family? Is it essential to work almost a week's worth of forced overtime without proper rest to move from extreme poverty to ordinary poverty?

These questions raise other, broader queries. What exactly are the rights of workers in the global marketplace? Who defines these rights? What are the obligations of employers? How should minimum wages and working standards be set? What is the proper role of unions? For the answers to these and other essential moral questions, we turn to the teaching of the church and the lessons of scripture.

WHAT THE CHURCH TEACHES

The Christian commitment to the rights of workers is as old as the Hebrew scriptures, dating to the Lord's intervention in a labor dispute between the Israelites and Pharaoh during the Egyptian captivity. The book of Exodus relates this story of worker justice in chapters 5 through 11. It is the prequel to the flight of the Israelites out of Egypt.

The Hebrews manufactured bricks for Pharaoh using straw, which he supplied for them. The time came when God told Moses to organize a religious festival in the desert, a three-day journey. When Moses asked Pharaoh to give the Hebrews a holiday to celebrate these holy days, he refused and complained of the laziness of the people, suggesting that they would use the time off for sexual pursuits and not religious observance ("Look how numerous the people of the land are already" [Exod. 5:5]). To punish Moses and the people, Pharoah ordered them to produce the same quota of bricks, but without the straw he normally supplied. As a social justice educator for the Archdiocese of New York, I once asked a group of parishioners, "What is Pharaoh doing?"[28] An assembly line worker replied, "Pharaoh has ordered a 'speed-up' "!

I think I met Pharaoh once, when I worked as lead organizer for the Brockton Interfaith Community in Brockton, Massachusetts. In 1992, the Raynham-Taunton greyhound dog-racing track near Brockton fired two women from their positions as clerks for refusing to work on Christmas. A lower court reinstated the women to their jobs, under a law protecting Massachusetts citizens celebrating Christian and Jewish holidays, but the state Supreme Court struck the law down in 1997 as discriminatory, as only two religions were protected. A small number of state legislators from Brockton (whose chief campaign contributor was the owner of the dog track) used parliamentary maneuvers to keep the new legislation protecting all religious holidays from coming up for a vote.[29] I convened a meeting with one of the recalcitrant House of Representatives members to discuss the matter with Brockton's clergy.

Rep. Geraldine Creedon arrived in jeans, eating candy throughout the meeting and asserting, "People don't even go to church on holy days!" I almost expected her to add, "Look how numerous the people of the land are already." The Brockton Interfaith Community clergy, decked in formal clerical dress, reminded her that the reason we were meeting was the firing of two women for refusing to work on Christmas, and the local clergy's experience of holy days was different from hers. Ultimately, we prevailed, and Rep. Creedon even switched her vote. But her dismissive attitude toward matters of faith stayed with me. "There goes Pharaoh," I thought as she left.

In Exodus, the Lord stands up for the Hebrews, causing ten plagues—from turning the rivers to blood to killing the first-born children of the Egyptians (the Passover). The Lord still intervenes on behalf of workers today by inspiring people of faith to insist that employers respect worker dignity and rights. The Catholic Church has a long record of standing up for workers, beginning, in modern times, with the publication of the first social justice papal encyclical *Of New Things* (*Rerum Novarum*) in 1891.

With *Of New Things*, Pope Leo XIII inaugurated the tradition of popes connecting the truths of scripture and natural law (universal law set by God and discovered by human beings in nature through the use of reason) to the challenges of modern times. The chief medium of this teaching has been the papal encyclical or letter to bishops, clergy, the people of God, and other persons of goodwill. It is one of the highest forms of church teaching. These official church teachings are compiled at the Vatican website (www.vatican.va) and address the relevance of the faith to issues of worker justice as well as peace, abortion, the economy, and international development.[30] The papal social justice encyclicals emphasize the social dimensions of sin, identified by Pope John Paul II in his encyclical *On Social Concerns* (*Sollicitudo Rei Socialis*) as "structures of sin."[31] The most recent papal encyclical is Pope Benedict XVI's *Charity in Truth* (*Caritas in Veritate*), promulgated in 2009.

Worker justice has figured prominently in each social justice encyclical, and the full body of teaching has been summarized in both the *Catechism of the Catholic Church* and the *Compendium of the Social Doctrine of the Church*. The *Catechism* notes first that through work, we participate in God's ongoing creation of the universe[32]: "In work, the person exercises and fulfills in part the potential inscribed in his nature. The primordial value of labor stems from man himself, its author and beneficiary. Work is for man, not man for work."[33] In other words, we bring dignity to work because we are made in the image of God, and this dignity must be respected—through salary and benefits, but also working conditions and proper time for rest. This section continues, "Everyone should be able to draw from work the means of providing for his life and that of his family, and of serving the human community,"[34] a clear call for a living wage.

The *Catechism* emphasizes the importance of solidarity among workers, but also among employers and employees,[35] which requires some degree of mutual respect. Like much of Catholic teaching, the *Catechism* emphasizes the importance of both rights and responsibilities. In the sphere of work, these include:

- The right to work: The *Catechism* calls for all societies to help every citizen find work and promote access to employment "without unjust discrimination."[36]

- The responsibility to work: While work is a right, it is also a duty. We are responsible to honor the Creator by using the gifts and talents God has given us to promote the common good through our labors.[37]

- The right to a just wage: A "just wage" is "the legitimate fruit of work," and "to withhold it can be a grave injustice." With a nod to the most vulnerable workers, the *Catechism* concludes the teaching by stating, "Agreement between the parties is not sufficient to justify morally the amount to be received in wages."[38]

- The right to strike when necessary: The *Catechism* upholds the right of workers to strike, "when it cannot be avoided, or at least when it is necessary to obtain a proportionate benefit. It becomes morally unacceptable when accompanied by violence, or when objectives are included that are not directly linked to working conditions or are contrary to the common good." Note that the right to strike is linked to several responsibilities here.[39]

♦ Responsibilities of owners and managers: While the *Catechism* upholds the right to economic initiative, private property, and profits,[40] it also stresses the responsibility of owners and managers for "the economic and ecological effects" of business operations. "They have an obligation to consider the good of persons and not only the increase of profits," the teaching states.[41] Finally, the *Catechism* concludes, "It is unjust not to pay the social security contributions required by legitimate authority."[42]

These teachings apply equally to all employers, especially to the church itself, which must teach by example in addition to catechesis.

The *Compendium of the Social Doctrine of the Church*, developed by the Vatican Pontifical Council for Justice and Peace, also summarizes this teaching, enhancing it with additional quotes from scripture, the papal encyclicals, and the documents of the Second Vatican Council. The *Compendium* employs scripture to underscore the right to a living wage and timely payment, an emphasis to be developed more in the next chapter. The sections on the rights of workers,[43] which give renewed attention to the right to "rest from work," note that "these rights are often infringed, as is confirmed by the sad fact of workers who are underpaid and without adequate representation. It often happens that work conditions for men, women, and children, especially in developing countries, are so inhumane that they are an offence to their dignity and compromise their health."[44]

The *Compendium* also takes on the fallacy that the social doctrine of the church is somehow optional or peripheral. "The Church's social doctrine is . . . the thought of the Church, insofar as it is the work of the Magisterium, which teaches with the authority that Christ conferred on the Apostles and their successors: the Pope and the Bishops in communion with him."[45] The *Compendium* later adds, "Insofar as it is part of the Church's moral teaching, the Church's social doctrine has the same dignity and authority as her moral teaching. It is authentic Magisterium, which obligates the faithful to adhere to it."[46]

In 2012, building on the success of the *Compendium*, the Pontifical Council for Justice and Peace issued a reflection on the *Vocation of the Business Leader*, which challenged business leaders "to engage the contemporary economic and financial world in light of the principles of *human dignity* and the *common good*"[47] (original italics). The document offered an assessment of the challenges of the global economy, including globalization and the mobility of capital that has characterized the sweatshop economy.[48] *Vocation of the Business Leader* also put forward specific "practical ethical principles for business" which encourage the business leader to be an innovator, promoting human dignity and the common good, rather than a speculator or exploiter.[49]

Catholic social teaching has also been applied by individual Catholic bishops and bishops' conferences to local situations. The U.S. Conference of Catholic Bishops (USCCB) has developed teaching resources on Catholic social doctrine for the United States, proper to its own role. The U.S. bishops summarize Catholic teaching on the dignity of work and the rights of workers as follows:

> The economy must serve people, not the other way around. Work is more than a way to make a living; it is a form of continuing participation in God's creation. Employers contribute to the common good through the services or products they provide and by creating jobs that uphold the dignity and rights of workers—to productive work, to decent and just wages, to adequate benefits and security in their old age, to the choice of whether to organize and join unions, to the opportunity for legal status for immigrant workers, to private property, and to economic initiative. Workers also have responsibilities—to provide a fair day's work for a fair day's pay, to treat employers and co-workers with respect, and to carry out their work in ways that contribute to the common good. Workers, employers, and unions should not only advance their own interests, but also work together to advance economic justice and the well-being of all.[50]

Benedict XVI put his own stamp on Catholic social doctrine regarding workers and globalization in his 2009 encyclical *Charity in*

Truth. In this teaching letter, Benedict first affirms the teaching of his predecessors, especially Pope Paul VI, whose 1967 encyclical *On the Development of Peoples* (*Populorum Progressio*) was the first Catholic social teaching document on international development. He goes on to say that "Once profit becomes the exclusive goal, if it is produced by improper means and without the common good as its ultimate end, it risks destroying wealth and creating poverty."[51] Echoing John Paul II, he also excoriates "the scandal of glaring inequalities" in both rich and poor countries.[52] In this encyclical, the pope calls for strengthening workers' associations[53] and the development of economic activity that respects human rights and is "directed towards the pursuit of the common good."[54] Benedict insists throughout the encyclical that "justice must be applied to every phase of economic activity."[55]

SIGNS OF HOPE

It is this commitment to justice, worker rights, and the common good that produced a large crop of Catholic "labor priests" in the twentieth century, men like Msgr. George Higgins, Jesuit Fathers John Corridan and Ed Boyle, Msgr. Jack Egan, and Fr. Martin Mangan, clerics with a special call to respond to the concerns of working-class Americans (watch the film *On the Waterfront* to see one in action). Since 1924, this teaching has also inspired hundreds of thousands of Catholics to join the worldwide Young Christian Workers' movement. Today it spurs Catholic participation in local workers' centers and coalitions affiliated with Interfaith Worker Justice, among other signs of hope.

Catholic social teaching on worker justice also produced a generation of Catholic students who demanded an end to sweatshops in the 1990s, spurring the development of the first "codes of conduct" for apparel producers. Some of these codes proved effective, others not. In the early years of the twenty-first century, students at 180 faith-based and secular universities convinced their respective schools to join the Worker Rights Consortium (WRC), an independent watchdog organization that monitors factories where collegiate apparel is manufactured with input from local labor unions, human rights groups, and other nongovernmental organizations (NGOs). The WRC now blows the whistle at abuses, but it also publicly praises those manufacturers who treat workers ethically and pay a living wage, like Knights Apparel, whose Dominican Republic factory is a model of what a justly managed apparel factory could be, with a unionized workforce and wages three times what the average apparel worker makes in the Dominican Republic.[56]

Even Catholic grade schools have begun to demand "sweat-free" school uniforms. The Archdiocese of Newark, led by then Archbishop Theodore McCarrick, inserted an antisweatshop clause in all vendor contracts in 1998. "We want to look at everything we buy, to make sure we're not contributing to injustice and indignity in the workplace," Archbishop McCarrick said at the policy's inception. The contracts continue to affect uniform purchases of over fifty thousand students in the archdiocese, and many other schools have followed suit.[57]

Another sign of hope has been the impressive growth of the Fair Trade movement. It used to be that when people learned about the plight of workers and commodity producers, they asked, "What should we boycott?" Now, consumers interested in purchasing certified ethically produced value-added items like handicrafts, soccer balls, chocolate products, and wine can do so by buying products with a Fair Trade label bestowed by one of the major Fair Trade certifying organizations. Most Fair Trade products are agricultural commodities such as coffee, cocoa, sugar, tea, and bananas, but we are beginning to see more convergence in certain areas of the "sweat-free" and Fair Trade movements as both grow in strength and motivate a growing population of consumers interested in making ethical consumer choices.[58]

One outcome of the "sweat-free" movement is the growth of independent, nongovernmental certification and auditing programs like the WRC. Another of these organizations is Verité, an NGO that works with some of the largest companies in the world to stop the worst abuses of the global economy. Verité partners with businesses to identify existing or potential problems in their supply chains and provides consulting to these companies to identify how to ethically respond to these problems. CEO Dan Viederman explained,

"Companies can no longer assume that they do not have problems in their supply chains, or that if they do, that they can't solve them."[59]

Verité works with businesses that have made a commitment to examining the conduct of their suppliers and contractors, so its impact is limited by the willingness of businesses to undergo this level of scrutiny. Yet the number of companies willing to take on such reflection is growing, thanks to legislation like the California Transparency in Supply Chains Act, passed in 2010.[60] This law requires all retailers and manufacturers who do business totaling more than $100 million (which would include "big-box" stores accused of contracting sweatshop labor, like Walmart and Target) to share information about what they are doing to eradicate slavery and human trafficking from their direct supply chains. While this law does not cover many of the abuses described in this chapter, it is getting businesses in the door of Verité and other auditors and moves the bar of transparency a little higher.

Groups like Verité appeal to business leaders to make decisions that promote ethical decision making in the global economy, but some shareholders are taking matters into their own hands as well. The Interfaith Center on Corporate Responsibility (ICCR) brings the collective investing power of the faith community to bear in the world of business. Its Catholic members include several major Catholic health care systems, Catholic Relief Services, Christian Brothers Retirement Services, Mercy Investment Services, and a score or so of religious orders.

They approach businesses not just as do-gooders, but also as owners. Almost all religious organizations own shares of stock, through their endowments' pension funds (you probably do too, through your college or retirement savings plan). The ICCR organizes that collective power of ownership among its members and promotes "justice and sustainability through transformation of the corporate world"[61] The ICCR has identified eight issue areas as priorities, including "supply chain monitoring," where sweatshops come into play.

ICCR brings its power to bear on these issues in part through shareholder resolutions, brought forward at a company's annual meeting. These resolutions are typically opposed by management and usually fall far short of a majority, but it often takes only 10 percent of a vote to get the attention of management and alter a company's direction. Research indicates that the average shareholder vote in favor of global labor standards proposals rose each year from 2001 to 2004, the years for which we have data.[62]

In 1995, when the global sweatshop issue began to gain national prominence, the ICCR entered the fray with shareholder resolutions at Nike and Gap shareholder meetings. Rev. David Schilling, a United Methodist Church minister who serves as ICCR's director of human rights and resources programs, explained, "These resolutions never passed, but they eventually got [management] to the table."[63] Today, ICCR is able to obtain meetings with corporate leaders on supply-chain issues quite easily, and the number of shareholder resolutions offered in this area has declined dramatically as codes of corporate conduct and efforts to ensure compliance have increased. Although many factories in the developing world resemble those profiled at the beginning of this chapter, Schilling sees signs of improvement at the brands that ICCR works with closely, particularly those that have increased the number of unannounced inspections and audits. In addition, those companies that partner with local NGOs to monitor compliance get consistently more reliable information than those who bring in outside staff.

Walmart, for example, debuted its first "Global Responsibility Report" in 2001, a "flimsy" effort, noted Schilling. But its most recent edition, a lengthy, detailed document, indicates that over half of the factories it contracts with were audited with unannounced inspections. For Rev. Schilling and ICCR, unannounced audits are the difference between effective and ineffective codes of conduct. In reality, the same global companies may have both model factories and troubled links in their supply chains. How its local audits are structured and who the partners are on the ground are key variables affecting the outcomes of these audits.[64]

But the future of corporate global responsibility, Schilling insists, is not in fine tuning the audit system—it is in developing "robust factory-level communications and feedback mechanisms,"[65] meaning workers, line supervisors, and managers coming together to educate workers about their rights, discussing and addressing issues of concern to workers. The ICCR and its partners call this approach "Dynamic Social Compliance" (DSC). The ICCR worked with McDonald's Corporation, the Walt Disney Company, the Catholic socially responsible investing firm Domini Social Investments, the Missionary Oblates of Mary Immaculate (Cardinal Francis George's religious order), and four other religious and secular organizations to develop Project Kaleidoscope, a pilot program based on DSC that concretizes its communications and feedback mechanisms and tests its ability to promote increased justice and respect for human dignity in the supply chains.

Project Kaleidoscope facilitators lead team exercises and discussion among these groups within the factories "to identify factory strengths, opportunities for improvement, and potential solutions to issues."[66] Among the ten Chinese factories that participated in the pilot (each with varied histories of compliance with corporate codes of conduct), improvement was seen in the areas of timing paydays, living conditions, and number of working hours. One chronic audit issue in many of the factories, failure to pay for required insurance, completely disappeared.

When companies like McDonald's and the Walt Disney Company, spurred on by stockholders, insist on justice throughout the production process and require ethical conduct in the supply chain, their overseas factories comply, perhaps at first just to keep the contracts. "If the factory wants to be a long-term supplier, they have an incentive," Schilling explained. Over time, he pointed out, the increased productivity, quality of workmanship, and decreased turnover will demonstrate that the implementation of DSC is good for business as well as promoting respect for human dignity.[67]

These efforts to address the treatment of low-income workers in the poorest countries have begun to make a difference. As the initial boycotts and shareholder actions made an impact, businesses began to take notice of faith-based worker advocacy organizations before such tactics came into play. But even these admirable efforts to change the worst dimensions of the global economy have still fallen far short of the vision of integral human development laid out by Pope Benedict and found in the *Catechism*. The most desperate workers in the world need our help, even if they are an ocean away.

But as we will see in chapter 3, many of them are already knocking at our door.

DISCUSSION QUESTIONS

1. Would it be better if sweatshops stayed open or closed? Why?

2. Select a product in your home. How far can you trace where it is manufactured and by whom? Work as a group with friends or family if you can.

3. What Catholic teachings on the dignity of work and the rights of workers were you familiar with before you read this chapter? Did any teachings surprise you?

4. How does the outcome of the Hameem Factory fire of 2010 compare with the outcome of the Triangle Shirtwaist Factory fire in 1911?

5. Can we assume that sweatshops are a stepping-stone to better working conditions and living wage jobs in LDCs?

GO MAKE A DIFFERENCE

1. If you are a college student or graduate, find out if your college is part of the Worker Rights Consortium. If not, why not?

2. If you are a high school student, teacher, or campus minister, find out if your school purchases "sweat-free" uniforms and apparel. If your school does not have a supplier's code of conduct, develop one.

3. Where do you purchase coffee, tea, and chocolate? Approach these merchants about selling Fair Trade products (check out online resources at www.fairtradeusa.org). If they already do so, be sure to thank them!

3

Immigrant Workers:
The Most Vulnerable among Us

Eduardo Jaramillo felt lucky to have a job. He collected recyclables in San Francisco's Mission District before he was hired as a dishwasher and janitor at the Viva Portofino restaurant. He told the *San Francisco Chronicle* he knew he wasn't being paid the overtime he was due after working up to twelve hours a day, six or seven days a week. His weekly checks totaled just $320–350. The total didn't add up right. But, he said, "I needed my job."[1]

Three months later, Jaramillo had had enough, and quit, filing a claim for $2,674 with the state labor commissioner. When Jaramillo filed the claim, his boss just laughed at him. When he bumped into the man some days later, "He yelled at me that he's going to have me deported," Jaramillo said. The case has yet to be resolved.[2]

SIGNS OF THE TIMES

Eduardo Jaramillo's case is not unique—it is part of a growing epidemic of wage theft against low-wage workers in the United States. Employers steal workers' wages in different ways. Minimum-wage and time-and-a-half-for-overtime laws are frequently ignored, with few consequences for offending employers. Workers are improperly misclassified as exempt from overtime regulations. Many are inappropriately classified as contractors. An alarming number of employers steal tipped workers' tips, and many do not pay the tipped workers minimum wage. A high number of low-wage workers do not get paid for all of the hours they work, and some do not get paid at all. All told, the volume of wage theft suggests the nation is retreating from the commitments made to American workers in the wake of the Triangle Shirtwaist Factory fire (see chapter 1).

Undocumented migrants are the hardest hit. Like Eduardo Jaramillo, they are especially vulnerable because of their lack of documenta tion and therefore are typically afraid to report abuses to law enforcement authorities. Many undocumented migrants come to the United States out of desperation, aiming to support families living in poverty with the cash remittances they send home. The flood of cheap corn that followed the implementation of the North American Free Trade Agreement in 1994 pushed many Mexican farmers and farm workers off the land and into the United States.[3] They left one experience of the violence of globalization in their native land (the inability to provide for their families) and found another (wage theft) in a new and unfamiliar country.

When farmers and farm workers slip into the United States and locate work, they typically take on jobs U.S. citizens prefer not to do: picking our crops, doing landscaping, child care, and day-labor construction and repair. Sometimes it is said that undocumented immigrants take jobs away from American citizens. The United Farm Workers has put this notion to the test through its "Take Our Jobs" campaign, encouraging U.S. citizens who visit their website to apply to replace an immigrant worker in the fields. So far, there have been few takers, other than comedian Stephen Colbert.[4]

How Common Is Wage Theft?

In September 2009, a nationally recognized team of academics working on behalf of three research organizations (Center for Urban Economic Development, University of Illinois at Chicago; National Employment Law Project; UCLA Institute for Research on Labor and Employment) released the largest study ever undertaken on wage theft. Over forty-three hundred low-wage workers were interviewed in thirteen languages by sixty-two field staff, throughout New York City, Chicago, and Los Angeles.[5] In all, undocumented migrants made up 38.8 percent of workers interviewed,[6] a representative sample of the urban low-wage workforce.

The study found widespread and systematic wage violations across many sectors of the low-wage urban economy. Apparel and textile workers, beauty, dry cleaning and general repair workers, maids and housekeepers, retail salespersons and tellers, building maintenance workers, and factory and packaging workers all experienced a 25 percent or higher incidence of minimum-wage violations in the week prior to the study.[7] When controlled for citizenship and immigration status, the study found that among undocumented immigrants interviewed:

- 37.1 percent experienced minimum-wage violations in the week prior to the study. The rate for men was 29.5 percent; the rate for women was 47.4 percent.[8]

- 84.9 percent experienced overtime violations in the week prior to the study. The sex of workers did not make a significant difference in the rate of overtime violations.[9]

- 76.3 percent experienced working "off the clock" violations in the week prior to the study, meaning they were not paid for some of work they had performed during the previous week.[10]

The widespread incidence of wage theft was not limited to undocumented immigrants. Overall, documented immigrants had a 21.3 percent incidence of minimum-wage violations, a 67.2 percent incidence of overtime violations, and a 68.9 percent incidence of "off the clock" violations, all within the week prior to the study. For U.S. born low-wage workers, the rates were smaller, but still appalling: 15.6 percent experienced minimum-wage violations, 68.2 percent reported overtime violations, and 67.0 percent reported "off the clock" violations.[11] The average worker lost $51 per week, out of $339 in earnings. This level of wage theft translates to $2,634 annually, 15 percent of true annual earnings of $17,616.[12] What would you do with a 15 percent raise? What would a person living in poverty do? That 15 percent difference must be understood as one of the true costs of low prices.

When Eduardo Jaramillo told the *San Francisco Chronicle* he feared that his former employer would make good on a threat to have him deported, he had grounds to be afraid. The study found high percentages of employer retaliation against workers who complained of wage theft. Among workers who made complaints, 62.1 percent experienced one or more forms of illegal retaliation. The most common forms of retaliation were threatening to call immigration authorities, firing or suspending workers, and threatening to cut workers' hours or pay.[13] Among those who did not step forward with complaints, 20 percent said they held back because of fears of such retaliation.[14]

Previous studies have found similar results, in rural and suburban locales as well as urban areas. In Kim Bobo's landmark book, *Wage Theft in America*, the director of Interfaith Worker Justice catalogues research on wage theft prior to 2009. Her findings include:

- ◆ 25 percent of tomato producers, 35 percent of lettuce producers, 51 percent of cucumber producers, 58 percent of onion producers, and 62 percent of garlic producers hiring farm workers stole workers' wages.

- ◆ Almost half of day laborers have had their wages stolen.

- ◆ 100 percent of poultry plants steal workers' wages (through industry-wide practices like not counting time spent donning protective clothing as work).[15]

A high percentage of undocumented migrants work in these areas: farm work, day labor, and poultry processing. Nevertheless, Bobo notes, "Although some of the worst wage theft occurs when immigrant workers aren't paid minimum wage or aren't paid at all, the largest dollar amounts are stolen from native-born white and black workers in unpaid overtime."[16]

Wage and Hour Division Fails to Protect Low-Wage Workers

How can it be that basic worker protection laws are so flagrantly violated? Isn't the government supposed to enforce these laws? The U.S. Government Accountability Office (GAO) looked into this question from July 2008 to March 2009, investigating complaints about the Wage and Hour Division (WHD) of the Department of Labor. The WHD is the branch of government responsible for protecting workers from violations of the law concerning compensation. Analyzing not only existing cases, but also posing as fictitious workers and employers, the GAO studied the performance of the WHD in responding to the most common forms of wage theft. The results were shocking— revealing an agency inadequately staffed but also mishandling cries for help, sometimes demonstrating gross negligence and even fraud. For example:

♦ Of the ten fictitious cases, only one was judged to be handled appropriately. Three of these cases were never investigated, including one that alleged children were operating dangerous heavy machinery during school hours.[17]

♦ In several real and fictitious cases, when employers agreed to pay back stolen wages, cases were closed without verifying that the wages were paid—even when complainants called back several times to report that they had not received the wages.[18] In one real case, an employer offered to pay for minimum wage and overtime violations but not for stolen tips. WHD did not accept the offer but closed the case without pursuing the stolen tips.

♦ If employers refuse to pay back stolen wages, WHD staff can recommend to management that the case receive a full, in-depth investigation. But in two out of the three fictitious cases in which an employer refused to pay, staff simply told complainants they had a right to sue if they wanted. One investigator responded to pleas for more help by responding, "I've done what I can do, I've asked her to pay you and she can't . . . I can't wring blood from a stone," and then suggested the complainant contact his congressman to ask for increased funding for WHD.

♦ Some investigators lied to complainants about progress on their cases or the reasons for lack of progress.[19]

♦ In one actual case, two garment workers filed complaints "alleging that their former employer did not pay minimum wage and overtime to its workers."[20] In its investigation, WHD learned the employer made employees sign a document attesting that they had been paid "in compliance with the law" before receiving their paychecks. On the next day, an investigator went to the factory and took pictures. No further action was taken until two months later when a second investigator went to the factory. It was empty! A realty broker in the area said that he did not believe the company had relocated, so WHD declared the case closed. GAO auditors working on this report quickly found the factory, three miles away, using publicly available documents.[21]

As you might surmise, WHD has a serious backlog of cases that preclude initiating investigations within six months. GAO investigators found backlogs of seven to eight months at one regional WHD office and thirteen months in another.[22] These backlogs are troubling not just because low-wage workers are not being paid. The statute of limitations to collect back wages under the Fair Labor Standards Act is "two years *from the date of the employer's failure to pay the correct wages*" (italics added for emphasis).[23] However unfair this provision may sound, given the backlog of cases, federal courts have still enforced the statute of limitations, regardless of how long it took WHD to investigate the case.

Although the report *Wage and Hour Division's Complaint Intake and Investigative Processes Leave Low Wage Workers Vulnerable to Wage Theft* came out in 2009, most of the incidents covered took place during the George W. Bush administration. Hilda Solis, the newly arrived secretary of labor in the Obama administration, embraced GAO's findings on March 25, 2009, and announced the hiring of 250 new investigators: 150 funded through a reordering of budget priorities and 100 financed by the 2009 stimulus bill. Secretary Solis also promised to "reinvigorate the work of this important agency,"[24] which many observers saw as a call for retraining investigators to prevent the abuses catalogued in the GAO report.

But, by the end of 2011, the stimulus funding wound down and the climate in Washington became one of cutbacks, not expansion. Wage theft, as we have seen, affects all workers, but undocumented immigrant workers most of all. And it's much more than a few unscrupulous or misinformed employers cutting corners. The 2009 three-city study demonstrated that wage theft has become a form of institutionalized violence against low-wage workers within our society, and for low-wage workers, the 15 percent loss in salary can be the difference between poverty and getting by. Wage theft also hurts the overall economy because workers can't spend stolen wages.

Because of the lack of law enforcement, an unfair choice is put before those employers who do comply with the law. Their choice is this: they can continue to obey the law, but face competition from those who lower their operating costs through wage theft, or they can adopt the same methods in order to stay competitive. The "race to the bottom" is therefore not simply overseas—it is here in the United States.

Wage theft against undocumented immigrants (as well as documented migrants and U.S. citizens) is a cruel dimension of the violence of globalization. But even more brutal is the victimization of day laborers, the vast majority of whom are undocumented migrants. Employers victimize day laborers not only through widespread wage theft, but also through the flagrant disregard of workplace safety laws.

Day Laborers: The Most Vulnerable Workers in America

According to the 2006 National Day Labor Study, funded by the Ford Foundation and researched by four scholars of urban poverty, on any given day approximately 117,600 workers are employed as day laborers in the construction industry as carpenters, roofers, painters, and drywall installers, gardeners and landscapers, as farm workers, cleaners, movers, child care, and restaurant workers. The study found that 80 percent of all U.S. day laborers were from Central America or Mexico. Nearly half of all day laborers had been victims of total wage theft in the two months prior to the survey; that is, they had been completely denied payment for work completed. Additionally, 48 percent were found to be paid below minimum wage; 28 percent were insulted or threatened by employers; 27 percent were abandoned at the worksite by their employer; and 18 percent were subjected to direct violence by their employer.[25]

A second, Associated Press investigation found that hazards facing Mexican workers in the United States claim the life of a worker every day. Workers die cutting tobacco in North Carolina, cutting beef in Nebraska, cutting trees in Colorado, trimming grass in California, falling from roofs in New Jersey, being crushed in collapsing trenches, and being crushed in machinery.[26] The Occupational Safety and Health Administration (OSHA) of the Department of Labor has found that 95 to 99 percent of the time, the death had resulted from noncompliance with an OSHA regulation that would have prevented the fatal injury.[27]

During the boom years of residential construction, immigrant workers did not fare well. In 2002, more Mexican workers in the construction industry died of fatal falls than from any other cause. Those who survived falls suffered paraplegia, quadriplegia, and brain damage. The Centers for Disease Control and Prevention (CDC) has reported that Hispanic workers face a far greater chance of being killed in the workplace than any other demographic group. Nearly one-third of fatal work injuries in construction occurred among Hispanic workers, and the number of Hispanic worker deaths from falls increased 370 percent from 1992 to 2006, CDC research indicates.[28]

Since 1971, OSHA has been requiring residential builders to implement occupational safety and health programs to comply with safety standards related to fall protection. However, it takes time to work safely. Because time is money, frequently decisions are made by builders to save time, even at the risk of endangering workers' lives. It is very rare for an immigrant framer or roofer to have received the proper training related to fall protection, and it is rare that they use reliable fall protection while working at heights.[29]

There are some construction practices that collectively institutionalize violence. For example, on a construction site, the general contractor is the company that runs the job. The general contractor hires a contractor who may hire a subcontractor to do the work. But the general contractor representative, usually called the superintendent, is the top manager. When a worker gets injured because the superintendent permitted the work to be done unsafely in violation of safety standards, the general contractor may be sued for negligence. However, the general contractor can get the job done quicker and cheaper if he or she permits the contractor or subcontractor workers to do so in violation of safety standards. It takes time and costs money to work safely.

In order to work quickly and to protect themselves from the cost of lawsuits, general contractors will require a contractor or subcontractor to buy insurance to cover the expenses of a lawsuit. So, when catastrophic injury or death occurs, the general contractor has protected his or her economic interests. He or she can then require or permit the contractor or subcontractor to work quickly and unsafely but not worry about the welfare of the workers or any legal liability. This is simply a method of institutionalizing violence.

When a worker falls from a roof or through an unguarded stairway opening, the general contractor may be sued by the injured worker for not requiring the subcontractor to install fall protection. In order to avoid the cost of a lawsuit, the general contractor will often require the subcontractor to purchase liability insurance or sign a contract with an "indemnification" or "save harmless" clause requiring the subcontractor's insurance company to pay for the cost if injury occurs. So the general contractor is protected from economic harm but permits the worker to be exposed to physical harm. Again, institutionalized violence.

There is also a good chance that an injured immigrant worker will not receive medical care. The National Day Labor Study found that more than half (54 percent) of day laborers who had been injured on the job did not receive medical care for their injury. They found that only 6 percent of injured day laborers had medical expenses covered by their employer's workers' compensation programs. The employers simply deny coverage or threaten workers with nonpayment of wages or other forms of retaliation should they attempt to file a workers' compensation claim.[30] The 2009 three-city study of wage theft also found alarming levels of retaliation against workers injured on the job.

The 2009 wage-theft study included many sectors of the low-wage economy, not just construction, and 12 percent of the respondents experienced "a serious on-the-job injury," defined as one that *should* receive medical attention, during the previous three years of work, but only 8 percent of those seriously injured filed a workers' compensation claim for their most recent injury. Forty-three percent of seriously injured respondents said they were required to work despite the injury, 30 percent said their employer refused to help them with the injury, 13 percent were fired after the injury, and 4 percent were threatened with deportation.[31] Only 40 percent of employers paid part or all of the medical bills for those seriously injured; 6 percent had the bills paid by workers' compensation. The majority of seriously injured workers were responsible for the bills themselves.[32]

It is easy for the general contractor or builder to get away with violating the law because there are so few OSHA inspectors, fewer than 1,200 nationwide,[33] compared to over 7,200 fish and game wardens in the United States.[34] Even if OSHA investigates a fatal accident, the fine will likely be minimal. And the great majority of the time OSHA fails to fine builders even though administrative procedures say it should. OSHA is supposed to pursue willful violations of its standards that result in death, but it rarely follows its multiemployer citation policy.[35] OSHA, like WHD, is affected by the priorities of the president and the limitations of its budget.

Immigrant workers are often employed by temporary labor agencies. They are sent to work in a factory and paid minimum wage or just a bit more. The factory owner will often find it cheaper to use workers from the temporary agencies than to pay all of the federal, state, and workers' compensation costs normally associated with labor costs of workers on the payroll. When temporary workers get injured, they may be threatened by a representative of the temporary labor agency with being reported to immigration and being sent to their country of origin if they file a workers' compensation claim or lawsuit. These workers are the most desperate and compliant of workers in the United States. They will rarely complain of being exposed to workplace hazards, although they are often exposed to risks of serious or catastrophic injury. Examples of recent injuries suffered by immigrant workers due to violations of OSHA standards include:

- A woman's hair was caught on a pulley under a belt conveyor, which ripped her scalp and face off.

- A man was required to clean a screw conveyor while the power was on and had his foot amputated.

- A worker fell while working on a roof of a new house under construction and died. He wasn't provided with a full body harness with a lanyard and lifeline.

- A worker fell and suffered paralysis while working from a scaffold without a guardrail.

- A worker was buried and died when a trench collapsed.[36]

- One hundred seventeen workers, mostly Mayan immigrants, were hospitalized at a recycling plant in New Bedford, Massachusetts, after exposure to a still unidentified chemical.[37]

Many workers, especially immigrants and members of racial minorities, are required to work while exposed to a variety of industrial toxins, fall hazards, machine hazards, electrical hazards, and so on.

Industrial decision makers usually know of the dangers of the workplace but too often decide not to spend the money to control the hazard. When a worker suffers amputation, lung disease, cancer, a heart attack, or heatstroke, it is an act of violence. It is institutionalized violence because the U.S. political, economic, and legal system is designed in such a way that when a worker is catastrophically injured, sickened, or killed, the culprits do not have to pay the full cost of the injury, disease, or death. Instead of the system providing companies with incentives to prevent worker injury, it provides disincentives. For there to be incentive to prevent injury, the primary culprit, the employer should be required to pay the full costs of the injuries. As the system and contracts are designed, those costs are shifted to the workers, their families, and to the hospitals if treatment is given. The culprit gets a "free ride" on the backs of the workers, their families, and hospitals. This combination of pressure to produce profit, lax law enforcement, and the assignment of responsibility through contracts illustrate how violence against immigrant workers has been institutionalized.

The United States has a long history of taking advantage of immigrant labor. Immigrants built the rails, skyscrapers, and dams. They toiled in slaughterhouses and factories. Immigrant children worked in the mines and the mills. But over the years, by organizing, workers fought for the end of child labor and for the enforcement of safety and health protection laws. Such laws are now in place and should provide justice to all workers, including the recently arrived.

WHAT THE CHURCH TEACHES

Catholic teaching on wage theft and immigration originates in the Hebrew scriptures, matures in the letters of the New Testament, and addresses the modern age through Catholic social doctrine. In the Torah, when Moses offers the Deuteronomic code, or "second law" of God, to the people of Israel, he includes the admonition "You shall not defraud a poor and needy hired servant, whether he be one of your own countrymen or one of the aliens who live in your communities. You shall pay him each day's wages before sundown on the day itself, since he is poor and looks forward to them. Otherwise he will cry to the Lord against you, and you will be held guilty" (Deut. 24:14–15). Note the class of worker described—the immigrant day laborer!

In Leviticus, Moses passes on more of God's law, including several rules of conduct relating to purity. Among them is "You shall not withhold overnight the wages of your day laborer" (Lev. 19:13). Again the Lord lifts up the day laborer as the most vulnerable of workers. A strong stand against wage theft is also present in the New Testament, in the letter of James, who writes, "Behold, the wages you withheld from the workers who harvested your fields are crying aloud, and the cries of the harvesters have reached the ears of the Lord of hosts" (James 5:4). This injunction and the laws pronounced in Deuteronomy and Leviticus undergird Catholic teaching on wages. Broadening the context from simply agricultural, service, or day labor, the *Catechism of the Catholic Church* asserts, "To refuse or withhold (wages) can be a grave injustice."[38]

The focus on the immigrant or "alien" day laborer in Deuteronomy is part of an overall emphasis on hospitality toward strangers, aliens, and migrants in the Hebrew scriptures. This weighting of charity (what is given out of love) and justice (what is due a person) toward immigrants begins in the book of Genesis (18:1–10) when Abraham provides lavish hospitality to three strangers and continues into the laws of the Covenant Code pronounced by Moses in Exodus 23:9: "You shall not oppress an alien; you well know how it feels to be an alien, since you were once aliens yourselves in the land of Egypt." This preferential option for immigrants appears again in Leviticus 19:33–34: "When an alien resides with you in your land, do not molest him. You shall treat the alien who resides with you no differently than the natives born among you; have the same love for him as yourself; for you too were once aliens in the land of Egypt," and Deuteronomy 10:19: "So you too must befriend the alien, for you were once aliens yourselves in the land of Egypt."

In the New Testament, the childhood narrative of the Gospel of Matthew places the Holy Family as refugees in Egypt, indentifying Christ with migrants throughout the world. And Jesus' description of the Last Judgment in the Gospel of Matthew calls to mind those who have given immigrants cups of cold water or meals, not to mention visited them in jails and detention centers: "I was hungry and you gave me food, I was thirsty and you gave me drink, . . . in prison and you visited me" (Matt. 25:35).

Rooted in scripture and natural law, Catholic social doctrine upholds and affirms the church's commitment to caring for migrants of all kinds. The *Catechism* states "The more prosperous nations are obliged, to the extent they are able, to welcome the foreigner in search of the security and the means of livelihood which he cannot find in his country of origin."[39] At the same time, public authorities are responsible for determining the legal basis for immigration, and immigrants should respect local laws and traditions once they migrate.[40] Lest we fall into the trap of believing that Catholic concern for immigrants is limited to legal, documented migrants, John Paul II offers an important clarification in his apostolic exhortation on the church in North, South, and Central America, *Ecclesia in America*, noting that immigrant rights must be respected "even in cases of non-legal immigration."[41]

The *Compendium of the Social Doctrine of the Church* offers a succinct summary of Catholic social doctrine on immigration, summarizing the papal encyclicals and documents of Vatican II:

> *Institutions in host countries must keep careful watch to prevent the spread of the temptation to exploit foreign labourers, denying them the same rights enjoyed by nationals, rights that are to be guaranteed to all without discrimination* [original italics]. Regulating immigration according to criteria of equity and balance is one of the indispensible conditions for ensuring that immigrants are integrated into society with the guarantees required by recognition of their human dignity. Immigrants are to be received as persons and helped, together with their families, to become part of societal life. In this context, the *right of reuniting families should be respected and promoted* [original italics]. At the same time, conditions that foster increased work opportunities in people's place or origin are to be promoted as much as possible.[42]

This last instruction has been described as championing "the right not to migrate," the notion that beyond respecting the rights of immigrant workers, we should be working to eliminate the "push" factors that drive people to leave family and homeland. In the United States, it is commonly known that the Catholic Church supports the right of persons to migrate, but this right is mitigated by the responsibility of nations to control their boundaries to promote the common good. Yet the church's support of the right of a person to remain in her or his native place is less well known, even among immigrant advocates.

This concern for conditions in sending countries is one reason the Catholic bishops of Mexico and the United States came together in 2003 to address the issue of immigration, bringing together their considerable experience with immigration from Mexico to the United States. In their joint statement, *Strangers No Longer: Together on the Journey of Hope*, the two national bishops' conferences addressed the phenomenon of globalization and migration as it affected the two countries. Offering a thorough review of Catholic social doctrine and scripture regarding immigration, the bishops noted five key themes:

1. Persons have a right to find opportunities in their homeland.

2. Persons have the right to migrate to support themselves and their families.

3. Sovereign nations have the right to control their borders.

4. Refugees and asylum seekers should be afforded protection.

5. The human dignity and human rights of undocumented migrants should be respected.[43]

These principles of Catholic social doctrine, as well as church teaching on wage theft, undergird church efforts to help the group of workers who have been the most vulnerable since the time of Moses—immigrant workers.

SIGNS OF HOPE

Wage-Theft Victims Fight Back with Workers' Center Help

The days of the full-time "labor priest" may have waned, but today Catholic clergy and laity come together with people of all faiths to stand with workers, helping them understand and act upon their rights while seeking public policy solutions that respect the dignity of work and the rights of workers. Interfaith Worker Justice (IWJ), a national organization based in Chicago, has been at the forefront of these efforts. Since the founding of IWJ in 1996, forty-five local religion and labor groups have been founded to help the religious community address the issues faced by low-wage workers. These organizations respond to specific cases of worker rights violations, develop partnerships between local faith communities and the labor movement, help workers exercise their rights to form unions, and advocate for public policies that promote and secure the rights of workers.

In dialogue with both immigrant and native-born workers, IWJ affiliates have also developed workers' centers, spin-off organizations that provide services for low-wage workers, organize them, and engage in public policy advocacy. These workers' centers have become beacons for victims of wage theft, who often have nowhere else to turn. Rebecca Fuentes, coordinator of the Workers' Center of Central New York, leads one such organization.

On September 4, 2010, Fuentes received a call for help that would eventually shake the region. She was shopping with her mother when the phone rang. On the other line was a social worker from University Hospital in Syracuse—two Mexicans working at the New York State Fair had been treated for infected bed-bug bites and dehydration. They needed a ride back to the fair. Could she help?[44]

Fuentes called Pat Rector, a member of the Central New York Labor–Religion Coalition, and the two women went to the emergency room to meet the workers. There, she met Rosales Rios and another worker. After picking up the two men's prescriptions, they set out to find a pharmacy open on a Saturday night.

The long ride to the pharmacy gave Fuentes and Rector a chance to hear Rios's story. The 23 year-old Durango, Mexico, native had met a recruiter from the United States back in Durango who promised $10.71 per hour to work U.S. carnivals throughout the summer. Work at home had been scarce, and only paid about $5.00 a day. Working in the United States on an H-2B temporary visa would help him support his wife, three-year-old son, three younger brothers, and parents.

What Rios and eighteen other Mexican workers found inside the New York State Fair's "Peter's Fine Greek Foods" tent was more chamber of horrors than a pleasant summer job. The men worked sixteen to eighteen hours per day making chicken gyros and other Greek foods, with one fifteen-minute break and one meal daily. They slept nine to ten men per trailer on bed-bug-infested mattresses. One day they worked twenty-four hours straight. For this effort, they were eventually paid $1.00 per hour.[45]

According to the criminal complaint filed by Thomas Kirwin, a Homeland Security Immigrations and Customs Enforcement agent, when Rios complained to the owner, Pantelis (Peter) Karageorgis about not being paid his full wages, Karageorgis threatened the workers with firing (resulting in automatic deportation, according to the terms of the H-2B visa), cutting their pay (to what level below $1.00/hour, the criminal complaint does not say), preventing them from ever returning to or working in the United States again, and canceling their visas and having them deported. He also called Rios and other workers who became ill or injured, "pussies."[46]

After filling the prescriptions, Fuentes and Rector took the men out for bean burritos (they could no longer stomach chicken). Fuentes recalled Rios crying as he showed them a picture of his son. "I never imagined that you would find this kind of thing in a place like a fair," she said.[47] That night Rector could not sleep. She had seen poor treatment of workers over the years, but this was the worst. She had to do something.

At 5:30 on Sunday morning, Rector called several other members of the Labor–Religion Coalition and invited them to a Labor Day prayer service at the fair. She also left messages with contacts at the area WHD office. Later, Ruth Beltran, a WHD investigator, arrived at the fair (on her day off—providing an example of the contrast between WHD's responses before and after the GAO report). Beltran spent the next two days investigating and interviewing fair workers during their few breaks. Several were treated for dehydration at the fair infirmary after their interviews. Some had lost up to fifteen pounds during their time at the New York State Fair.[48]

On September 9, Karageorgis was arrested by Immigration and Customs Enforcement agents. When confronted with the provisions of the law he violated, he blamed his attorney and recruiters. Karageorgis was ultimately fined $50,000 by WHD and ordered to pay back wages of $115,900.88. A civil class action lawsuit is still pending. As a result of this case, the New York State Department of Labor developed and now distributes at fairs Spanish-language brochures specifying the rights of fair workers. In addition, the Mexico-based Centro de los Derechos del Migrante reaches out to Mexican workers *before* they come to the United States, helping potential guest workers understand their legal rights at the outset and know whom to turn to for help when these rights are violated.[49]

If it were not for the Workers' Center of Central New York and the New York Labor–Religion Coalition, this case would have gone unnoticed, as just one more unchallenged incident of wage theft against immigrant workers. It takes organized people of compassion and charity, working together with local and federal law enforcement agencies, to stop wage theft. This case is a good place to start in considering how wage theft becomes institutionalized in particular sectors of the economy. Imagine you are a business owner, and your competitor is paying his workers $1/hour. What kind of pressures does that put on you? When a significant number of employers get away with wage theft, perverse incentives arise and sinful structures victimize low-wage workers, especially immigrant workers. In order to combat these sinful structures, some workers' centers are augmenting their efforts to enforcing existing laws with new public-policy initiatives.

Increasing the Effectiveness of Law Enforcement

Successes like the Karageorgis case energize workers' centers and their allies, but the sheer scope of the wage-theft epidemic often leaves victims' advocates exhausted. The scarcity of law enforcement resources can be frustrating. In states like Florida, which lacks a statewide department of labor, employers who commit wage theft are answerable mainly to the understaffed WHD and its notorious southeast office, which came under heavy criticism in the GAO report. Under the current system, wage-theft victims have to get in

Coalition of Immokalee Workers demonstrators demand Chipotle restaurants join its Fair Food campaign.

line behind thousands of others as the clock ticks on the two-year statute of limitations.

Working with legal advocates, immigrant rights groups, unions, and university researchers, South Florida Interfaith Worker Justice cofounded the Florida Wage Theft Task Force in 2006 to explore new ways to fight wage theft. Members of the task force have utilized a number of strategies including direct conciliation (settling a dispute outside of the courts) of claims by member organizations, public shaming of chronic offenders, and education of low-wage workers about their rights and what to do if they become victims of wage theft. Their biggest success to date has been the 2010 passage of Miami–Dade County's Wage Theft Ordinance, which brings the resources of the county to bear on claims of wage theft.

To implement the ordinance, the Miami–Dade County Department for Small Business Development (SBD) developed a process for conciliating claims. If the worker and employer cannot work out a settlement mediated by SBD, a "hearing examiner" judges the case.

If the examiner finds the employer guilty, the employer must pay the wages owed, plus two times those wages as damages.[50] This latter provision sends a message to other employers that they must pay employees properly.

Although the ordinance passed unanimously, there has been pushback by some elements of the statewide business community, particularly the National Federation for Independent Businesses, a construction lobby, and the Florida Retail Federation. A bill was introduced in both houses of the Florida legislature that would strike down the Miami–Dade County ordinance and prohibit Florida cities and counties from passing their own wage-theft laws, but so far, attempts to pass it have been stymied.[51] SFIWJ has been working hard to protect the ordinance and help advocates who have passed antiwage-theft laws and ordinances, in San Francisco; New York; Fayetteville, Arkansas; and Grand Rapids, Michigan. The states of Illinois and Texas are watching carefully.

New data from a Florida International University Center for Labor Research and Studies Report, *Wage Theft in Florida: A Real Problem with Real Solutions,* strengthened SFIWJ's resolve to protect the wage-theft ordinance. The study found a continued high prevalence of wage theft, especially for workers in the accommodation and food-service industry, a mainstay of the South Florida economy. The study, which focused on Miami–Dade and Palm Beach counties, also noted that the incidence of wage theft has increased since the advent of the Great Recession,[52] underscoring the need for new strategies and tools to stop this form of institutionalized violence.

Immokalee Workers Promote Fast-Food Justice

The Immokalee workers know something about developing new strategies. As farm workers, these tomato pickers in southwest Florida are not subject to the overtime pay provisions of the Fair Labor Standards Act (FSLA). Those employed by small farms with six or fewer employees are not even covered by the minimum-wage standards. Injustice against farm workers, an almost entirely immigrant workforce, has been a staple of journalistic exposes since Edward R. Murrow's 1960 Thanksgiving Day documentary *Harvest of Shame.* But farm worker justice has been elusive, in part because farm workers lack the legal protections that other classes of workers in the United States enjoy.

In 2001 the Coalition of Immokalee Workers (CIW) decided that they had had enough of falling real wages and, in some cases, degrading working conditions. They announced a boycott of Taco Bell for its refusal to consider providing for a penny-a-pound increase in wages for tomato pickers. At the time, workers earned 40 cents for each thirty-two–pound container they filled, the same wage they had earned in 1975.

The boycott grew in strength as religious groups including the U.S. Conference of Catholic Bishops' Catholic Campaign for Human Development and the National Council of Churches lent their support. Over three hundred religious and secular universities supported boycotts, and twenty-one colleges removed or blocked Taco Bell from doing business on campus. After four years of the boycott, Taco Bell's parent corporation, Yum! Brands, Inc., agreed to the penny-a-pound increase and added language in its supplier code of conduct indicating that "indentured servitude" would not be tolerated.[53]

Next target: McDonald's. A similar boycott, buttressed by strong religious and student involvement, ensued. In 2007, not long after the Adrian Dominican Sisters, the Jesuits of the New Orleans Province, and the Sisters of Charity of the Blessed Virgin Mary cosponsored a shareholder resolution to require McDonald's to apply its overseas suppliers code of conduct to the tomato fields of Florida, McDonald's agreed to the penny-a-pound increase, updated its supplier code of conduct, and agreed to independent monitoring.[54] After a bruising one-year battle with Burger King, that hamburger giant agreed to an increase of 1.5 cents per pound, the extra half-cent earmarked for payroll taxes and administrative costs for tomato growers.[55]

Even with these agreements negotiated, the Florida Tomato Growers Exchange (FTGE), the association representing 90 percent of the state's tomato growers, balked at passing the raise on to tomato pickers. Citing "antitrust" concerns, a representative of the growers' association told the *New York Times*, "I think its un-American when you get people outside your business to dictate terms of business to you, to tell you to do something that your lawyers tell you is illegal."[56] Most legal experts scoffed at the growers' reasoning, and the association eventually dropped its threat of $100,000 fines for growers that cooperated with the fast-food giants in passing the raise on. Former Republican governor Charlie Crist also weighed in, supporting the Fair Food Campaign and admonishing the FTGE for its intransigence.

The penny-a-pound effort has now grown into what the CIW calls its Fair Food Campaign. The Fair Food Campaign has targeted and won over several food-service industry leaders like Bon Appé-tit, Sodexo, Compass, Chipotle Mexican Grill, and Aramark, as well as Whole Foods Supermarket and Trader Joe's. By 2012, boycotts and negotiations involving grocery giants Kroger and Ahold (Stop & Shop, Giant) had begun, in earnest. CIW continues to receive awards and attention for its successful efforts to unite consumers and immigrant farm workers to extract some measure of justice for vulnerable immigrant workers.

"Fair Trade Plus" Products: Eliminating the "Push" Factor

Fair Trade certified products have also become a means to alleviate the "push" factors that make people abandon their homes to escape poverty. Producing Fair Trade commodities like bananas, quinoa, and especially coffee affects migration rates by offering farmers a guaranteed price, immune from commodity-market fluctuations, and calculated to provide a living wage. Fair Trade coffee is usually sold to consumers by development-minded roasters, who package and sell the coffee to consumers willing to pay a little more for a premium product that lifts families out of poverty. Despite the widespread availability of Fair Trade coffee, the demand worldwide has not kept up with production. Only 20 percent of coffee that meets Fair Trade standards is sold at the Fair Trade price of $1.26 per pound,[57] an important concern when the market price currently stands at 60 to 70 cents per pound.[58]

Just Coffee, a Catholic Relief Services partner based in Chiapas, Mexico's poorest state, takes the Fair Trade model an additional step. For many years, Fair Trade coffee farmers earned the Fair Trade price of $1.00–1.50 a pound for their labors, an improvement on the low of 18 cents per pound they earned in 2001 selling conventional coffee, but still a small percentage of what you might pay for organic Fair Trade coffee. But by roasting and packing the coffee at their facility in Agua Prieta, a small border city near Tucson, Arizona, the co-op brings in $5–6.00 per pound after expenses, a model that has come to be known as "Fair Trade Plus." The "dirty little secret" of Fair Trade coffee is that most of the money is made by roasters through the roasting and packaging process. Just Coffee's model captures those profits for the farmer.

For the thirty-five families in Chiapas who co-own Just Coffee, Fair Trade Plus has meant the difference between poverty and a living wage, between immigration to the United States and remaining in their native place. It's a small number of people, but their business model is already being replicated in other Mexican Fair Trade coffee projects. It's a sign of hope that recalls Pope Benedict's call for "hybrid forms" of business that seek profit but also pursue "social ends," as described in his encyclical *Charity in Truth*.[59]

Benedict described these kinds of businesses as "civilizing the economy."[60] It is hard to imagine the pope writing these words without reference to slavery in our global economy, for what society can rightfully call itself "civilized" when it benefits from the labor of slaves? From global sweatshops and the structured violence of wage theft and lax safety standards against immigrants in the United States, we now turn to one of humanity's greatest scourges: slavery.

DISCUSSION QUESTIONS

1. Were you surprised at the prevalence of wage-theft experienced by low-wage workers? Why or why not?

2. Have you ever been a victim of wage theft? Do you know someone who has been a victim of wage theft? How did you or they feel? What did you or they do?

3. Why does the phrase "for you were once aliens yourselves in the land of Egypt" appear so frequently in the Hebrew scriptures?

GO MAKE A DIFFERENCE

1. Contact the closest workers' center or Interfaith Worker Justice affiliate and ask how you can help.

2. Gather youth of the parish to discuss their experiences in the workplace—even affluent youth have worked low-wage jobs. Conduct a workers' rights training session for youth or adult workers in your parish.

3. If your parish sponsors a fair, obtain a list of companies utilizing foreign labor from your state department of labor. Set up a meeting with vendors to discuss the parish "code of conduct." If you don't have a parish code of conduct, work with your pastor to develop one.

4. Research ethically produced and union-made products on the web. Three good places to start are responsibleshopper.org, shopunionmade.org, and fairtradefederation.org.[61]

5. Is your own parish practicing wage theft? Are parish workers misclassified as consultants? Are nonexempt workers paid overtime? Do janitors and yard-service workers (even if they are contractors) get paid minimum wage or higher, and do they get paid overtime when appropriate?[62] Find out and discuss with your pastor and finance council.

4

Modern-Day Slavery

It began with a cow and $650. Narayan had borrowed the equivalent of $300 from Mr. Vasu to purchase the livestock, at once a sign of and means to prosperity in India.[1] In return, he agreed to work in Mr. Vasu's brick kiln until he repaid the loan. Narayan calculated about a year's time to meet the terms. When his sister Maya approached Narayan about needing a cash advance to take care of some urgent needs, he thought of Mr. Vasu. Other relatives expressed similar needs, and for a loan of $650, five young couples and their three uncles began working in the brick kiln, Maya's share of the loan totaled $30. For such a small amount of money, she and her husband, Ajay, believed, it would not take long to discharge the debt.

The family of thirteen moved into its quarters at the kiln, a single room, which they nicknamed "the stable." Work began at 6:00 a.m. The women packed mud and straw into wood forms, while the men moved the molds in and out of the hot kiln. Mr. Vasu drove the family of workers with verbal and physical abuse. If they produced less than a thousand bricks in a day, he would say, "You lazy dogs! Why were you so slack today!" and if they produced more than a thousand, he would berate them, saying, "You manipulative cheats! Don't expect to be paid for more than a thousand bricks." Random physical violence became commonplace. On one trip to the well for a drink of water, Mr. Vasu struck Maya on the right ear and said, "Maybe that will help you forget about your thirst!"

Early on, the family ran out of food, and Maya's cousin approached Mr. Vasu about going to the market and purchasing more provisions. Mr. Vasu hit her several times with a stick, yelling, "I will tell you when it's time to go to the market!" The family went hungry for a day, and when the trip was finally organized, Mr. Vasu warned the shoppers, "If you do not come back, I will make this place a living hell for those who are left behind." For the first time, Maya realized she was not free to leave.

After six months, Maya asked for an accounting of the debt. She was astounded to learn that after half a year of labor, her debt had *doubled*. "As you can see," Mr. Vasu explained, handing Maya a ledger, "You have incurred interest on your initial loan. I have also given you a substantial amount of money to pay for your food." After a pause, he smiled and added, "It looks like you are going to have to work harder."

Maya and her family continued their labors. When they exceeded their quota of bricks for the day, Mr. Vasu gave them no credit for their efforts to "work harder." When orders slowed, the kiln would shut down for a few weeks, and Mr. Vasu would tell the men to do chores around the compound, for which they received no compensation, even as interest on their debt continued to accrue. Meanwhile, the women would accompany Mr. Vasu to clean the village temple he built as a gift to the community.

Once inside, they learned the temple's depraved secret—it doubled as a brothel, and it became their role to service local men. Restrained and raped repeatedly, Maya left the temple completely broken. She and her cousins hid their shame and told no one what had happened when they returned to the brick kiln, afraid of further reprisals. They quietly continued their brickmaking, afraid of additional "cleaning" duties at the temple.[2]

SIGNS OF THE TIMES

Modern-Day Slavery

Slavery like Maya's debt bondage exists throughout the world and supports the lifestyle of elites in poor countries and most everyone in developed nations. Slaves from all over Africa, Asia, and Latin America work as maids for the well-to-do in cities and suburbs throughout the world—even in the United States. Slaves in Bangladesh may have cut and sewn your clothing. The cocoa in the chocolate you enjoy may have been harvested by child slaves in the Ivory Coast. Slaves working in India may have made your carpet. In the United States, farm workers have been found working under armed guards as field slaves.

Slaves may have made bricks for the factory in China that manufactured your television. They may have grown the rice that fed the
woman who wove the cloth of your curtains. Slaves work mineral
mines in the Congo. They harvest bananas in Honduras. In Brazil,
slaves may have produced the sugar for your table or the beef on
your plate. Slaves manufacture jewelry in Pakistan. Slaves in Angola
may have mined the diamond in your engagement ring. The gold in
the ring may have come from Mali, where slaves assist gold miners.

In scores of countries, enslaved children have been organized
into begging rings, as portrayed in the film *Slumdog Millionaire*. The
drug trade throughout the world also benefits from slave labor, particularly in Colombia. All over the world, slaves work as prostitutes,
fetching high prices both from sex tourists abroad and in U.S. and
European brothels. In many instances of slavery overseas, slaves
have been trafficked from still-poorer countries.[3]

"Slavery." It sounds so harsh, doesn't it? But the people you will
meet in this chapter are not sweatshop workers; they do not put in
a lot of overtime, or work for a demanding boss. They are not child
laborers. They do not work in "slave-like conditions"; they *are* slaves.
Reliable sources estimate the number of slaves in the world as some-
where between twenty-five and thirty million human beings, a
majority of whom are women and children.

Abolitionist Kevin Bales, president of Free the Slaves, acknowl-
edges that modern-day slavery sometimes defies clear definition,
but, he notes, common elements are present. In evaluating whether
working conditions amount to slavery, we should ask the question,
"Can the person walk away from the situation without fear of violence?" Then we should ask, "Was the person paid either nothing or
compensated at a bare subsistence level?"[4] Modern-day abolitionists distinguish between four main types of slavery: chattel (from the
word "cattle") slavery, debt bondage, sex slavery, and forced labor.[5]
The most common types of modern slavery are often categorized as
"human trafficking," a useful legal term but one that must never be
used to obscure what these forms of institutionalized violence are:
slavery.

We are most familiar with *chattel slavery* because it is part of
our American history. The *legal* buying and selling of persons who

become their master's property was banned in the United States in 1865 by the Thirteenth Amendment to the Constitution. Globally, the legal buying and selling of human beings has been almost entirely extinguished. In only a few places in the world, such as the African nation of Mauritania, is chattel slavery legal.[6]

Debt bondage, however, remains a common form of slavery in some parts of Asia despite its illegality. In the Indian subcontinent, for example, if people like Maya incur (or inherit) a debt they cannot repay, they might be held as slaves until the debt is paid off. But the arrangement is rigged against the debtor. Usurious interest rates and charges for food and housing quickly accrue and ensure that the debt is never fully paid. The obligation is then passed on to the next generation. Whole families and even entire villages have fallen into debt bondage, while laws prohibiting the practice go unenforced.[7]

Sex slavery has drawn millions of women and girls into a nightmare of degrading activity and almost certain illness from sexually transmitted diseases like HIV/AIDS. Many sex slaves were kidnapping victims or fell prey to bogus immigration schemes. They tend to come from the poorest countries in their region of the world. Sex slaves service up to forty men per day in "sex tourism" brothels in the United States, Europe, and parts of Asia, particularly Thailand.

Forced labor is a matter of public policy in China and North Korea, where speaking one's mind can result in time served in a "labor camp." This form of slavery is not limited to totalitarian states, however. Forced labor can be found in agricultural, industrial, and service industries in both rich and poor countries. The slave's experience usually includes abandoning her or his native country, crossing borders, and entering into a situation from which she or he cannot escape.[8] In some countries, child soldiers under threat of physical harm fight on behalf of the nation or a rebel group. Chapter 8, on institutionalized violence against women and children, discusses this dimension of forced labor at length.

Many people are surprised to learn of the resilience and growth of slavery. Despite greater democracy present in the world today, the work of the United Nations, increased enforcement of international law, and stronger coordination among regional bodies like the European Union and African Union, more slaves walk the earth now than in 1860.[9] Kevin Bales offers a three-part explanation for the explosion of modern-day slavery, beginning with the dramatic drop in the price of slaves.

Bales explains that the price of slaves has fallen for three reasons. First, population growth after 1945 brought four billion more people onto our planet. The "supply" of human beings is now greater than any other time in history. Second, neocolonialism (see chapter 2) and the advance of globalization grew the global economy tremendously throughout the past fifty years, but its benefits were not shared equally. The billion or so people living on $1.25 per day were simply "left behind, stuck in the subsistence poverty of the past, or worse."[10] Those "left behind" are the people most vulnerable to slavery: Indians in rural villages far from urban high-tech jobs and the glitz of Bollywood, Africans who farm and herd in countries where HIV/AIDS is widespread and infant mortality high, Latin Americans who populate the unincorporated outskirts of their largest cities.

Finally, Bales points to widespread corruption in developing countries. "In Western Europe, Canada, and the United States," he writes, "slavery happens *in spite of* the efforts of the police, but in many countries slavery flourishes *because of* the work of the police [original italics]." In a world where slavery is now largely illegal, it generally flourishes only where police and public officials turn a blind eye. Bales points to Pakistan as a case in point. In 1988 Pakistan established a law against debt bondage, but not one person has been convicted since its passage, despite several important cases that resulted in the freeing of slaves. In India, the anti-debt-bondage law has been on the books since 1976, but not one slaveholder has served the prescribed three-year jail term (although a few have been fined the equivalent of $2). In some countries, like Thailand and Russia, slaveholder payments follow each step of the police chain of command, on up to government officials. Corruption has become so widespread that law enforcement agencies have developed a retooled mission: *protecting* widespread violations of the law.[11]

These three factors, the global population explosion, persistent global poverty and inequality, and corruption, are responsible for the twenty-first-century explosion of slavery. The great supply of very poor, exploitable people has created a veritable "buyer's market" for slaves. Bales estimates the cost of a slave in 1850 at $40,000, adjusted for inflation, while in many places around the world, less than $100 can fetch a slave today. This precipitous drop in price has also affected the way slaves are treated. Bales writes, "Slaves today are treated like cheap plastic ballpoint pens, the kind we all have in our desk drawers or pockets. No one worries about the care and maintenance of these pens or about keeping a careful record of their whereabouts. No one files a deed of ownership for these pens or sends out a search party if one goes missing. No one takes out insurance on these pens. These pens are disposable, and, because they are so cheap, so are slaves."[12] These insights inspired Bales's term "disposable people."

Slaves who get sick, become injured, or begin to question their status

> are dumped—or worse. The young woman enslaved as a prostitute in Thailand is thrown out onto the street when she tests positive for HIV. The Brazilian man tricked and trapped into slavery making charcoal is tossed out when the forest is razed and no trees are left to cut. The boy in India who spends all day rolling bidi cigarettes is dumped or sent back to his family if he is injured or ill, and the slaveholder will try to take another child in his place. The young woman in Ghana who has been exploited, sexually abused, and impregnated again and again by a trokosi priest, will be sent back to her parents when the priest tires of her or her health breaks down. Enslaved domestic workers around the world will be discarded when their "family" moves to another city or country.[13]

But the abuse of slaves is more than negligence—it's also a means of control. As Jesse Sage and Liora Kasten describe, slaveholders use both physical and emotional cruelties to keep slaves in line and, above all, prevent escape. Modern-day slavemasters "whip, stab, gag, pull out hair and sting with electric prods."[14] They belittle and ridicule slaves until the slaves are so subservient as to lose their own identity. Slavemasters will rename slaves or refuse to use their true names to reinforce that loss of identity. Each one of these abuses is aimed at breaking the slave's will—like breaking a horse—and ensuring compliance.[15]

Drissa and the Chocolate Factory

Slavery taints many of the products we use every day, but no product has elicited such outrage as that which occurred in 2000, after the discovery of child slaves working in Ivory Coast cocoa farms, where almost half of the world's cocoa is produced.[16] Kevin Bales had set out to film child slaves harvesting cotton for a film version of his book *Disposable People*. When he and the filmmakers reached the Ivory Coast, they learned that nineteen teenage boys had just been freed from slavery on a cocoa farm.

The boys were from Mali, a poor nation on the Ivory Coast's northern border, where half the population lives on $1.25 a day or less. They had come to the Ivory Coast looking for work. Three hundred miles from home, in an alien country where they did not speak the language, the teens turned to a local labor recruiter for help. He sold them into slavery.[17]

The teenagers were transported to a farm, far away from view of anyone who might question why they were not in school and never seen with their parents. They worked every day, from sunup to sundown, collecting cocoa pods that one day would be transformed into chocolate bars, a product with which they were unfamiliar. If they grew tired and rested, they were beaten. One of the boys, Drissa, is photographed in Bales's book *Ending Slavery* with numerous welts on his back from whipping.[18] For months, the boys ate nothing but bananas, causing vitamin deficiencies.

Whippings for runaways dissuaded thoughts of escape. In addition, the farmer who held the boys explained he had put a spell on each one of them. If they escaped, "they would be paralyzed and easily recaptured."[19] But one boy did break the purported spell and escaped to a nearby town, where he was able to reach a diplomat from Mali. The official enlisted the help of local police and freed the boys shortly before Bales's camera crew arrived.

Successive teams of journalists have found more child slaves in the cocoa farms of the Ivory Coast. Sometimes called "plantations" in the media, these farms are typically ten acres or less in size. In the

2010 documentary *The Dark Side of Chocolate*, Danish filmmakers U. Roberto Romano and Miki Mistrati found scores of children on Ivory Coast cocoa farms.[20] Like Drissa, all of them were from Mali. The filmmakers traveled to Zegoua, Mali, a southern border town where smuggling sojourns are staged. Public buses bring newly enslaved children to Zegoua; then smugglers traffic groups of ten to twelve slaves into Korogho, Ivory Coast, after transferring in Zegoua. There, they sell the children to individual farmers and plantation owners from a "safe house."

The trafficking of enslaved children through Zegoua has grown so widespread that local bus drivers have been moved to action. Idrissa Kante, secretary of the Sikasso Driver's Union, explains in the film that since 2003 he has rescued hundreds of children. Kante recorded each child's name and circumstance in a notebook. On camera, he leafs through page after page: 132 entries in 2006 (97 boys, 35 girls) and 140 in 2007 (99 boys, 41 girls). In addition, in 2008–2009 he rescued over 150 children. During the filming of interviews with bus company officials, a bus driver rescues a twelve-year-old girl named Mariam Marico. She had traveled from a small, rural village some two hundred miles away, responding to a promise of work. Her return home should be a happy ending, but the viewer fears for the girl. Wounds on her leg suggest some form of abuse at home, and we know she is returning to extreme poverty. She says, "My parents will be angry with me because I did not bring back any money." The bus driver weeps after she departs.

The filmmakers traveled to a village in Mali not far from the border with the Ivory Coast, where 130 children aged twelve to fifteen have been abducted and never seen again. The village chief looked into the situation and became convinced that the children were being sold into cocoa slavery at a nearby market and then transported by motorcycle across the border. In the film, a smuggling transfer from bus to motorcycle is caught on camera.

Later, Malian research assistants outfitted with hidden cameras and microphones slipped into random Ivory Coast cocoa plantations and farms, looking for evidence of child slaves. On screen, footage of numerous children (unrelated to farmers) harvesting cocoa was spliced with the unequivocal denials of a cocoa company executive.

A government official's denials were also captured, including his assertions that the children riding the buses into the Ivory Coast were "on vacation." In the film, footage follows of children performing various farm chores. A voice-over dryly states, "These children are definitely not on vacation."[21]

No one can view *The Dark Side of Chocolate* and maintain that child slavery in cocoa production has been eradicated. But that is what many chocolate companies continue to insist, even as they stymie certification measures for slave-free chocolate. Almost a decade elapsed between the filming of the two documentaries. One might expect greater progress in the eradication of child slavery.

The outcry that followed *Disposable People* resulted in the 2001 passage in the U.S. House of Representatives of an amendment to an agriculture appropriations bill sponsored by Rep. Elliot Engel (D-NY), allowing the Food and Drug Administration to require a "no child slavery" label on chocolate products.[22] Cocoa industry lobbyists, including former Senators Bob Dole (R-KS) and George Mitchell (D-ME),[23] responded quickly, fiercely opposing Tom Harkin's Senate bill. They argued against the "no child slavery" label, maintaining first that American chocolate companies could not be expected to make and enforce rules in a foreign country, and second, if they did not use the slave cocoa, their competitors would do so, and therefore undercut their business.[24] Cocoa company executives ultimately yielded, agreeing to voluntary steps, or a "protocol," in exchange for Senator Tom Harkin's (D-IA) pulling the Senate version of the Engel Amendment.

The Harkin-Engel Protocol put the cocoa industry on record as working toward "credible, mutually acceptable, voluntary industry-wide standards of public certification, consistent with federal law" by 2005. Compliance would be monitored by human rights groups, businesses, and unions working together through an international foundation.[25] When the 2005 deadline passed with no industry-wide standard adopted, it was extended to 2008. When this deadline passed in 2008, it was extended again to 2010. Yet some progress has been made in implementing the protocol. For example, in September 2010, the labor ministers of Ghana and the Ivory Coast, along with the president of the National Confectioners Association, signed

Justin Herron and Grace Chow Grund of Montclair, New Jersey, sell Fair Trade Chocolate at Terra Café to combat child slavery. The Fair Trade market and café is located at the town's public library. Justin is a member of the Fair Trade Club at Montclair High School, and Grace is the proprietor of Terra Café.

a Declaration of Joint Action to Support Implementation of the Harkin-Engel Protocol, aiming to reduce child slavery by 70 percent by the year 2020. Hilda Solis, secretary of the U.S. Department of Labor, announced a U.S. commitment of $10 million to "remediate children caught in the worst forms of child labor."[26] In 2012 Hershey announced new commitments to purchase cocoa from certified sustainable producers far less likely to be utilizing child slaves. Even so, as of 2013 no industry-wide standard has been adopted.

The public outrage of the past decade, following revelations of child slavery in cocoa farming, has brought needed attention and some progress, but we are still far from a covenant for slave-free certification. Perhaps the force of law found in legislation like California's

Transparency in Supply Chains Act (see chapter 2) and in the original Engel Amendment is needed. Ultimately, the California law may have more of an impact on child slavery in the cocoa industry than the Harkin-Engel Protocol.

At this time, the burden remains on the chocolate companies to implement the protocol they agreed to over a decade ago. We put a man on the moon in less than ten years. We found Osama Bin Laden in less than a decade. Ten years seems time enough to eradicate child slavery in the chocolate business. Consumers of chocolate in the United States (are you one?) must demand that the chocolate companies finish the job.

Sex Slavery on the Balkan Trail

The enslavement of children tears at our sense of justice in the world, but the enslavement of women and girls for sexual exploitation provokes ever greater outrage. According to the U.N. Office on Drugs and Crime, 1,920,000 people worldwide are trafficked as sexual slaves, and only one out of a hundred victims is ever rescued.[27] Eastern Europe has become a center for sex tourism and the trafficking of women and girls into Western Europe and the United States for sex slavery. Why? Because poor white women and girls live there.

The journalist E. Benjamin Skinner spent a month undercover in Romania, studying the sex trade from within. There, one-third of the population lives in poverty, and many women, who flocked to Bucharest in search of work, have become sex slaves. Skinner drove through neighborhoods where sex clubs have proliferated like fast-food franchises in American suburbs. He walked down streets where "Sex—fifty Euros!" is the standard greeting. He met one man who offered him three months' use of a sex slave in exchange for a used car.

Skinner visited the Gara de Nord railway station in Bucharest, where a thousand orphans, deinstitutionalized after communism, live in the sewers but emerge to service sex tourists and local men. The older children serve as pimps and reward compliant younger children with candy and glue for sniffing. There, Skinner received a tip on where he could buy a girl and continued on to a Roma (Gypsy) ghetto in Bucharest.

When he reached the Bucharest address, Skinner haggled with the Roma proprietor for some time until they reached agreement. The brothel owner would not sell any of his slaves, but he would take a reliable used car in exchange for three months' use of a young woman with Down Syndrome. It was all Skinner could do to control his nausea and stay in character.[28]

Building on Skinner's participant-observer experience, David Batstone explains the reach of the sexual enslavement of Eastern European women in his book *Not for Sale,* drawing attention to the "Balkan Trail." According to his research, thousands of women are abducted annually throughout Eastern Europe and distributed to brothels throughout the world. Their journey usually begins in one of the republics of the former Soviet Union. Smugglers traffic the newly enslaved through Romania to one of the former Yugoslav republics, then to Albania, and on to Italy. From Italy, the women are typically moved to one of the more prosperous European Union countries, though many end up in the United States, the Middle East, or one of Asia's red-light districts. Batstone describes a moment in Bangkok, Thailand, which demonstrates the reach of the Balkan Trail:

> As soon as night falls, a flood of blond girls wearing mini-skirts and heavy makeup ambulate the Muslim quarter. It's a bizarre scene—these eastern European women weaving along the sidewalks amid a sea of Muslim women wholly covered in black burkas. The Muslim men, meanwhile, don white pants, white shirts, and white hats. The white is meant to represent purity of intention and action.[29]

It's hard not to question the "purity of intention and action" of some of these men, given the demand they have created for Balkan Trail survivors.

Batstone traces the beginnings of widespread sexual slavery in Eastern Europe to the fall of the Soviet Union. Under communism, many problems existed, but unemployment was minimal, and the social safety net caught most on their way down. During the rocky transition to capitalism in the 1990s, a small number of people amassed great wealth, while the vast majority faced rising unemployment, without the safety net communism once offered. With the police state withering away throughout the former Soviet republics, organized crime stepped in to fill the power vacuum. Many of the new crime bosses were former Communist Party leaders.[30] Nearly all had some connection to the Russian Mafia.[31]

These newly minted mafiosi noted the disproportionate impact of unemployment on women in the former Soviet republics, which ranged from 70 to 80 percent, depending on the country. Many were desperate for work. Predators affiliated with organized crime preyed on the dreams of many of these young women—to live a prosperous life in Western Europe. With promises of jobs, "recruiters" lured young women and teenage girls into abductions, and their Balkan Trail journey began.

Today, sex slavery is a problem throughout the world, not just in Eastern Europe and the countries to which their sex slaves are exported. Nearly every country profiled in the 184 profiles found in the 2011 U.S. *Trafficking in Persons Report* supplies, transports, or receives sexual slaves—even the "good" Tier One countries. Sex slaves make up almost half of all slaves in the world and a significant number of the estimated 17,000 slaves in the United States.[32] As noted above, almost two million sex slaves live in bondage, and only about 1 percent ever escape this ugly manifestation of the violence of globalization.

Twenty-First Century American Field Slaves

Many Americans would concede that some forms of sexual slavery persist, but the notion of field slaves under armed guard harvesting crops would, to their ears, sound like a scene out of a history book. Could forced labor happen today in the United States? Just ask Miguel,[33] a Mexican worker enslaved in 2004 in the orange groves of south Florida. Back in Mexico, Miguel's son developed cancer, and Miguel's $60 per-week salary only began to cover copayments for treatment. Miguel borrowed $300 to get to the U.S. border with some friends and then "looked around and asked around for somebody who would give us a ride across and who we could work for; someone who could pay for our ride and then we could pay them back."[34]

That somebody was Ramiro Ramos, who made the arrangements for the illegal crossing in exchange for a pledge from the men to work off their transportation costs by picking oranges for him on behalf of several farmers. When the workers arrived at his orange grove, Ramos's brother, Juan, provided an orientation: "Look, if you want to work here, you're gonna work here, and it's hard work. You gotta work, you gotta be motivated, and you gotta cut oranges, and you gotta harvest those oranges, you gotta use a big heavy knife. And if any of you a-holes try to leave without paying your ride, that's when I'm gonna really f-k you up."

The Ramoses charged for room, board, and check cashing, and these costs began to pile up alongside Miguel's debt. He worked from sunup to sundown harvesting oranges, getting paid by the bucket. A day's work yielded only $28, hardly enough to begin paying down the ballooning debt.

Juan Ramos suspected one of Miguel's friends of planning to escape. Miguel overheard the younger Ramos talking on a cell phone, threatening to throw the man into an alligator-infested pond. Miguel and his friends caucused. They needed to find a way out, but they were afraid—forty men guarded them.

Miguel's story is not unique. Whether we realize it or not, whether we want it or not, slave labor supports the lifestyle of most of us in developed countries. People like Miguel, Maya, and the other workers profiled in this chapter subsidize elites in their own countries and most everyone in developed countries. Modern forms of slavery such as debt bondage and forced labor give us lower prices but violate human dignity and provide an even lower bottom toward which businesses can race.

WHAT THE CHURCH TEACHES

Let's face it—the Catholic Church has a mixed record on slavery. Until the publication of Vatican II's *Pastoral Constitution on the Church in the Modern World* (*Gaudium es Spes*), church teaching on slavery varied according to shifting theological currents and the economic interests of Catholics. The church never completely embraced the "peculiar institution," but it also never fully condemned slavery. All the way back to the time of the apostles, some letters of Paul suggest continuity with long-standing secular, pagan, and Jewish traditions of enslavement, while others imply abolitionist sympathies. Paul admonished slaves to "be obedient to your human masters with fear and trembling" (Eph. 6:5), but he also encouraged Philemon to regard the slave Onesimus as a "a brother" in Christ (Phil. 1:16) and insisted that in Christ Jesus "there is neither slave nor free person (Gal. 3:28)."

Some early saints, like the freed slave St. Patrick,[35] preached for the abolition of slavery or limiting its duration, but generally, the church staked out a middle ground, calling for humane and just treatment of slaves, but not demanding the outright abolition of slavery. St. Thomas Aquinas argued for slavery as a punishment for crimes and spoke against aiding runaway slaves. At the same time, he advocated for slaves' rights to food, rest, marriage or celibacy, and the raising of children.[36]

Through the 1400s, the church held to variants of Aquinas's formulation, even as some church leaders pushed for abolition. At times popes, religious orders, and clergy would own slaves; in other eras, priests, brothers, and sisters formed religious orders to free slaves. Meanwhile, a consensus against the enslavement of Christians—even the recently baptized—began to emerge in the fifteenth century.[37]

The dawn of colonialism, with its voracious appetite for slave labor, vastly expanded Christian ownership of slaves, and this development brought new pressures on the church to reaffirm the right to own slaves. The church returned to condemning "unjust" slavery but not slavery itself. As late as 1866 (over three years after Abraham Lincoln's Emancipation Proclamation), Pope Pius IX affirmed the right of slaveholders to buy, sell, and otherwise exchange slaves, subject to Aquinas's conditions of justice within slavery.[38] The Jesuits in the United States owned slaves well into the nineteenth-century, as did the Carmelites, the Sisters of Charity, and the Sisters of Loretto in Kentucky.[39]

However, nineteenth century abolitionist currents were already changing the direction of church teaching on slavery. At the 1815 Congress of Vienna, Pope Pius VII joined the consensus calling for the suppression of the slave trade. In 1839, Pope Gregory XVI issued a bull (a formal papal communication) condemning new enslavements and slave trading. He also forcefully denounced slavery in general but offered no call for emancipation.[40] Pope Pius IX's 1866 affirmation of slaveholders' rights confused matters further. But when Brazil abolished slavery in 1888, the last predominantly Catholic slaveholding nation turned away from chattel slavery, leaving little opposition among the faithful to growing Catholic antislavery sentiment.

The eventual consensus against all forms of slavery finally entered into official church teaching in 1965, at the close of the Second Vatican Council. *The Pastoral Constitution on the Church in the Modern World* stated, "Whatever violates the integrity of the human person, such as mutilation, torture . . . whatever insults human dignity . . . slavery . . . the selling of women and children . . . they are a supreme dishonor to the Creator."[41] What Vatican II called an "infamy" and a "supreme dishonor," John Paul II later declared "intrinsically evil" in his 1993 encyclical *Veritatis Splendor*, or *The Splendor of Truth*.[42]

This shift in the characterization of slavery, from "supreme dishonor" to "intrinsically evil," is important because church teaching now defines slavery as *always* wrong, regardless of circumstances or intentions. It may have taken awhile, but contemporary Catholic social doctrine now places slavery and the trafficking of women and children on a par with the worst offenses against human life and dignity: homicide, genocide, abortion, euthanasia, voluntary suicide, and torture. John Paul's discussion of slavery allows for no exceptions and certainly leaves open no possibility for any form of slavery that could be considered just.[43] Benedict XVI has affirmed this teaching in several speeches and homilies, calling for action against human traffickers.[44]

The *Catechism of the Catholic Church*, updated in 1995, incorporates these latter documents into its treatment of slavery, framing the teaching in reference to the seventh commandment, "You shall not steal":

> The seventh commandment forbids acts or enterprises that for any reason—selfish or ideological, commercial, or totalitarian—lead to the *enslavement of human beings* [original italics], to their being bought, sold and exchanged like

merchandise, in disregard for their personal dignity. It is a sin against the dignity of persons and their fundamental rights to reduce them by violence to their productive value or to a source of profit.[45]

The 2004 *Compendium of the Social Doctrine of the Church* affirms the teaching of the *Catechism*, but also decries "the painful reality of . . . ever new forms of slavery such as trafficking in human beings, child soldiers, the exploitation of workers, illegal drug trafficking, prostitution."[46]

The United States Conference of Catholic Bishops has brought attention to the problem of human trafficking in the United States.[47] Writing in 2007, the bishops noted that the estimated 17,500 slaves in the United States are preyed upon in part because of the lack of comprehensive immigration reform (consider the slaves working in Florida's orange groves), a challenge that still remains.[48] In their "Call to Action" on human trafficking, the bishops present what the church has to offer the modern abolitionist movement: "As a global institution which is present in source nations as well as countries that serve as markets for human trafficking, the Catholic Church is well-positioned to identify and rescue survivors of human trafficking."[49]

SIGNS OF HOPE

As the U.S. bishops note, the global reach of the Catholic Church brings many strengths to its response to modern-day slavery. The church has a presence in almost every nation in the world, through diocesan Catholic Charities and Caritas agencies, parishes, and the leadership of bishops and bishops' conferences. The church's global reach includes countries that send, transport, and receive slaves. Some Catholics are slaves; some, sadly, own slaves; and some work for businesses that knowingly or unknowingly use slave labor. Catholic Relief Services (CRS), together with local partners, operates antitrafficking programs in thirty-six countries.[50] Today's church is abolitionist and collaborative in its efforts to stop human trafficking, partnering with the best antislavery organizations throughout the world to produce concrete signs of hope. Some of these partners emerged out of evangelical Christian missionary work, like the International Justice Mission.

International Justice Mission: Liberating the Captives

In Luke's Gospel, when Jesus opened the scroll in his hometown synagogue and read, "The Spirit of the Lord . . . has sent me to proclaim liberty to captives" (Luke 4:18), he gives Christians a compelling rationale and mandate to liberate slaves. Maya and her family (see chapter opening) were ultimately freed from debt bondage in the brick kiln (and the temple) by the International Justice Mission (IJM). IJM is a U.S.-based NGO founded by evangelical Christian missionaries and human rights activists.

After repeated sexual violations in the temple and one set of rapes of the wives in the presence of their husbands, Maya's family committed to a plan of escape. Her husband overheard Mr. Vasu telling his son about an upcoming overnight festival. When the Vasus departed, Maya and her family clambered over the iron fence surrounding the slave compound and stole away to the nearest bus station. They caught the next bus to their home village, but they feared bounty hunters would soon arrive. After reuniting with relatives in their home village, they agreed it would be safer to hide with more distant relatives on the other side of their province.

As expected, Mr. Vasu responded vindictively to the rescue. He abducted and tortured three of Maya's relatives in the temple in retaliation for their escape. He allowed one, Uncle Amar, to look for the fugitives while Vasu continued to torture the others, threatening them with death if Amar did not return. When Amar arrived at the family hut where Maya was staying, she could hardly recognize him because of the bruises and ritual head shaving he experienced at the hands of Mr. Vasu's thugs. Stricken with guilt over the treatment of their kin, and anticipating the execution of the two still held hostage, the family hatched a plan. Village leaders who heard their story pointed the family toward IJM, a trusted antislavery organization working in the region. Maya and seven members of her family traveled to a safe location where they gave testimony about their treatment. Two days later, IJM staff joined local police in a raid on the kiln compound.

Rescuers liberated a dozen slaves, including the hostages. The next day, Maya and her family visited the local magistrate, who gave them a document that certified they owed nothing to Mr. Vasu. They were free to go, and as freed debt-bondage slaves, they were eligible for many government benefits, including a lump sum of cash.[51] Mr. Vasu currently awaits trial for "wrongful confinement, physical abuse and torture, rape, and forced labor."[52]

But Mr. Vasu would not have faced prosecution at all were it not for the efforts of IJM. Despite all of the evidence, police conducting the raid refused to arrest him. It was only after two years of IJM's relentless activity, presenting multiple testimonies from victims and demanding greater consequences than merely freeing his slaves, that Mr. Vasu faced any legal consequences. In India, the official response to debt bondage appears to be "free the slaves *and* the slaveholders." The mixed results in this story underscore Kevin Bales's analysis suggesting corruption as the third leg keeping modern slavery aloft. Surely police knew that illegal activity was occurring at the temple—so many local men participated. But it took a Christian abolitionist organization's involvement to move the criminal justice system into action.

Maya's family returned to their home village where they continue to support themselves at a subsistence level through agricultural work. They still fear encounters with Mr. Vasu, his cronies, or one of the men who raped them, but their lives are better. They have resolved never to borrow money again.

Maya was able to return to her own village, but IJM finds that this is not always best for freed slaves. They may continue to be targets for slavery. Freed sexual slaves, particularly, sometimes anticipate that shame and abuse await them at home, and liberation will only be achieved in a new, supportive environment.

IJM has freed two thousand slaves in South Asia alone, and it provides a number of aftercare programs such as shelters, food distribution, counseling, and protective services. The organization also helps freed slaves obtain government home loans and enroll children in public schools. Ninety-four percent of former slaves who participate in these aftercare programs stay out of slavery for good.[53]

Guilt-Free Chocolate Prevents Slavery

The efforts of IJM and other abolitionist groups who free slaves directly are admirable, but other signs of hope exist in the global economy that reduce the *demand* for slave labor. Divine Chocolate is a good example. Divine Chocolate is a Fair Trade certified chocolate brand produced by the Day Chocolate Company, partially owned by the Kuapa Kokoo cocoa cooperative in Ghana. Kuapa Kokoo represents 35,000 cocoa-producing members from 1,650 villages. Together with the Body Shop, a British NGO called Twin Trading, the British government, and others, Kuapa Kokoo founded Divine Chocolate in 1998 to raise small-scale cocoa farmers out of poverty. The cooperative now imports cocoa beans from war-torn Sierra Leone as well.[54] Other Fair Trade chocolate bars exist, such as Green & Black's Maya Gold bar,[55] but Divine takes the Fair Trade model a step further.

Divine Chocolate is a "Fair Trade plus" operation; that is, the farmers own a share of the value-added production: the chocolate bar we purchase. The additional monies collected from Fair Trade chocolate buyers (much of the cooperative's cocoa beans are still sold at conventional terms) has helped Kuapa Kokoo to invest in school construction, clean water and sewage facilities, and develop income-generating projects for cooperative members in other areas of the economy.[56]

In the past decade, Divine Chocolate has expanded greatly. Sales are strong in Europe, and in 2006, Lutheran World Relief invested $270,000 to cofound Divine Chocolate, USA, an American spinoff. CRS has selected Divine as its designated Fair Trade chocolate brand. CRS now markets Divine Chocolate to 67 million U.S. Catholics.

The success of Divine Chocolate raises an important question. Chocolate makers have committed to developing certification standards to assure consumers the chocolate they enjoy is not produced by slave labor. But doesn't Fair Trade chocolate already do that—and more? By certifying that the chocolate sale provides a living wage for producers, the Fair Trade label goes a step further. So why don't chocolate makers simply adopt the Fair Trade certification as their slave-free standard?

Cadbury was the first chocolate company to make this connection, announcing in the spring of 2009 that its popular Dairy Milk bar would be 100 percent Fair Trade certified in Great Britain and Ireland by the end of the year. Mars followed suit not long afterward, promising that Kit Kat bars in the same region would be manufactured with Kuapa Kokoo Fair Trade certified cocoa beans.[57] But the same companies have not done so in the United States.

One positive development, though only just the beginning, is the January 30, 2012, announcement by Hershey, explaining that its Bliss and Dagoba products would use chocolate sourced from Rainforest Alliance certified farms and plantations.[58] The Rainforest Alliance focuses on how farms are managed—looking at eco-sustainability, of course, but also ensuring fair treatment of workers and, certainly, rooting out slavery. Hershey later added a commitment to purchase 100 percent of its cocoa from certified sustainable sources like the Rainforest Alliance by 2020.[59] With additional consumer pressure, we could expect the other chocolate companies to follow suit, especially those currently selling Fair Trade products in the United Kingdom and Ireland.

Awareness of Fair Trade certification, though growing, is still limited. Dunkin' Donuts uses Fair Trade expresso beans in all of its U.S. expresso drinks, but rarely advertises its good corporate citizenship. Most Fair Trade coffee beans are ultimately sold on conventional terms; the demand simply is not high enough. Consumer interest in Fair Trade chocolate is even weaker. Chocolate companies in the United States face popular demand to certify their product as "slave free," but not Fair Trade. The growth of Divine Chocolate is indeed a sign of hope, but it must be accompanied by greater use of Fair Trade (or Rainforest Alliance) cocoa by the largest chocolate companies if cocoa farmers are to reap the sweetest justice.

Enlisting Tourism Workers to Fight Sex Slavery

One of the most touching moments of the film *The Dark Side of Chocolate* occurs when bus driver Idrissa Kante recounts the hundreds of children he rescued from traffickers in the first years of this century. Hope broadens and deepens when we meet ordinary people responding to evil with heroism. Yet what about the many people across our nation and abroad who see the signs of sex slavery but, like Cain, ask, "Am I my brother's keeper?" And what about the people who profit from such activity?

Faith-based corporate responsibility organizations like the Interfaith Center on Corporate Responsibility (ICCR), profiled in chapter 2, engage businesses in these questions of moral obligation in the global economy. We saw how the bus drivers organized their response to the trafficking of child slaves; what is the role of hotel workers and management in a hotel used by sex traffickers? Do airlines bear any responsibility toward discouraging sex tourism? Tour operators?

These questions have motivated the efforts of the Tri-State Coalition for Responsible Investment, an ICCR member representing forty Catholic religious orders and dioceses, to engage the travel industry on issues of human trafficking and sexual slavery. Their interest in the issue originated from member religious orders with experience ministering to the victims of sexual slavery. These sisters had witnessed firsthand the horrors of the sex trade and believed the tourism industry had a responsibility to respond to slavery facilitated—wittingly or unwittingly—by their businesses.[60]

In 2006, the Tri-State Coalition began discussions with hotel chains and airlines about signing onto "the Code," a code of conduct for travel and tourism businesses aimed at protecting children from sexual exploitation. Scandinavian tour operators created the Code in 1999, and its growth was initially confined to Europe. At first, as Sr. Pat Daly, OP, director of the Tri-State Coalition, explained, lawyers for American hotels and airlines stymied efforts to encourage U.S. travel companies to sign onto the Code. Making such a written public commitment, they argued, would increase company liability for human trafficking employees might not notice.

Initially, the Tri-State Coalition encouraged the management of Delta Airlines and the Wyndham Hotel Group to take internal steps like developing company policies and training employees about human trafficking. At the same time, the Sisters of Mercy, a Coalition member, began to develop shareholder resolutions on human trafficking for Delta Airlines. These resolutions brought Delta back to the table, and after several years of negotiations, in

March 2011, Delta became the first major airline in the world to sign the Code.[61]

No such strategy was needed for the Wyndham Hotel Group. In April 2011 members of three gangs and the owners of a Wyndham-franchised Travelodge in Oceanside, California, were indicted for human trafficking and prostitution. The incident so incensed Oceanside native Tim Rosner that he developed an online petition calling for Wyndham to develop effective policies on human trafficking and sexual slavery. Fourteen thousand people eventually signed the petition.[62] In July of 2011, Wyndham withdrew its objections and signed the Code, joining Hilton Worldwide, which signed on in April.[63]

The Code of Conduct for the Protection of Children from Sexual Exploitation in Travel and Tourism commits "suppliers of tourism services" to the following actions:

1. To establish an ethical policy regarding commercial and sexual exploitation of children.

2. To train the personnel in the country of origin and travel destinations.

3. To introduce a clause in contracts with suppliers, stating a common repudiation of commercial sexual exploitation of children.

4. To provide information to travelers by means of catalogues, brochures, in-flight films, ticket slips, home pages, etc.

5. To provide information to local "key persons" at the destinations.

6. To report annually to the NGO End Child Prostitution, Child Pornography, and Trafficking of Children for Sexual Purposes (ECPAT) International.[64]

Very few American companies signed on to the Code initially, and liability-conscious lawyers and marketing directors concerned about association with sexual slavery dissuaded those businesses sympathetic to the issue of sexual slavery from signing. But thanks to shareholders like the Sisters of Mercy and consumers like Tim Rosner, industry leaders have finally come to the table and signed. Tri-State Coalition leaders hope the legal ice is now broken, and the Code can become a U.S. travel industry standard.

Church-Funded Immokalee Workers Rescue Miguel

In this chapter, we have encountered Christian abolitionists who rescue slaves, learned how to promote justice for cocoa farmers and child slaves through the implementation of the Harkin-Engel Protocol and the promotion of Fair Trade chocolate, and discovered how people of faith have put their investments to work to influence the travel industry to fight sexual slavery. We now turn to the church's investment in promoting solidarity among low-wage farm workers in the United States to fight modern-day slavery.

When we left Miguel and his friends, they realized they were trapped. The men picked oranges from sunup to sundown, with little impact on their border-crossing debt. As they began to despair, two organizers arrived from the Catholic Campaign for Human Development–funded (CCHD) Coalition of Immokalee Workers (CIW). CIW organizers Lucas Benetiz and Laura Jamino appeared six months after Miguel fell into slavery. Responding to rumors of the conditions migrants working for the Ramoses experienced, Benetiz and Jamino slipped onto the property and into the workers' quarters, asking a lot of questions. Miguel held back, fearing the two worked for Ramos, but he took their card, nevertheless. Another month passed as the workers debated what to do. Finally they agreed to reach out to the CIW, biding their time, and waiting for the right moment.

Holy Week came and Ramos gave the men a few days off. Miguel saw an opportunity. But two other workers ran off, and the Ramoses' guards became suspicious, paying more notice to their comings and goings. Miguel took to carrying a pair of scissors in his boot for protection.

On the pretext of buying food for Holy Week, two of Miguel's friends went to the local supermarket. There, they called the CIW and arranged for a rescue. CIW organizers picked them up at the supermarket, and minutes later, Miguel saw an unfamiliar car drive up. Recognizing Lucas Benetiz, Miguel jumped into the car, and in a cloud of dust, sped to freedom.

Today, as a certified victim of human trafficking, Miguel is working in the United States legally. "Things are much different now," he said. "I'm working eight hours a day, but I'm working for a boss who pays me, and I get to work eight hours, no more or less, and now I'm working on my own will. . . . I know if I want a day off that he's gonna give me a day off, and I know that if I want to work ten hours, I can work ten hours, but it's not because I'm being forced to." Miguel's son's condition has improved, but he continues to require essential medicines. Miguel sends part of his paycheck every month to help pay for the treatments. Four years after his border crossing, Miguel is thankful for the chance to provide for his son, but he misses his family. He is also grateful to the CIW for liberating him from slavery.

Miguel's rescue was just one of the many actions the CIW has taken against modern-day slavery. For the CIW, fighting slavery is more than just dramatic rescues. Its approach also includes assistance in the federal prosecution of slave rings entrapping hundreds of farm workers. For example, in January 2008, CIW research led to the arrest of Antonia Zuniga Vargas, accused of holding over a dozen Mexican and Guatemalan workers on her farm. According to their indictment, Vargas and others arrested "threatened the immigrants, held their identification documents, created debit accounts they couldn't repay, and hooked them on alcohol to keep them working. They made them sleep in box trucks and shacks, charged them for food and showers, didn't pay them for picking produce, and beat them if they tried to leave." Chief Assistant U.S. Attorney Doug summarized, "Slavery, plain and simple."[65]

The CIW has assisted federal prosecutors in nine of these cases, involving over a thousand workers. Their mission is to eliminate the market conditions that allow slavery to flourish. When slavery is tolerated, it creates pressures on "good" employers to lower their labor costs by adopting the same methods. Vigorous prosecution sends a message: slavery will not be tolerated in the United States.

The Florida Modern-Day Slavery Museum has taken that message on the road. Developed by the CIW, the museum is a portable collection of photos, court documents, and artifacts relating to cases like Miguel's. In 2010, the museum toured the Northeast inside a white Freightliner truck outfitted as a replica of the trucks utilized in a 2008 slavery operation.[66] One of the workers traveling with the museum was Romeo Ramirez, a friend of Miguel's, who helped federal prosecutors gather evidence to prosecute the Ramoses.

The Coalition of Immokalee Workers' mobile Modern-Day Slavery Museum tours the United States, telling the story of immigrant workers' forced labor in the twenty-first century.

During their trial for conspiracy, extortion, and possession of firearms, the Ramoses offered an interesting defense—they weren't the only ones involved, why should prosecutors single them out? Why not arrest the growers who hired them? Why not take legal action against Tropicana, who bought the lion's share of the oranges? It took the jury a day and a half to convict the Ramoses, who were sentenced to twelve years in prison. But part of the Ramoses' defense affected Judge K. Michael Moore. In his final remarks at the sentencing hearing, Judge Moore encouraged law enforcement officials to go beyond prosecuting contractors like the Ramoses and to investigate greater actors in the supply chain, because "others at a higher level of the fruit picking industry seem complicit in one way or another with how these activities occur."[67]

Judge Moore's statement rings true. Each of the signs of hope presented in this chapter suggests we adopt a multifaceted approach to ending slavery, stepping beyond dramatic rescues and piecemeal prosecutions. We who are outraged by the institutionalized violence of slavery need to support such a comprehensive effort, enforcing the laws on the books and providing aftercare services to former slaves. We also must educate businesses in every sector about slavery and secure their commitment to marketing slave-free products. Finally, we need to develop open and transparent systems to verify the slave-free claims of businesses, with measurable consequences for those who do not. A certified slave-free orange? Judge Moore is asking for nothing less, and neither should we.

Modern-day slavery is one of the more brutal dimensions of the violence of globalization, sharing the church's "intrinsically evil" label with the worst violations of God's law. These sins include torture, assassination, terrorism, and other affronts to human life and dignity deemed always wrong, regardless of intention or circumstances. We now turn to the role of torture and assassination in the global economy, another troubling "intrinsically evil" manifestation of the violence of contemporary globalization.

DISCUSSION QUESTIONS

1. How are slaves able to "hide in plain sight"? Why don't we see them?

2. If you were a slave, what might prevent you from fleeing?

3. Why has it taken so long to implement the Harkin-Engel Protocol?

GO MAKE A DIFFERENCE

1. Invite the CIW's Museum of Modern Slavery to come to your parish, diocese, city, town, or school. More information is available at the Coalition of Immokalee Workers' website.[68]

2. Show the film *The Dark Side of Chocolate* at your parish, school, or public library.[69] Be sure to have opportunities for action available afterward!

3. Write to your favorite chocolate company requesting full implementation of the Harkin-Engel Protocol. Use the forms and addresses found on the Stop Chocolate Slavery website.[70]

4. Sell Divine Fair Trade chocolate in your next fund-raiser or work with Catholic or public schools in your area to switch to Fair Trade chocolate fund-raisers. SERRV International's website provides details.[71]

5

Torture and Assassination

Sr. Dorothy Stang ambled up a small hill in the heart of the Amazon forest, toward a meeting of small-scale farmers. The government of Brazil had guaranteed their right to cultivate sustainable crops in two large land reserves straddling the Trans-Amazonian Highway, but loggers and ranchers had other ideas. They felled trees, sold the timber, and planted cattle grass in the area in defiance of the law. With demand for timber and beef high, a great deal of money stood to be made. Local police were easily bribed, and the area was too remote to command attention from the federal government. The farmers felt increasingly vulnerable, as hired hands working for ranchers Vitalmiro Basros de Moura and Regivaldo Pereira Galvão increasingly raided their homes, issued threats, and sometimes burned homes to the ground.

The morning's meeting would address the latest house burnings. Sr. Dorothy hoped the farmers would stand their ground, having received assurances from federal officials that the farmers had the weight of law on their side. The road curved at the top of the hill. Two men stepped out from behind the trees, Rayfran das Neves Sales and Clodoaldo "Eduardo" Carlos Batista. Sr. Dorothy invited Rayfran and Eduardo to the farmers' meeting, to learn about the boundaries of the land reserve. Perhaps they would stop throwing cattle grass seed around the farmers' lands, an action for which she had scolded them just the day before. Spreading cattle grass meant that Moura and Galvão would soon try to seize the property. She believed the two hired hands had a lot in common with the farmers, settlers who had come to the Amazon seeking relief from extreme poverty. The real thugs were ranchers like Moura and Galvão.

Sr. Dorothy opened her bag and produced a map indicating the boundaries of the land reserve. The men ignored her. Folding up the map, she shook hands with Rayfran and Eduardo and turned to go.

"Sister!" Rayfran shouted, drawing his gun. Sr. Dorothy froze. A full minute passed. "Well, lady," he said, cocking the gun, "If we don't settle this business today, we'll never settle it."

"Don't do this," Sr. Dorothy said. "Don't shoot me." She reached for her bag.

"Take your hand out of your bag! Is that a gun there or what?" Rayfran shouted.

"I have no gun," the seventy-three-year-old nun replied. "My only weapon is this." Sr. Dorothy smiled, removed her Bible from the cloth bag, opened it to Matthew 5, and read:

"Blessed are the pure in heart, for they will see God.

"Blessed are the peacemakers, for they will be called children of God.

"Blessed are those who are persecuted for righteousness' sake, for theirs is the kingdom of heaven."

"Well, lady," Rayfran responded, "that's enough of that."[1]

The assassin fired one shot to the stomach, then another to the shoulder, from a short distance. Then, standing over Sr. Dorothy, he fired four rounds to the head, emptying the revolver provided by Moura.[2] As her blood flowed into the red clay of the Amazon, Sr. Dorothy gave up her life, joining Archbishop Oscar Romero, the Jesuit martyrs, the women missionaries of El Salvador, and thousands of labor union leaders, catechists, and human rights activists in Latin America martyred by the violence of globalization.

SIGNS OF THE TIMES

Martyr of the Amazon

Sr. Dorothy's Amazon journey began with a 1974 invitation from the Bishop of Marabá, Brazil, to the Sisters of Notre Dame de Namur of Dayton, Ohio, inviting the nuns to minister within a sprawling region of small settlements. Along with Sr. Becky Spires, Sr. Dorothy quickly became enamored with the people and followed pioneers heading westward to start a new life. In no time, her role evolved from simply catechizing and organizing base communities[3] to organizing the community to defend itself from land grabbers.

Sr. Becky described the challenges facing the two sisters and the Brazilian settlers, beyond clearing land, building shelters, and planting crops:

> First of all it was the land grabbers. They would wait until the migrants had cleared a little patch of land and then they'd come in and claim it. Threaten people, wave their guns around, burn down the settlers' houses. So we got all the little communities together, documented everything, drew up petitions, and did all we could to publicize the plight of the settlers. As a church we took our stand with the people. We started teaching them about their rights, helping to establish farm workers' unions, giving literacy classes.[4]

The conflicts over land introduced Sr. Dorothy to the issue that would characterize her ministry for the next thirty years.

By 1982, Sr. Dorothy began to feel unsafe in Marabá. Her work on behalf of poor settlers had made her many enemies among powerful logging and ranching interests. Whenever the loggers and ranchers tried to illegally deforest an area, Sr. Dorothy would intervene, bringing in federal authorities, trying to protect the settlers' homes from destruction. Sometimes she was successful, sometimes not. When Sr. Dorothy's name was included in a locally published "hit list,"[5] she knew it was time to go. She met with Bishop Dom Erwin of the Diocese of Xingu, who encouraged her to travel to the Transamazon East, a poor region located in the Amazon forests of Brazil, on one side of the new Trans-Amazonian Highway. "It's the end of the world there," he said. "The people haven't got so much as a place to lay their bones."[6]

With the dawn of construction on the Trans-Amazonian Highway in 1972, the government opened up new lands to settlers with the slogan "land without men for men without land." The highway runs through the western states of Brazil, integrating these regions with the rest of the country, and with neighboring Colombia, Peru, and Ecuador. First the settlers came, but in due time loggers and ranchers followed, as global demand for wood and cattle grew, stirring up the same kinds of conflicts Sr. Dorothy had left behind in Marabá.

Most of Sr. Dorothy's ministry, in the 1980s, comprised organizing Bible studies, constructing schools, training teachers, and simply building community—creating new festivals like "Farmers Days." She helped settlers process the foods they produced, obtaining a rice-hulling machine so the settlers' rice crops would command a better price at market, and canning equipment for tropical fruits. She had a special interest in the empowerment of women of African and Native American descent, who often lacked self-confidence after years of inferior treatment.[7]

For over twenty years, Sr. Dorothy developed this ministry, becoming ever more beloved among the poor—and more reviled among the loggers and ranchers. But by the turn of the century, the government of Brazil had become a stronger partner, awarding settlers two large tracts of land on either side of the Trans-Amazonian Highway. Federal law forbade logging and ranching on these lands to preserve the character (and ecological benefits) of the Amazon forests. Yet within a year, loggers began paying settlers to leave, harassing those small farmers who remained with threats of violence. In just three years, the number of sawmills in the area increased from two to twenty-three, and once again, the Amazon forests were under siege.

In 2004, another published "hit-list" placed a $20,000 bounty on Sr. Dorothy's head. A rumor circulated that a group of ranchers and loggers had met in January 2005, at a hotel in Altamira, to discuss a final solution—she would be assassinated.[8] Ranchers Vitalmiro Bastos de Moura and Regivaldo Pereira Galvão later hired Rayfran and Eduardo to kill Sr. Dorothy for $25,000. After the killing, Rayfran and Eduardo were quickly arrested, tried, and convicted within the year.[9] But it took six separate trials over a period of five years, to convict Moura and Galvão, who are currently serving twenty-eight and thirty- year sentences, respectively.[10] None of the others suspected in the broader conspiracy, including the mayors of the towns of Anapu and Porto de Moz, has been prosecuted.[11]

Neocolonialism and the School of the Americas

There was a period when business interests could count on most Latin American governments to take care of obstacles like Sr. Dorothy

Sr. Dorothy Stang defended the rights of indigenous people living in the Amazon rainforests from 1974 until her assassination in 2005.

Stang. Indeed, at times in the 1970s, Sr. Dorothy feared she would be killed by the Brazilian soldiers who branded her a communist. Such was the neocolonial approach of U.S. Cold War allies to do-gooders and troublemakers ministering to the vast numbers of the poor in Latin America. Sadly, the United States was complicit with, and even advocated, torture and assassination in Latin America during this period. Agents of many Latin American governments tortured and killed multitudes of innocent victims—including priests and women religious.

In the 1970s, revolutions to overthrow violent dictators spread throughout Central America and some countries of South America. In Nicaragua, a bloody revolution overthrew Anastasio Somoza, one of the most brutal dictators in Latin America. Civil wars plagued El Salvador and Guatemala, with unrest developing in Honduras and Panama as well. The United States and the Soviet Union played out the last decades of the Cold War on this tropical chessboard.

To prevent revolutions in Central America and provide stability for American companies doing business there, the U.S. government provided millions of dollars of military aid to compliant Latin American governments. The United States also trained Latin American military leaders at its School of the Americas (SOA) in various techniques to suppress opposition to government policy, including torture from 1982 to 1991.[12] This training had its roots in CIA Cold War research on mind control in the 1950s and 1960s.

According to the historian Alfred McCoy, throughout the 1950s and early 1960s, the CIA financed and conducted secret research on "mass persuasion and the effects of coercion on individual consciousness."[13] In short—mind control. The CIA spent several billion dollars in this area, supporting psychology departments in fifty-eight universities.[14] The basic torture techniques that resulted from this research included the use of stress positions (self-inflicted pain created by, for example, standing with arms extended for long periods), mock executions, sensory deprivation, and sexual humiliation.[15]

In 1963, the techniques were codified in a secret manual known as the *KUBARK Counterintelligence Interrogation*. By 1967, the CIA operated some forty interrogation centers in Vietnam utilizing these techniques—and still more disturbing tactics passed on from the Middle Ages.[16] The KUBARK manual served as a model for the CIA's *Human Resource Exploitation Training Manual* used in the 1980s in Honduras.[17] Florencio Cabellero, a CIA-trained Honduran interrogator, told the *New York Times* that he and others were taught "to study the fears and weaknesses of the prisoner. To make him stand up, don't let him sleep, keep him naked and in isolation, put rats and cockroaches in his cell, give him bad food, serve him dead animals, throw water on him, change the temperature."[18] Such tactics served as the interrogational palate of SOA's graduates of the 1980s.

Torture and the School of the Americas

The SOA utilized six manuals of torture from 1982 to 1991. They advocated execution of guerillas, extortion, physical abuse, and coercion. SOA leaders kept the manuals secret until 1996, when they were disclosed by a Pentagon rattled by Rep. Joseph Kennedy's (D-MA) inquiries and rumors Kennedy had obtained copies of the manuals. Rep. Kennedy conducted a five-year campaign to close the school, once remarking, "According to the Pentagon's own excerpts, School of the Americas' students were advised to imprison those from whom they were seeking information, to 'involuntarily' obtain information from those sources—in other words, torture them: to arrest their parents; to use 'motivation by fear;' pay bounties for enemy dead; execute opponents; subvert the press; and use torture, blackmail, and even injections of truth serum to obtain information."[19]

The SOA originated at Fort Amador in the Panama Canal Zone in 1946 and was known as the Latin American Training Center—Ground Division. Four years later, it was renamed this time as the U.S. Army Caribbean School. In 1963, it was again renamed the U.S. Army School of the Americas, and in 1985, the school moved to Fort Benning in Columbus, Georgia. In 2001, under pressure to close, it was renamed the Western Hemisphere Institute for Security Cooperation (WHISC).

The SOA has trained more than 55,000 commissioned officers, cadets, noncommissioned officers, and government civilians from twenty-two Latin American countries. Many of its graduates were responsible for ordering or participating in assassinations, torture, and massacres. For many years, Roy Bourgeois, a Maryknoll priest, educated, organized, and protested to bring attention to and force the closing of SOA. Bourgeois was a decorated naval officer who gradually came to understand how the military in Latin America was being used to intimidate the poor and eliminate those demanding justice. He founded the School of the Americas Watch as a national movement to close the SOA.

Joining Bourgeois as the first SOA Watch director, Vicky Imerman, also a veteran, helped substantiate the allegations of oppression and violence against the SOA, researching Army documents for evidence. Imerman found that forty-six of the sixty six officers cited for major atrocities in Latin America were trained in torture and assassination at the SOA. Among the atrocities inflicted by SOA graduates are the following, as reported in James Hodge and Linda Cooper's *Disturbing the Peace*:

- Two of the three men responsible for Archbishop Oscar Romero's murder in El Salvador were trained at the SOA. Two days after Archbishop Romero's assassination, the Reagan administration pushed through a multi-million-dollar aid program to El Salvador. Two months later, the Salvadoran Army massacred six hundred unarmed peasants at the Sumpul River. "Most were women and children, many of whom were hacked to death and fed to dogs."[20] In March 1993, the United Nations–sponsored Truth Commission of El Salvador cited Colonel Ricardo Pena Arbaiza, trained at the SOA, for this atrocity.[21]

- Three of the five men accused of the 1980 rape and murder of U.S. missionaries in El Salvador (Sr. Ita Ford, Sr. Dorothy Kazel, Sr. Maura Clark, and Jean Donovan) were trained at the SOA. One of the three was General Carlos Vides Casanova, the former defense minister of El Salvador, who was a guest speaker at the School of the Americas five years after the murders.[22]

- Ten of the twelve officers who oversaw the El Mozote massacre were trained at the School of the Americas. At El Mozote, U.S.-trained Salvadoran troops shot, hanged, and decapitated more than nine hundred peasants, mostly women and elderly villagers.[23]

- Nineteen of the twenty-six cited in the assassination of six Jesuit priests, their cook, and her daughter in El Salvador were trained at the SOA.[24] U.S. Army Major Eric Bucklan reported that he was told Colonel Guillermo Alfredo Benavides helped plan the murders. Bucklan, a U.S. military advisor, "had knowledge of the scheme well in advance of the assassinations."[25]

◆ General Hector Gramajo, an SOA graduate, was defense minister in El Salvador when Sr. Dianna Ortiz was kidnapped.[26] She had been teaching Mayan children to read and write. She was taken to a "clandestine prison where she was gang-raped, burned more than a hundred times with cigarettes, and lowered into a pit with the bodies of 'children, women, and men, some decapitated, some lying face up and caked with blood, some dead, some alive—and all swarming with rats.'"[27] In 1995, U.S. District Judge Douglas Woodlock found that Gramajo was aware of and supported widespread acts of brutality committed by personnel under his command, resulting in thousands of civilian deaths.[28]

◆ Father James "Guadalupe" Carney, a former Jesuit missionary in El Salvador, was tortured and thrown out of a helicopter on orders of General Gustavo Alvarez Martinez, an SOA graduate, the same year President Reagan awarded the general the Legion of Merit.[29]

◆ Guatemalan Bishop Juan José Gerardi released a 1998 report entitled *Guatemala: Nunca Más* (Never Again), which implicated the Guatemalen army and its paramilitaries in almost 90 percent of the atrocities committed in Guatemala. "SOA graduates figured prominently among the officers cited for abuse. Two days after releasing the report, the bishop was assassinated."[30]

◆ Hundreds of peasants in Colombia were killed and dismembered in the Trujillo chainsaw massacre. The executions were carried out by SOA graduate Major Alirio Antonio Urena Jaramillo. The crimes were reported by a U.S. Army informant, Daniel Arcila. In his report, Arcila said that victims were tortured before being killed. Their fingernails were pried off, their feet were cut, salt was poured into their wounds, they were burned with a blowtorch on different parts of their body, and their skin was peeled off. The men were emasculated and their penises and testicles put in their mouths. Finally, they were quartered with a chainsaw.[31]

◆ More than three thousand political opponents of Chilean President Augusto Pinochet were kidnapped, tortured, and executed during the 1980s. Most of Pinochet's security forces were trained at the SOA.[32]

Unrelenting pressure from Catholic parishioners, university students, and religious orders, combined with leadership from Massachusetts congressmen Joseph Moakley and Joseph Kennedy, led to the banning of the torture and assassination manuals in 1992 and a successful 1999 U.S. House of Representatives vote to cut off funding for the SOA.[33] Though this amendment failed to reach the Senate floor by an 8–7 committee vote, the message was clear: torture and assassination in the name of advancing American political and economic interests would no longer be tolerated. The SOA could not continue as an academy for despots.

Congress and the Clinton administration responded in December 2000 with a compromise unsatisfying to anti-SOA activists. The SOA would close but then reopen as the Western Hemisphere Institute for Security Cooperation. Protests continued, but the civil wars that plagued Latin America into the 1990s wound down, reconciliation processes commenced, and government atrocities diminished dramatically. WHISC appointed a Catholic bishop, Most Rev. Robert Morlino, to the board of visitors of the school,[34] along with "labor priest" Rev. Clete Kiley,[35] and the locus of the torture debate shifted to the "War on Terror." Today, only 5,000 people attend November's annual SOA Watch protest, down from over 17,000 just a few years ago.[36] SOA Watch continues to demand the outright shutdown of WHISC, but although significant changes in U.S. policy have been won, the symbolic victory of closing the school has proved elusive.

Outsourcing Torture and Assassination

Given the changes in U.S. policy, when workers and peasants become taciturn, and business interests need defending today, to whom are the wealthy and powerful of Latin America to turn? Sr. Dorothy Stang's story implies a new strategy—the outsourcing of torture and assassination to local thugs. Two cases now working their way through the American court system suggest an even wider contracting of torture and assassination to terrorist organizations.

The relatives of 387 murder victims, including some church and labor leaders, sued Chiquita Brands International in 2007 for its financial support of the right-wing United Self-Defense Forces of Colombia (AUC), known for its death squads and massacres, in addition to drug trafficking. The United States designated the AUC a terrorist organization in 2001. Chiquita admits that it paid the AUC $1.7 million in "protection money" from 1997 to 2004 and agreed to pay a fine of $25 million for its violation of U.S. antiterrorism laws.[37] A second lawsuit holds Chiquita responsible for the deaths of five American missionaries, an earlier killing committed by the left-wing Revolutionary Armed Forces of Colombia (FARC),[38] an earlier recipient of Chiquita "protection money." Both lawsuits assert that Chiquita's support of the two terrorist organizations extended beyond cash payments to the smuggling of weapons.[39]

For its part, Chiquita denies anything more than paying protection money to keep its employees safe—the cost of doing business in a violent region of the world. But, the head of the AUC, Carlos Castano, said he "told Chiquita executives in a meeting that the money would be used to drive out the guerillas and protect the company's interests."[40] Those allegedly killed, and in some cases tortured, by the AUC include "trade unionists, banana plantation workers, political organizers, and social activists," as noted by Judge Kenneth Marra.[41] Chiquita's defense has not yet persuaded any judge to dismiss the lawsuits. As the first case worked its way through the courts, more families joined, and the number of plaintiffs now exceeds 2,100 families.[42]

Did Chiquita order the deaths of every one of the estimated ten thousand people killed in the banana-growing region of north Colombia over the past decade? Not likely. But could the protection payments and alleged favors like gun running have encouraged the AUC to eliminate some meddlesome community leaders working contrary to Chiquita's economic interests? Perhaps, especially if these leaders were also considered problematic by the AUC, and herein lies the most dangerous possibility. In the absence of Latin American governments willing to torture and kill church and labor leaders, it is possible that some businesses may now turn to organized crime and terrorist organizations to eliminate troublemakers like Archbishop Romero, Sr. Dianna Ortiz, the Jesuit martyrs, Sr. Dorothy Stang, and so many thousands of labor union leaders, catechists, and human rights activists. Torture and assassination may yet become the latest service in the global economy to be outsourced.

WHAT THE CHURCH TEACHES

The development of the church's teaching on torture follows the same evolution as its teaching on slavery. The use of torture by the Inquisition in the Middle Ages is well known. Pope Innocent IV authorized the use of torture in 1252 by proclamation of the papal bull *Ad Extirpanda* to facilitate the confessions of heretics. The pope admonished inquisitors to use torture only in circumstances in which they were convinced of the accused's guilt, to use these methods only once, and to never cause loss of life or limb. Like slavery, torture was legal, but subject to conditions of justice.[43] By the mid-nineteenth century, however, the notion that torture was ever permissible gave way to the current teaching, found in the *Catechism of the Catholic Church.*

Today's *Catechism* places torture in the category of "intrinsically evil" actions—behavior that is always wrong, regardless of one's intentions. The *Catechism* states, "*Torture* [original italics] which uses physical or moral violence to extract confessions, punish the guilty, frighten opponents, or satisfy hatred is contrary to respect for the person and for human dignity."[44] The *Catechism* follows this teaching with an apology of sorts for past behavior and telegraphs lessons learned:

> In times past, cruel practices were commonly used by legitimate governments to maintain law and order, often without protest from the Pastors of the Church, who themselves adopted in their own tribunals the prescriptions of Roman law concerning torture. Regrettable as these facts are, the Church always taught the duty of clemency and mercy. She forbade clerics to shed blood. In recent times it has become evident that these cruel practices were neither necessary for public order, nor in conformity with the legitimate rights of the human person. On the contrary, these practices led to ones even more degrading. It is necessary to work for their abolition. We must pray for the victims and their tormentors.[45]

The *Compendium of the Social Doctrine of the Church* affirms this teaching in the post–9/11 context, noting:

> In carrying out investigations, the regulation against the use of torture, even in the case of serious crimes, must be strictly observed: [quoting John Paul II] "Christ's disciple refuses every recourse to such methods, which nothing could justify and in which the dignity of man is as much debased in his torturer as in the torturer's victim." International juridical instruments concerning human rights correctly indicate a prohibition against torture as a principle which cannot be contravened under any circumstances.[46]

That final phrase summarizes Church teaching on torture: it is wrong, regardless of time, place, or purpose, and must be opposed by all disciples of Jesus Christ.

Church teaching on assassinations is a bit more nuanced. Although the fifth commandment, "You shall not kill" (Exod. 20:13) is quite clear, some conditions allow for the taking of human life, for example a "just war."[47] Although the targeting of civilians is prohibited under the "just war" doctrine,[48] the killing of military figures, up to and including a head of state, is permitted. For example, several religious figures, including the Protestant theologian Dietrich Bonhoeffer, participated in the failed plot to assassinate Adolf Hitler, an action considered as a means of protecting innocent life. On the other hand, if the conspirators had tortured members of the Nazi Party to obtain the Führer's whereabouts on a particular day, that action would be considered sinful, as torture is never justified. Our own nation's return to the practice of torture from 2001 to 2008 should be considered in light of this teaching.

SIGNS OF HOPE

Perhaps this has been a hard chapter to read. The brutal reality of torture and assassination in our world challenges the capacity to hope. But hope—the confidence that God will deliver on God's promises— is found in church basements, in university meeting spaces, in rectory living rooms, wherever people of faith come together and say

"No—human beings are made in the image and likeness of God, and torture for any reason must be eliminated." Signs of hope featured in this chapter focus on the abolition of both state-sponsored and privately outsourced torture and assassination.

Stopping State-Sponsored Torture

It was the American return to the practice of torture that put the issue of torture high on the U.S. Catholic Bishops' public policy priorities in the early 2000s. Working through the National Religious Campaign Against Torture (NRCAT), the USCCB has, since 2006, stood with three hundred religious organizations, representing mainline and evangelical Protestant, Orthodox Christian, Jewish, Muslim, Hindu, and Buddhist communities, among others, to demand an end to the practice of torture. The coalition achieved its highest legislative priority after three years of vigorous activity, when President Obama signed an executive order banning the use of torture (or in the language of the executive order, "any interrogation technique or approach, or any treatment related to interrogation, that is not authorized by and listed in Army Field Manual 2 22.3") on January 22, 2009.

Since this important victory, NRCAT has worked to promote awareness of torture and increase the number of Americans "who believe that torture is always wrong, without exception."[49] The organization has also urged Congress to pass a law making President Obama's executive order on torture the law of the land and advocated to curtail the use of solitary confinement by state and federal prisons for extended periods of time, especially for mentally ill inmates. On the international front, NRCAT has urged the U.S. State Department to develop a "Torture Watch List" of nations engaged in torture and target foreign aid to support efforts to end the use of torture in those countries.[50] The Catholic members of NRCAT have developed an educational tool, *Torture Is a Moral Issue: A Catholic Study Guide*, for use with parish and other study groups.[51]

For decades, many Catholic organizations also sponsored chapters of Amnesty International, an international human rights organization known for its letter-writing campaigns on behalf of victims of torture and death row inmates as well as legislative advocacy against torture and the death penalty. In 2007, Amnesty International abandoned its neutral stance on abortion and adopted policies supporting the worldwide decriminalization of abortion, a decision at odds with Catholic teaching. As a result, USCCB president Bishop William Skylstad wrote to Amnesty International on August 23, 2007, to express dismay at the decision to "promote worldwide access to abortion." He noted, "in promoting abortion, Amnesty International divides its members (many of whom are Catholics and others who defend the rights of unborn children)."[52] In the words of the *Catechism*, the Church "has affirmed the moral evil of every procured abortion,"[53] and considers abortion an intrinsically evil action, like torture, genocide, and homicide.

Most Catholic organizations immediately disaffiliated with Amnesty International. Some groups disappeared altogether, but others adopted new names, like the University of Notre Dame's "Human Rights Notre Dame." Disaffiliating with Amnesty International was simple for the students. Laying out the details of a new relationship to Amnesty International was not. Could the new Human Rights Notre Dame group use Amnesty International resources in its work on cases of torture overseas? The Student Activities Office first ruled no but reversed itself weeks later, maintaining that simply learning about the work of Amnesty International and acting in concert on campaigns in accord with church teaching was not the same as affiliating as a chapter, with the full endorsement of all of the organization's work that affiliation would imply.

Human Rights Notre Dame has severed contact with Amnesty International's regional office, but continues to use Amnesty International's website as a source for its "urgent action" alerts on torture and death penalty cases. The student group also draws from Oxfam International sources, and uses Catholic Relief Services materials for its Fair Trade campaign. Providing effective educational materials and promising vehicles for action was a challenge in the transition but is not so anymore.[54]

Thus far, no Catholic organization has emerged from the vacuum created by Amnesty International's decision, but the Interreligious Campaign Against Torture has risen in prominence. The church has sent a strong message to Amnesty International about its new abortion policy by closing Catholic institutional chapters, but groups continue, unaffiliated, under new names. Many (though not all) still make use of resources from Amnesty International to some degree. On the whole, the mission to stop torture and the use of the death penalty continues in countless Catholic institutions, regardless of the policy changes of Amnesty International or any similar secular organization.[55]

Another sign of hope is the Torture Abolition and Survivors Support Coalition International (TASSC), founded in 1998 by Sr. Dianna Ortiz (see above section on the SOA) and other torture survivors "to end the practice of torture wherever it occurs and to empower survivors, their communities wherever they are."[56] TASSC operates a campaign to end torture much like the NRCAT, but its strength lies in the stories of its members, torture survivors who testify at congressional hearings, for example. Its Truth Speakers Program also brings torture survivors to church groups, community forums, advocacy groups, high school classes, and universities throughout the world to tell their stories. TASSC's documentary *Breaking the Silence* brings many of those same stories to DVD.

The popular Christian social justice reflection and action organization JustFaith Ministries teamed up with TASSC, the NRCAT, and Pax Christi USA to develop a JustMatters study module, an eight-session exploration of the past and present use of torture and its hoped-for demise. The two-and-a-half hour sessions include the testimony of survivors, documentation on the use of torture in the United States and abroad, and theological reflections on "Following Jesus, Our Tortured Brother."[57] The lesson plans devote about one-third of the discussions to taking "decisive moral action" against torture. The experience is open to both graduates of JustFaith's core thirty-week experience and those who have not yet participated.

Ending Torture and Assassination in the Private Sector

NGOs like the Interreligious Campaign Against Torture and the TASSC rightly celebrated President Obama's 2009 executive order banning torture by the CIA, but the assassination of Sr. Dorothy Stang and Chiquita's "protection" payoffs suggest that the banning of torture by governments is not enough. Businesses and business leaders in the global economy must also be held accountable for their out-sourcing of torture and assassination. Two important aspects of law cited in this chapter bear reviewing.

Under the Anti-Terrorism Act of 2005 (U.S. Criminal Code, Title 18, USC 2332), if a U.S. citizen is murdered in another country, the killers or coconspirators can be tried in U.S. federal courts and pun-ished with either the death penalty or a prison sentence. Lesser sen-tences apply for attempted murder.[58] If such a law had been in place in 1980, the five Salvadorans accused of murdering Sr. Ita Ford, Sr. Dorothy Kazel, Sr. Maura Clark, and Jean Donovan could have been tried in the United States as terrorists.

An older law, the Alien Tort Statute (ATS), has figured promi-nently into the Chiquita lawsuit. The over-two-hundred-year-old law "allows foreigners to sue in American federal courts if their claims involve violations of U.S. treaties or the 'law of nations.' "[59] It's not the first time plaintiffs have invoked the ATS over human rights viola-tions, but few of these cases have resulted in convictions. The ATS and the Anti-Terrorism Act are complementary, though passed over two hundred years apart. One law protects Americans living and working in foreign countries (Anti-Terrorism Act); the other protects citizens of foreign countries from the actions of U.S. companies (ATS).

Without laws such as these, people of faith and others con-cerned about such torture and assassination would have far less recourse to legal action. Businesses respond to different kinds of pressures than governments do, so laws that carry heavy monetary liability may be the best response to the outsourcing of such abuses. The development of these laws is itself a sign of hope. Whether they are governmental or corporate, we need multiple levels of change to stamp out these most brutal elements of the violence of global-ization. Nothing less would be fitting memorial to Sr. Dorothy and her fellow martyrs.

DISCUSSION QUESTIONS

1. Should Sr. Dorothy Stang have left the Trans-Amazon when she found she had a price on her head, as she did at Marabá years earlier?

2. Is the use of mind-altering substances in interrogations a form of torture? Are such practices justified to protect innocent lives and the economic interests of our country?

3. Does the church's historical practice of torture make us more credible, less credible, or have the same degree of credibility as other organizations in the public debate on torture?

GO MAKE A DIFFERENCE

1. Organize an affiliate group of the National Religious Campaign Against Torture in your parish, school, or college. Visit www. nrcat.org for more details.

2. Hold an event at your parish, school, or college to raise awareness of Catholic teaching on the use of torture.

3. Organize a group to study and discuss the JustFaith module "In the Steps of the Crucified: Torture Is Never Justified." More information is available at www.justfaith.org.

6

Violence against
God's Creation

Han Zongyuan had high hopes for his three-year-old daughter Tian-tian. Every choice he made over the last four years expressed his dreams for her, including his decision to work at Zhejiang Haijiu Battery. The work at the factory was difficult and dangerous, but his income soared when he took the job. He now owned a home across the street from the factory. China's foray into capitalism had truly improved his life.

But a recent blood test revealed that his daughter had very high levels of lead in her blood—enough to permanently lower her I.Q. and cause irreversible damage to her nervous system. Zongyuan told the *New York Times*, "At the moment I heard the doctor say that, my heart was shattered. We wanted this child to have everything. That's why we worked so hard. That's why we poisoned ourselves at this factory. Now it turns out the child is poisoned too. I have no words to describe how I feel."[1]

Stories like Zongyuan's echo throughout China and other rapidly developing nations taking the sweatshop route to reducing poverty. The factories that brought them some measure of prosperity have also poisoned the environment, harming ordinary workers and their families. In addition, carbon emissions from these factories have made China the leading producer of "greenhouse gasses" contributing to the warming of the planet and consequent climate change. Other less developed countries (LDCs) hoping to follow China's path out of poverty will only exacerbate these problems, degrading God's creation on land, sea, and air. This chapter will explore violence against creation, relevant church teaching, and signs of hope from communities of faith and others of good will.

SIGNS OF THE TIMES

The Poisoning of God's Creation

Millions of Chinese share Han Zongyuan's grief over environmentally based illnesses. As the country has developed, pollution has contributed substantially to making cancer the leading cause of death.[2] The World Health Organization estimates that air pollution causes 656,000 premature deaths each year in China.[3] Half a billion Chinese lack access to clean drinking water.[4] Over 40 percent of state-monitored rivers are classified as "unfit for human contact."[5] Only 1 percent of city residents breathe air that the European Union would consider safe, and these urban dwellers rarely see the sun.[6]

What is most insidious about China's lead-poisoning epidemic is the role of government. China's central and provincial governments consistently deny and minimize the vast scientific and medical evidence of lead poisoning in nearly every industrial center. In 2011, the international NGO Human Rights Watch issued a scathing report on lead poisoning in China, *My Children Have Been Poisoned: A Public Health Crisis in Four Chinese Provinces*. Human Rights Watch based its report on current medical research along with interviews with fifty-two parents and grandparents of children who suffer from lead poisoning in four Chinese provinces. The organization's staff also interviewed the family of a female factory worker who died of lead poisoning and six children with lead poisoning.

The study noted that lead poisoning among children has become one of the most common pediatric ailments in China, as children tend to absorb about 50 percent of the lead they are exposed to, compared to 10–15 percent for adults. Exposure typically occurs from inhaling factory smokestack exhaust in the air, but exposure can also occur from factory workers bringing fine particles of lead home in their clothing. Many Chinese villages are organized around heavy industry, like lead smelting factories, so residents tend to live in close proximity to lead processing.

Under Chinese law, children under the age of fourteen living within one kilometer of these businesses are eligible for free lead testing, an acknowledgement of heavy metal pollution, but the testing is not advertised. Human Rights Watch discovered that parents who had their children tested often could not obtain the results. Others were shown initial results but denied access to follow-up tests. One grandmother's experience was representative:

> [My granddaughter's] first test, done at the hospital in our local town was 18 ug/dL [micrograms per deciliter of blood, almost double the normal level].[7] We went back for another test, which we had to pay for ourselves. The doctor said her results were fine. We didn't believe him, so we asked to see the results, but he wouldn't give them and just said the results were fine. We don't have any power to force him to give them to us so we don't know what her true result is now.[8]

On the whole, it appeared as if the local clinics offered blood tests to better inform the government, not their patients. Doctors administered blood tests in some communities without even informing people they were testing for lead.

In places where clinics were more forthcoming with results indicating abnormally high levels of lead, doctors frequently gave children's parents dietary advice only. But doctors offered this counsel inconsistently. Prescriptions to "eat more apples" in one province yielded to "drink more milk" in another. Rarely did doctors offer medicine beyond foodstuffs like garlic. Even when young people were hospitalized, few medical interventions took place.[9]

The Human Rights Watch report shines a light on just one dimension of China's environmental catastrophe, but the lead-poisoning epidemic represents in microcosm the overall consequences of environmental pollution in China. Lightly regulated factories bring jobs and economic growth to China, but they also poison creation, including factory workers and their families. Despite some recently enacted environmental laws, local and central government officials frequently look the other way because their highest priority is economic growth. These same officials often have a financial stake in companies that pollute.[10] Local elites and consumers in developed countries will continue to get the products they need at reasonable prices, but the "true cost" will be borne by families like the Hans.

Lead poisoning is just one example of the environmental challenges posed by globalization. Another growing problem, spurred by the demands of the global economy, is the legacy of e-waste. U.S. electronic waste—our discarded computers, televisions, cell phones, etc.— grows with every new computer or phone we purchase. Increasingly, we upgrade our electronics before they wear out or break, tossing out the old models. And every one of these items contains hazardous substances, safely contained during normal use, but released when the product is broken open or burned.

I was relieved when, after a computer upgrade, I learned that my New Jersey town recycled computers, mobile phones, televisions, and other electronics.[11] No more would I fret about old circuit boards leaking heavy metals into the groundwater under landfills. My four year-old clunker (which still functioned, but with lots of quirks) would be *recycled!* Meaning what?

The truth is so far from what most Americans would call recycling as to suggest "greenwashing." First, a majority of American e-waste is "recycled" overseas. If, for example, a discarded computer still functions, it is typically shipped to West Africa for reuse. But many broken and barely functioning computers are commonly mixed in with the operational machines. These useless computers go straight to landfills like the Agbogbloshie Dump, near Accra, Ghana, [12] where young men and boys as young as five years old smash the items open to remove metal components.[13] Sometimes they burn rubber to separate worthless components from copper; in other instances, they sell the waste directly to local businesses, which extract precious metals and dump or incinerate what remains.

Used but functioning computers follow a different path. They are sold at a fraction of their original value, putting computers in the hands of those who might otherwise not have access, a positive development. But the reused computers have a shorter lifespan than new computers and will eventually meet the same fate as nonfunctioning machines. Now situated in a LDC, the American computer has virtually no chance of being recycled properly. What started as a good deed—donating an unneeded computer—then causes hardship, as the computer leaks lead, cadmium, and brominated flame retardants into the soil, air, and groundwater.[14]

The vast majority[15] of America's discarded electronics is shipped to Asia for recycling, to operations in China, India, Indonesia, Cambodia, Malasia, and Sri Lanka. As in Ghana, Asian recyclers remove items of value, such as gold or copper, but using methods like open-air wire burning and open acid baths. Both of these processes release lead into the environment. Recyclers burn or dump leftover components, releasing more lead, mercury, and cadmium into the atmosphere, soil, and groundwater.[16] Similar primitive "recycling" processes are employed in Mexico, where 20 percent of U.S. car batteries end up. As the batteries are broken for recycling, lead disperses in the form of dust and vapor during the melting process.[17] These emissions cause health problems in adults, but even more severe difficulties for children, born and unborn, whose nervous systems are still developing. For this reason, some leaders in the American pro-life movement have become involved in environmental activities promoting stricter regulation of toxic waste disposal.[18]

The environmental poisoning of children in developing countries is one more dimension of the violence of globalization. But outraged citizens of both developed and LDCs have demanded and won new rules to regulate e-waste and limit the effects of its toxicity on children and adults. Signed in 1992 and implemented in 1995 by ninety countries, the Basel Convention is one example of such actions. The Basel Convention compels signee nations exporting hazardous waste (including e-waste) to obtain informed written consent before shipping. Additional pressure from LDCs, Denmark, and the NGO Greenpeace led to the 1995 passage of an amendment (the Ban Amendment) to completely ban the shipment of toxic waste, including e-waste, to LDCs. The amendment will go into effect when 68 of the original 90 parties ratify it. Currently, 51 of the original parties have approved the amendment, and the Basel Action Network, an NGO specifically focused on the implementation of the Convention, estimates full ratification will take 2–3 more years.[19] There are currently 178 parties to the Convention, including the European Union and China. The United States has signed, but not ratified, the Convention, meaning that the Convention will not acquire the force of law in the United States until the Senate ratifies the agreement by a two-thirds majority vote.

The terms of the Basel Convention need not simply shift the location of e-waste dumping grounds. State-of-the-art processes can extract reusable metals from discarded electronic components, and recyclers can then properly dispose of what remains. Scientists note that these new forms of precious-metals recycling are much less harmful to the environment than mining itself. For example, the United States Geological Survey has stated that "one metric ton of computer scrap contains more gold than 17 metric tons of ore and much lower levels of harmful elements common to ores, such as arsenic, mercury, and sulfur."[20] Proper recycling of e-waste harms neither LDCs nor developed countries. And if all nations ratified the Basel Convention, recycling costs would create a level playing field in industry, since all companies would bear such expenses equally.

E-waste and lead poisoning are just the tip of the environmental iceberg we cruise toward. It would be easy to fill this book with retching examples of environmental degradation in pursuit of lower prices and higher profits, from the lagoons of pig excrement in the United States to the burning of mercury-laced coal in China, to the destruction of the Amazon rain forest for timber, and on and on. But we should also focus on what lies beneath the tip and is often ignored in public discussions of the environment: the three-fourths of the earth covered by water.

The Great Pacific Garbage Patch

Marta watched as a stranger dropped the empty Diet Coke bottle onto the Alameda, California, street. It looked hard to balance two bags while talking on a cell phone and crossing the street! To Marta's surprise, the woman did not stop, and the bottle rolled down a hill and out of sight. "Too late to get that one," she thought.

Marta imagined the journey ahead. The plastic bottle would continue to the bottom of the hill. Then the afternoon rains would wash it into a storm drain emptying into a local creek. The current would float the bottle to San Francisco Bay and out to sea. This Diet Coke bottle would ride the tide and ocean currents for thousands of miles to its final destination: the Great Pacific Garbage Patch.

Halfway between the California coast and Hawaii lies the North Pacific subtropical gyre, where ocean currents move slowly in a clockwise direction. What floats into a gyre's gentle whirlpool is unlikely to float out. The North Pacific subtropical gyre draws in plastic debris from the Pacific coasts of the United States, Mexico, and Japan, as well as ships crossing the ocean. It has come to be known as the Great Pacific Garbage Patch.

Competitive sailor and amateur oceanographer Charles Moore discovered the garbage patch in 1997. Moore was en route to California after winning third place in the Transpac competition, a sailing race from Los Angeles to Hawaii. On the return home, he decided to flip the motor on and take a shortcut through the peaceful currents of the gyre. Moore discovered what no person had yet seen—a swirling soup of plastic debris twice the size of Texas. Bottles and caps, cigarette lighters, forks, spoons, straws, toys, toothbrushes, tampon applicators, and wrappers, the detritus of everyday life, gently circled around. Beneath the surface, bits of plastic the size of rice grains called "nurdles" moved like plankton through the water. "It seemed unbelievable," he wrote later, "but I never found a clear spot. In the week it took to cross the subtropical [gyre], no matter what time of day I looked, plastic debris was floating everywhere."[21]

Gyres are found throughout the world's oceans, and five similar garbage patches have been identified: in the western Pacific Ocean; off the coast of Chile; near the western coast of Antarctica; the northwestern Gulf of Mexico; and the Atlantic's Sargasso Sea. Recreational divers and oceanographers have found numerous other smaller swaths of human jetsam throughout the world's oceans.[22]

These garbage patches are ugly, to be sure, but they are also deadly—to sea life and ultimately to humans. Plastic bags kill sea turtles, whales, and whale sharks when ingested, because they create blockages in creatures' digestive systems.[23] Seabirds, too, die when they ingest plastic, as it clogs their throats, gullets, and digestive organs. The United Nations Environment Programme estimates that the ingestion of plastic kills a million seabirds and 100,000 marine mammals each year.[24]

The physical violence to animals caused by the discarded refuse of the global economy is problematic, but even more troubling is its chemical violence. Plastic items do not biodegrade—they photodegrade into those tiny "nurdles" (in some countries they are called "mermaids tears," as they outnumber grains of sand on the beaches). Factories make all plastic consumer items, from combs to lawn chairs, out of nurdles. Even though many plastic objects have photodegraded, nearly every nurdle ever created (except for those that have been burned) is still with us, including 100 million tons floating in the oceans.[25] Those nurdles outweigh plankton in the Great Pacific Garbage Patch by a ratio of six to one.[26]

Nurdles are like sponges; they soak up whatever chemicals are present in seawater. They have a special knack for absorbing DDT (dichlorodiphenyltrichloroethane, an insecticide), PCB (polychlorinated biphenyl, a toxic fluid used in motors, capacitors, and transformers), and mercury. When zooplankton, mussels, and other plankton feeders mistake nurdles for plankton, these toxins enter their bodies. As larger creatures feed on the smaller ones, the chemicals make their way up the food chain into fish eaten by humans. That "wild, deep sea" fish you had for dinner last night may well contain more toxins than farm-raised fish.

Chemicals normally present in plastics like phthalates and Bisphenol-A (BPA)[27] also appear to be leaching into marine life that ingest nurdles. Scientists at the Agalita Marine Research Foundation have discovered the same toxic chemicals normally present in plastic items in fish tissues. Their conclusion? The chemicals come from the plastic nurdles the fish eat.[28] As with other toxics like DDT, these chemicals concentrate as they move up the food chain, until they arrive on the human dinner plate, a quiet, mostly unseen, manifestation of the violence of globalization. That discarded soda bottle in Alameda may be worth chasing down, after all.

In this chapter we have considered, thus far, the violence of globalization against God's creation in land and sea. Lead poisoning among children, the challenge of e-waste, and the massive quantities of plastic in the sea have been our focus. Now we turn to the air, and what may be the greatest threat to human life the planet has ever seen—global climate change.

The Challenge of Climate Change

I was eight years old when my father, a physical oceanographer, explained the warming of the earth to me.[29] It was 1974. President

Nixon had just resigned over the Watergate scandal. The Cold War still provoked nightmares of nuclear war. An epidemic of divorce was sweeping the country, and abortion was newly legalized. But Dad insisted that this newly discovered environmental problem might well threaten life on the planet as we know it. It may not be a stretch to say the last thirty-eight years has proved him right.

The basic science of climate change has not changed much since the 1970s, though it was called "the greenhouse effect" back then. Thermal radiation from the sun bounces off our planet, and heat-trapping gasses like carbon dioxide retain just the right amount of it for our planet to support life as we know it. Sometimes, these gasses are called "greenhouse gasses."

When we alter the mixture of gasses in the atmosphere, we change its heat-trapping properties. A broad consensus of scientists now agree that the human contribution of additional carbon dioxide and other greenhouse gasses to the atmosphere has resulted in higher temperatures and rising sea levels worldwide. The U.S. Catholic bishops have endorsed the findings of the Nobel Peace Prize–winning Intergovernmental Panel on Climate Change (IPCC)[30] and called on Catholics and others of goodwill to respond to their findings with prudence. The IPCC is a scientific organization which originated in the United Nations Environment Programme and the World Meteorological Organization. Its purpose is to review worldwide research on climate change, engaging thousands of scientists globally in the production of its reports. At this time, 194 countries are members of the IPCC. We have chosen to quote only the IPCC on the science of climate change because it summarizes the consensus views of many different studies, and the organization enjoys both a reputation for evenhandedness and the endorsement of the USCCB.

The IPCC's *Climate Change 2007: Synthesis Report* defines climate change as a "change in the state of the climate that can be identified"[31] by changes in temperature, sea level, and other properties of our climate. "It refers to changes over time, whether due to natural variability or human activity."[32] Using this definition, the panel investigated average air and ocean temperatures throughout the world over time, measurements of snow and ice covers, and various sea levels. Their conclusion is that "warming of the climate system is unequivocal"[33] (100 percent certain). The evidence, as captured in their mapping of air and sea temperature measurements, photographic evidence of ice sheets and glaciers, and measurements of changing sea levels does not allow for any other conclusion (though many nonscientists nevertheless do so). Indeed, the sum of all of the *natural* effects of the sun's activities and the earth's active volcanoes in recent years are likely (>90 percent) to have produced *cooling* effects on planetary temperatures, not warming.

In addition to greenhouse gasses, "feedback systems," or effects that become causes, amplify the rise in temperatures. For example, white snow reflects more energy back to the sun than a green and brown landscape, so snow melt causes more snow melt. The same holds true for water vapor. With increased temperatures, the amount of water vapor in the air increases, and so does the temperature. Fully understanding these feedback mechanisms—what they are and how they operate—continues to be one of the big challenges of climate-change science.[34]

The IPCC also points to weather events correlated with global warming, determining the likelihood that these phenomena are caused by higher temperatures: the increase in the number of hot days and nights (>90 percent), the increase in the number of heat waves (>66 percent), the increase in heavy rainfall in most areas (>66 percent, and the increase in incidence of very high sea levels (>66 percent). The panel also suggests that increased hurricane activity may be caused by the increase in temperatures, but because past data extends only to 1970, no clear answers can be offered.[35] Changes in the weather associated with global warming are the reason the term "global climate change" came into use—temperature alone does not capture the scope of the issue.

So what is causing climate change? The IPCC notes that greenhouse gas emissions (carbon dioxide, nitrous oxide, methane, hydrofluorocarbons, perfluorocarbons, and sulphurhexafluoride) "due to human activities have grown since pre-industrial times, with an increase of 70 percent observed between 1970 and 2004."[36] Some of these gasses were hardly present in nature before the industrial revolution.[37] The panel concludes that "there is *very high confidence* [original italics] (>95 percent) that the global average net effect of human activities since 1750 has been one of warming. "[38]

If the trends identified by the IPCC continue, many negative effects are anticipated. But we cannot project the future without knowing whether fossil fuels will be our main source of energy through the end of the century. In addition, we do not know what the effect of the 20 percent annual increase in air conditioner use in China and India will be on climate change. The gases emitted by air conditioners have thousands of times more impact on the heat-trapping properties of the atmosphere than carbon dioxide, which tends to get most of the attention.[39] Will air conditioning use in India and China come to rival that of the United States? Will a technological fix emerge? Stay tuned! Other uncertainties include world population and the economic growth rate in Africa and other parts of the world in the second half of the twenty-first century.

For this reason, the IPCC developed six different development scenarios,[40] each representing a different future snapshot of energy use, population growth, and economic development—each with its own output of greenhouse gases between today and the year 2100. None of the scenarios eliminates temperature rise and climate change, but the range is +3.2 degrees Fahrenheit to +7.2 degrees Fahrenheit, with a six-inch to about two-feet rise in sea level.[41]

All of these scenarios would bring about more droughts, heat waves, severe storms, stronger hurricanes, and more flooding. Some parts of the world (Greenland, for example) would see increased crop yields, while others (large areas of Africa and Asia) would see lower agricultural production and increased famine. The likelihood of all of these events is hard to predict, but the IPCC forecasts for extreme weather events throughout the planet range from 90 to 95 percent.[42]

Ninety to 95 percent. Former Vice President Dick Cheney once famously remarked, "If there's a 1% chance that Pakistani scientists are helping Al Qaeda build or develop a nuclear weapon, we have to treat it as a certainty in terms of our response." Thomas Friedman and others have suggested that, we should apply Vice President Cheney's "precautionary principle" to the arena of climate change.[43] If the best scientists in the world have reviewed all of the scientific literature and concluded that there is a 100 percent certainty that the earth is warming (with all of the catastrophic weather associated with warmer temperatures) and a 95 percent chance the phenomenon is in part human caused, we should take it seriously and fashion a prudent response. The USCCB calls for applying this virtue of prudence in their 2001 statement *Global Climate Change: A Plea for Dialogue, Prudence, and the Common Good,* a teaching document rooted in Catholic teaching on the care of God's creation, to which we now turn.

WHAT THE CHURCH TEACHES

Scholars and journalists have used many terms to describe the church's teaching on the care of God's creation: environmental justice, ecological justice, stewardship of creation, the promotion of the integrity of creation—but it's all the same teaching. Rooted in the Hebrew scriptures, Catholic teaching on the environment reaches all the way back to creation and God's description of the cosmos and humanity as "very good" (Gen. 1:31). The Creator charged human beings at their creation with "dominion" over the earth and its creatures, properly understood as stewardship, or a mission "to till it and keep it."[44]

Care of God's creation is the oldest strand of the Catholic social tradition. God's creation is "very good" and worthy of protection, care, and cultivation. As the psalmist sings (Ps. 24), "The earth is the Lord's and all it holds, / the world and those who live there; / for God founded it on the seas,/established it over the rivers." Our charge as stewards comes from the Creator, not from ourselves.

Other Hebrew scriptures underscore the dignity of creation, to the degree that creation itself is expected to join humanity in worship. Freed from the fiery furnace, Shadrach, Meshach, and Abednego offer this song of praise:

> Sun and moon, bless the Lord,
>   praise and exalt him above all forever.
> Stars of heaven, bless the Lord;
>   praise and exalt him above all forever.

Every shower and dew, bless the Lord;
   praise and exalt him above all forever.
All you winds, bless the Lord;
   praise and exalt him above all forever.
Fire and heat, bless the Lord,
   praise and exalt him above all forever.
Cold and chill, bless the Lord,
   praise and exalt him above all forever.
Let the earth bless the Lord,
   praise and exalt him above all forever.
Mountains and hills, bless the Lord,
   praise and exalt him above all forever.
Everything growing on the earth, bless the Lord,
   praise and exalt him above all forever.

(Dan. 3:62–67, 74–76)

Centuries later, none other than St. Francis of Assisi echoed their praise in his famous "Sermon to the Birds."

In 1213, torn by conflicting commitments to contemplative life and a more outward secondssministry of preaching, St. Francis began to doubt the purpose of his movement of priests, brothers, and sisters, now known as the Franciscans. Should Franciscans focus on prayer, solitude, and contemplation, or roam the earth, preaching the Good News to all? Fortified by an encouraging conversation with confidants Brother Sylvester and Sister Clare, St. Francis rededicated himself to preaching as a key dimension of the Franciscan way of life. In his excitement, he began to preach to a group of birds he encountered in a field in eastern Italy. Evoking the canticle of the men in the fiery furnace, St. Francis addressed the birds:

> My little bird sisters, you owe much to God your Creator, and you must always and everywhere praise Him, because He has given you a double and triple covering, and your colorful and pretty clothing, and your food is ready without your working for it, and your singing that was taught to you by the Creator . . . and you are also indebted to him for the realm of the air which He assigned to you. Moreover, you neither sow nor reap, yet God nourishes you, and gives you the rivers

and springs to drink from. . . . So the Creator loves you very much, since he gives you many good things. Therefore, my little bird sisters, be careful not to be ungrateful, but strive always to praise God.[45]

In this creative homily, Francis launched a ministry of friendship with creation (building on his childhood experiences of awe in nature) that included both biblical elements of stewardship and of creation's praise of God.

The *Catechism of the Catholic Church* builds upon the ancient biblical precepts, integrating the tradition of the church regarding human stewardship of creation. In its treatment of creation, the *Catechism* notes, "Respect for laws inscribed in creation and the relations which derive from the nature of things is a principle of wisdom and a foundation for morality."[46] The human person "occupies a unique place in creation," created by God "in friendship."[47] Because of this friendship, God provided the Ten Commandments, among them the admonition "Thou shalt not steal." The *Catechism* links the seventh commandment to human stewardship of creation:

> The seventh commandment enjoins respect for the integrity of creation. Animals, like plants and inanimate beings, are by nature destined for the common good of past, present, and future humanity. Use of the mineral, vegetable, and animal resources of the universe cannot be divorced from respect for moral imperatives. Man's dominion over inanimate and other living beings granted by the Creator is not absolute; it is limited by concern for the quality of life of his neighbor, including generations to come; it requires a religious respect for the integrity of creation.[48]

The *Catechism* goes on to discuss the ethical treatment of animals, staking out a moderate position—the use of animals for food and clothing is permissible, and medical experimentation on animals is morally acceptable as long as it does not cause needless suffering or death and "contributes to caring for or saving human lives."[49]

The *Compendium of the Social Doctrine of the Church* takes the general principles found in the *Catechism* and notes some of their application in the encyclicals of the popes, placing "the protection of the environment" squarely within the responsibility of all people "for the common good of the whole of humanity and for future generations also."[50] The *Compendium* assigns responsibility for environmental injustice to "man's pretension of exercising unconditional dominion over things, heedless of any moral considerations,"[51] and calls for humanity to preserve *"a sound and healthy environment for all"* [original italics].[52] The *Compendium* continues, drawing attention to the following dimensions of ecological justice:

- *"Individual property is not the only legitimate form of ownership. The ancient form of community property also has a particular importance* [original italics]. Fair land distribution is "an effective means for safeguarding the natural environment."[53]

- The area of agriculture *"merits special attention"* [original italics] because of its "significance in safeguarding the natural environment."[54]

- Economic development and growth must be compatible with the environment,[55] "respect the cycles of nature,"[56] and businesses must "contribute to the common good also by protecting the natural environment."[57]

- In making consumer choices, the faithful should take into account "the level of protection of the natural environment [in the place] in which [the company] operates."[58]

- Consumerism, with its promotion of "artificial new needs which hinder the formation of a mature personality," is "a threat to future generations, who risk having to live in a natural environment that has been pillaged by an excessive and disordered consumerism."[59] "Serious ecological problems call for an effective change of mentality leading to the adaptation of new lifestyles."[60]

- The poor bear the brunt of environmental injustice, "whether they live in those lands subject to erosion and desertification, are involved in armed conflicts or subject to forced immigration, or because they do not have the economic and technological means to protect themselves from other calamities" or live in polluted lands near cities.[61]

- Government has a key role in fostering ecological justice. The state should be guided by the human "right to a safe and healthy natural environment."[62] All people have a right to water, and "satisfying the needs of all, especially of those living in poverty, must guide the use of water and the services connected to it."[63]

- People cannot reduce "nature to a mere object to be manipulated and exploited," but we must also avoid going to the opposite extreme, to "divinize" the earth or creation and place nature *"above the dignity of the human person himself"* [original italics].[64]

- As St. Francis realized (see above), "Christian culture has always recognized the creatures that surround man as also gifts of God to be nurtured and safeguarded with a sense of gratitude to the Creator." [65] Human beings should not see themselves as separate from "the environment."

The Pontifical Council for Justice and Peace compiled the *Compendium* late in the papacy of John Paul II. Since its publication, Benedict XVI has affirmed its findings and developed teaching summaries for new contexts.

In his 2009 encyclical, *Charity in Truth* (*Caritas in Veritate*), Benedict emphasized many of the environmental themes captured in the *Compendium*, with a specific emphasis on the context of the global economy. After dispensing with neopagan trends, the pope emphasized the wonder nature inspires in people and stressed his hopes for an "intergenerational justice" that would take into account the care of God's creation. The pope also decried the hoarding of energy resources and its role in the exploitation of poor countries, calling for "technologically advanced countries" to lower energy consumption.[66]

Benedict proposed a "shift in mentality" that would foster lifestyles characterized by "the quest for truth, beauty, goodness, and communion with others for the sake of common growth."[67] He also drew stronger connections between care of creation and pro-life issues, stating,

> If there is a lack of respect for the right to life and to a natural death, if human conception, gestation, and birth are made

> artificial, if human embryos are sacrificed to research, the conscience of society ends up losing the concept of human ecology and, along with that, environmental ecology. It is contradictory to insist that future generations respect the natural environment when our educational systems and laws do not help them to respect themselves. The book of nature is one and indivisible: it takes in not only the environment but also life, sexuality, marriage, social relations: in a word, integral human development. Our duties towards the environment are linked to our duties towards the human person, considered in himself and in relation to others. It would be wrong to uphold one set of duties while trampling on the other. Herein lies a grave contradiction in our mentality and practice today: one which demeans the person, disrupts the environment, and damages society.[68]

With these words, Benedict placed questions of ecological justice squarely within the pro-life movement, an action with great practical consequences for church activity in the public square.

In 2010, Benedict again privileged the issue of environmental stewardship with a World Day of Peace Message devoted entirely to the care of God's creation. In the message's very title, the pope turned previous Catholic social doctrine on its head, morphing Pope Paul VI's bumper sticker phrase (and motto of the U.S. Bishops' Catholic Campaign for Human Development), "If You Want Peace, Work for Justice," to "If You Want to Cultivate Peace, Protect Creation."[69] Perhaps too many words for a bumper sticker, but still revolutionary in that Benedict gave new prominence in a new century to this sometimes overlooked dimension of Catholic social teaching. While the message contained no new teaching (all of its themes could be found in the *Compendium* and *Charity in Truth*), it thrust the church's teaching on environmental justice back in the spotlight and helped earn Benedict the moniker "the green pope."

Closer to home, the U.S. Catholic bishops have been active on many environmental issues, applying the teaching cited above to the concerns of our day, including mountaintop removal, pollution, alternative energy development and climate change. Two major pastoral letters have already emerged in this century. Bishops in southwest

Canada and the northwest United States issued *The Columbia River Watershed: Caring for Creation and the Common Good* in 2000[70] as an appeal for balance in sorting out economic development and environmental challenges. The USCCB released their pastoral statement *Global Climate Change: A Plea for Dialogue, Prudence, and the Common Good* in 2001.[71] The pastoral letter holds up well after more than a decade, and its call for prudence in the face of near consensus in the scientific community seems all the more prophetic as the number of Americans who doubt the scientific findings on climate change has increased since the early years of this century.

Fostering a "religious respect for the integrity of creation" is one element of Catholic teaching on the environment explained in the *Catechism* and further developed in the *Compendium* and the teachings of Pope Benedict. Millions of Catholics and other Christians, as well as other people of good will, have taken that teaching to heart and acted on behalf of environmental justice. We now turn to specific examples of these signs of hope.

SIGNS OF HOPE

From Garbage Audit to Solar Panels: One Congregation's Journey

Pastor Seth Kaper-Dale sliced open the bulging black trash bag with a razor blade and hoisted it up, spilling the contents onto the church lawn. "Ughhhh!" reacted one parishioner. "Oh—there's a diaper!" added another. Laughter filled the church yard. "You don't go to seminary for this," the clergyman remarked.[72]

Like a city mayor initiating a giant public works project, Kaper-Dale kicked off the Reformed Church of Highland Park's garbage audit with ritual flourish, opening the ceremonial first bag. The New Jersey congregation partnered with GreenFaith, a national interfaith organization devoted to issues of ecological stewardship, to examine ways to raise their commitment to environmental justice. The process began with a fun, but yucky, exercise: the garbage audit. Cameras caught it all for the 2007 documentary film *Renewal*.

Latex-glove-wearing congregants opened dozens of trash bags, separating the contents into piles by category of refuse. An Episcopal priest, the Reverend Fletcher Harper, executive director of Green-Faith, surveyed the piles of garbage. Food waste. Aluminum cans. Plastic bottles and containers, glass, paper, wrappers, paper cups, Styrofoam cups, and, of course, coffee grounds. Reverend Harper immediately noted the number of recyclable items, estimating that over half of the trash fell into this category, a typical proportion. Surveying the twin mountains of paper and foam cups, he asked, "What's the solution?"

The church responded with a plan to add clearly marked recycling bins, begin composting organic waste for the church garden, and drink from mugs during coffee hour. The church's men's group disarmed skeptics who envisioned dirty mugs piled high in the kitchen sink by committing to clean any unwashed mugs for one year. The congregation also took steps to increase their energy efficiency, bringing in a GreenFaith energy consultant, who, in short order, recommended replacing antiquated lighting with compact fluorescent bulbs and purchasing a new boiler to replace the current model (which ran 200 degrees too hot). But the church did not stop there, beginning an investigation into the promise of solar energy for church buildings.

As part of the larger stewardship reflection, Reverend Harper led an ecospirituality discussion, and an exercise to help parishioners look at their "ecological footprint." In the first dialogue, Reverend Harper asked church members, "When did you experience God in the natural world—and why has this experience stuck with you?" One woman shared a summer camp memory, watching the sun rise from the top of a mountain. "It's the closest to God I've ever felt," she said, evoking the mountaintop experiences of scripture.

In the second exercise, an eleven-year-old boy sat with the adults among several computer stations. "How often do you eat pork, beef, or other meats?" he read from the screen prompt. "Very often!" the boy responded, "Because I do like meat." He finished the questions and awaited the computer's assessment. "If everyone consumed like you, we would need 5.4 planets," he read, his voice trailing off glumly. "That's really shocking."

The film ends with the blessing of the church's new solar panels, the most complex effort adopted by the Reformed Church of

Highland Park. Pastor Kaper-Dale offered this litany of thanks, with his wife, copastor Rev. Stephanie Kaper-Dale, at his side, and surrounded by church members:

> "Consumption of 19.6 barrels of oil avoided."
> "Thanks be to God!" (*all assembled*)
>
> "Consumption of 11,153 pounds of coal avoided."
> "Thanks be to God!"

Congregations like the Reformed Church of Highland Park that take on a sustained reflection on environmental stewardship can also enroll in GreenFaith's certification program, leading to designation as a GreenFaith Sanctuary. The two-year process emphasizes leadership development and concrete actions in the areas of worship, religious education, spirituality, developing relationships with environmental justice leaders, and legislative advocacy. In addition, participating congregations must meet comprehensive stewardship requirements in building management, waste processing, and grounds maintenance. Traditional and social media spread their stories of hope. Specific requirements, translated to the Catholic context, include:

◆ Implementing six liturgies over two years focused on the care of God's creation.

◆ Offering six weeks of catechesis on environmental justice over the two-year period.

◆ Providing special formation on environmental stewardship for clergy.

◆ Organizing one interfaith religious–environmental activity per year involving at least three religions.

◆ Holding at least one meeting per year for two years with a local or regional environmental justice leader to identify ways the parish can support environmental justice initiatives.

◆ Conducting at least one environmental justice advocacy campaign with GreenFaith or the state or national Catholic Conference of Bishops.

- Fostering specific activities to reduce energy use in the parish and encouraging sustainable transportation practices.

- Integrating environmentally sustainable food practices into parish events and conducting activities to conserve water.

- Implementing sustainable grounds maintenance activities.

- Encouraging parishioners to adopt these practices at home.

- Publicizing all of these efforts through the parish bulletin and website, (arch)diocesan newspaper, websites, social media, and local television stations and newspapers.

GreenFaith aims not only to help the parish achieve all of these discrete accomplishments, but to also revitalize the faith community, help develop leadership, save money, and accomplish larger visions like solar installations, farmers markets, community gardens, or other goals the parish develops.

The Roman Catholic Church of the Presentation in Upper Saddle River, New Jersey, enrolled in GreenFaith's certification program not long after Dennis Foley joined the staff. "I had a Coke at lunch," Dennis recalled, "and I didn't know what to do with the can—there was no recycling." Staff conversations brought to the surface a desire to do more. "Being good stewards is part of our mission," agreed the pastor, Fr. Bob Stag. Coincidentally, within a week, twelve parishioners from the parish's peace and justice commission approached Dennis with the notion of an environmental ministry to promote ecological stewardship within the parish and educate the faithful.

The group initiated its Green Team ministry by examining the infrastructure of the parish, initiating a recycling program, installing solar panels, and swapping out obsolete fluorescent lighting for more efficient twenty-first-century bulbs. Two "green fairs" raised the profile of the new ministry, and they began to educate parishioners about the role of the faithful in caring for God's creation. In May 2011, GreenFaith approved the Church of the Presentation's application for the certification process. Boasting over 3,500 families, the parish is now the largest congregation participating in the certification program.[73]

The St. Francis Pledge

When Sr. Mary Schmuck represented the Sisters of Mercy NGO at the United Nations in the 1980s, she attended a U.N. Environment Programme (UNEP) workshop. A UNEP environmental educator "suggested getting the churches involved," she recalled. "So we did, and then it went interfaith." As the group developed, Sr. Mary noticed a pattern to the diverse faith leaders' conversations. "They were all talking about St. Francis!" she exclaimed. The universal appeal of St. Francis and his message stuck with her. Today, as a coordinator for Catholic Charities in the Bardstown, Kentucky, area of the Archdiocese of Louisville, Sr. Mary finds St. Francis at her side again, as she organizes parishes, schools, and universities to foster environmental signs of hope.[74]

Sr. Mary describes her environmental ministry as "part cheerleader, part gadfly, part tracker." On behalf of Archbishop Joseph Kurtz,[75] she encourages Catholic organizations to adopt the St. Francis Pledge, an environmental covenant developed by the Catholic Coalition on Climate Change. The St. Francis Pledge commits individuals and organizations to:

- **Pray** and reflect on the duty to care for God's creation and protect the poor and vulnerable.

- **Learn** about and educate others on the causes and moral dimensions of climate change.

- **Assess** how we—as individuals and in our families, parishes and other affiliations—contribute to climate change by our own energy use, consumption, waste, etc.

- **Act** to change our choices and behaviors to reduce the ways we contribute to climate change.

- **Advocate** for Catholic principles and priorities in climate change discussions and decisions, especially as they affect those who are poor and vulnerable.[76]

The Catholic Coalition on Climate Change developed the St. Francis Pledge to help educate and organize the Catholic community in the United States on the church's approach to climate change, captured by the three key themes of the 2001 USCCB pastoral letter on climate change. Executive director Daniel Misleh describes this approach as "one, a plea for the common good, two, a reminder that the poor and vulnerable are already suffering from climate disruption and will continue to do so, and three, that common sense and prudence dictate we act sooner than later, even in the face of some uncertainty." The coalition encourages those taking the St. Francis Pledge (over 7,000 individuals, parishes, schools and other organizations) to act on legislative priorities identified by the USCCB.

Nineteen Catholic entities in the archdiocese have taken the pledge. Together with other parishes, agencies, schools—and Archbishop Kurtz himself—they have put together an impressive list of accomplishments. Here's just a sample:

- Assumption High School in Louisville broke ground in September 2011 for an 8,800-square-foot athletics complex including solar panels, a wind turbine, a plant life roof for half the building, recycled building materials, and temperature, water, and energy-tracking sensors for student experiments.

- St. Willam Parish in London installed solar panels to help power the church and weatherized its stained glass windows.

- St. Gregory Parish in Samuels, Kentucky, sold reusable grocery bags with the parish logo to cut down on the use of plastic bags, benefiting the parish's Lend-a-Hand ministry.

- While building a new one-thousand–seat sanctuary, Louisville's St. Peter the Apostle Church constructed a one-hundred–seat chapel for daily Mass and other smaller liturgies, so the large space does not have to be heated and cooled as often. More trees will also be added to the property in the landscaping process.

- The archdiocesan communications office has prepared environmental-stewardship bulletin announcements and distributed them to every parish.

- Trinity High School in Louisville coated its roof with reflective paint to reduce its cooling needs and bounce some of the sun's radiant energy back.

- Bellarmine University in Louisville has installed a geothermal heating/cooling system and is collecting rainwater from its activities center roof to use in flushing toilets and urinals.

- Archbishop Kurtz has pledged to raise his thermostat two degrees higher in summer and lower it two degrees in winter.

Sr. Mary believes the St. Francis Pledge helps Catholics stay focused on church teaching and spirituality. "It's asking people in the spirit of St. Francis to promise to pray about taking better care of creation," she explained, "to study the whole of creation issues, to look at how I'm using resources and make some choices about being better about it. It's not just environmentalism; it's also taking care of the poor people who get hurt when we don't take care of creation."[77]

E-Stewards Tackle E-Waste

We learned earlier how e-waste poisons not only the earth, but also the scavengers and recycling workers in LDCs who extract valuable materials from our discarded computers, cell phones, monitors, and televisions. In support of the Basel Convention, the secular Basel Action Network developed a certification project called E-Stewards, launched in 2010, that independently verifies American companies' selection of U.S.-based recyclers who meet a set of criteria. These requirements include not disposing in landfills or incinerators, not using prison labor, and not exporting to LDCs. E-Stewards auditors review each company's policies and actions and those of recyclers every three years.[78]

E-Stewards accredited a score of businesses and foundations in its first year, including Bank of America, Capital One, Wells Fargo, and Samsung. A competing e-waste recycling standard, called R-2, was also launched in 2010. R-2 means "responsible recycling," but, according to the two environmental organizations involved in the early stages of R-2's development, the standards have not met expectations. The bone of contention is this: unlike E-Stewards, R-2 allows the export of e-waste to LDCs, and permits landfill disposal under some circumstances. R-2 also lets recyclers determine which chemicals need to be monitored to protect workers' health, rather than setting the standard.[79] Both the Basel Action Network and the

Electronics TakeBack Coalition withdrew from the development of R-2 when the recycling industry refused to address concerns in these areas.

The E-Stewards recycling standard assures consumers that every purchase they make with certified companies contributes to the solution to the world's e-waste problem. The E-Stewards standard could be likened to Fair Trade certification, where an informed consumer base demanded ethical behavior, certified by independent auditors. But E-Stewards is not just for the private sector. Several foundations received certification early on, and the reality is, nonprofits junk old equipment too. Imagine what would happen, on a global scale, if the Roman Catholic Church only did business with recyclers audited by E-Stewards. Total, comprehensive participation would likely require the involvement of the pope himself, a plausible notion, considering Pope Benedict's own legacy of teaching and action on the care of God's creation.

The Green Pope

When Benedict XVI was elected in 2005, few predicted that by the end of the decade he would be known as "the green pope." He earned this nickname not simply by updating Catholic social teaching on the care of God's creation (which he has done), but by putting environmental doctrine into practice in a way no other pope before him has done.

Woodeene Koenig-Bricker details Benedict's stewardship initiatives in her book *Ten Commandments for the Environment*. For example, in 2007, the Vatican became the first "carbon-neutral" independent state in the world, in part from the installation of solar panels on the roof of the Paul VI Auditorium (saving eighty tons of oil per year) and a reforestation project in Hungary that will, by greatly increasing the number of trees, convert significant amounts of carbon dioxide to oxygen. Coming attractions may include the installation of small windmills at the papal estate at Castel Gandolfo and a solar energy system for Vatican Radio.[80]

In the area of sustainability, Benedict has brought his environmental sensibility into planning World Youth Day. Past World Youth Days had generated appalling levels of trash. But today, one measure of the event's success is how *little* waste is generated. Cornstarch plates that disappear in water are one of the ways planners minimize the leftovers of such a vast assembly of young people. But don't expect Benedict to start hugging trees anytime soon. As noted earlier, the church's environmental ethic emphasizes the stewardship role of humanity, not deifying creation or declaring all of creation equal in God's eyes.

Under Benedict's leadership, the Pontifical Academy of Sciences has also expanded its own research on climate change. Long known for its objectivity and independence from state concerns, the academy convenes eighty of the top scientists worldwide, believers and nonbelievers alike, around specific scientific questions raised in the pursuit of truth. Over the past century, over fifty academy members have won Nobel Prizes in the sciences. The academy's most recent report on climate change, *Fate of Mountain Glaciers in the Anthropocene*, documents the loss of mass and length of mountain glaciers throughout the world.[81] The term "anthropocene" refers to the "manmade" epoch of geological time in which we live, when human influences on the environment often outweigh natural factors. The report concludes that "widespread loss of ice and snow" during this period accounts for about one-third of recent sea level rise.[82]

The contributions of this scientific arm of the Holy See demonstrate one more dimension of the environmental legacy of Pope Benedict XVI. From the Pontifical Academy to solar panels to World Youth Day to reforestation, no other pope has implemented the environmental teachings of the church in so many and such diverse ways as Benedict. If it could be said that he has a signature public issue, it is environmental stewardship. The stakes are high: the survival of our planet.

From creation we now turn to one of its bounties—food. In chapter 7, we narrow our focus to the impact of globalization on the politics of food. The lack of food security in so many parts of the world, along with new perils such as obesity and diabetes, lead us into further dimensions of the violence of globalization.

DISCUSSION QUESTIONS

1. Inventory the plastic in your house. Which plastic items could you live without? Which would it be difficult to live without? Is it better to cut down on plastic or recycle more?

2. How frequently should you upgrade computers and smart phones? What should you do with unwanted or unneeded devices?

3. How can nations work together to both care for God's creation and provide for the economic needs of their people?

GO MAKE A DIFFERENCE

1. Take the St. Francis Pledge. Start a parish, school, or university dialogue about taking the St. Francis Pledge together. How will you pray, learn, assess, act, and advocate?

2. Hold a garbage audit for your parish, school, or university. Discuss the results and implications for action.

3. Consider applying for GreenFaith certification. Speak to your pastor, principal, or university administrator about the possibilities.

7

The Politics of Food

Lochoro, a mother of five living in Uganda, is one of 925 million hungry people in the world.[1] "I have not cooked anything today," she told an interviewer from the evangelical Christian aid organization World Vision. "I don't even know what the kids are going to eat." Obtaining enough food for the family was difficult enough before the drought came, ruining most crops in the Karamoja region of northern Uganda. Now one million Ugandans living in Karamoja are hungry.[2]

Lochoro earns money by collecting rainwater and delivering it by foot to soldiers a few miles away, for about 25 cents a trip. She also sells firewood at a village market four miles away. Each log must be hand carried. If sales go well, she will purchase eight rats to cook for her family. "I smoke the rats," she explained, "cut them into pieces, and fry the meat—or boil it if I don't have cooking oil." If sales falter, the family goes hungry.

Lochoro has tried other ways of obtaining food. "I planted sorghum," she said, "but the drought came and killed the plants." Violence in Karamoja has exacerbated Lochoro's plight. Battles between rival gangs of cattle rustlers have displaced thousands of families. Cut off from their livelihoods, formerly well-fed people are becoming hungry.

Some have turned to cutting down trees (deforestation) to burn into charcoal to sell. Such enterprises produce enough money to eat for a day, but they also contribute to the desertification of the area. Desertification means less arable land, fewer crops, and more hungry people. Climate change has been linked to the drought itself; deforestation will only exacerbate Lochoro's troubles and those of the region.

SIGNS OF THE TIMES

Almost one billion people in the world are chronically hungry. While East Asia has seen significant drops in its extreme poverty rate (formerly over 50 percent, now 16.8 percent), sub-Saharan Africa's extreme poverty rate remains unchanged at 50.9 percent, according to the World Bank.[3] All available research indicates that poverty rates have decreased overall worldwide, but the absolute number of hungry and undernourished people has increased—to 925 million in 2010.

Reverend David Beckmann, president of Bread for the World, offers a moving portrait of hunger in his book *Exodus from Hunger*. Bread for the World is an ecumenical Christian organization (with a plurality of Catholic members) that offers a united Christian voice on hunger issues in the United States and throughout the world. Beckmann, a Lutheran pastor who worked for the World Bank for many years, describes hunger as the leading killer of children worldwide— more than any disease. "One child dies every three seconds in developing countries, and undernutrition contributes to at least a third of these deaths. Little children are weakened by chronic hunger, so they often die of simple maladies such as measles or diarrhea," he writes.[4]

Reverend Beckmann introduces the term "undernutrition" as a measure of hunger. "Undernourished people do not get enough food to provide their bodies with the calories they need," he explained, "They certainly can't afford a diet that would give them the vitamins and minerals that would keep them healthy." For example, a child with vitamin A deficiency who gets enough calories to stave off hunger is nevertheless at higher risk of fatality from measles and gastrointestinal infections, and many also go blind from this form of undernutrition.

Extreme poverty offers further deprivations that exacerbate the effects of hunger. "Undernourished families . . . drink water from unsanitary sources," Beckman adds. "Their bodies are weakened by untreated disease. They don't know how to write or add, which makes planning ahead and smart farming difficult. They live in huts that don't fully protect them from the elements."

Beckmann connects hunger and the disproportionate suffering of women and girls, who "have the least education. They work long hours. They [like Lochoro] walk miles each day with heavy loads of water and firewood. In many cultures, they wait to eat until after the men and boys have had their fill."

Most Americans have some notion of the problem of world hunger—many of us grew up on public service announcements for global charities, the "We Are the World" and "Do They Know It's Christmas" ensemble songs, and the drama of the Live Aid and Live 8 concerts. But awareness of suffering does not always translate to understanding its causes. Many Americans still believe persistent myths about hunger. Food First, an organization founded by Frances Moore Lappe to address the causes of hunger, has developed a comprehensive list of facts and myths, culled from decades of research by its Institute for Food and Development Policy. Foremost among these myths is the notion that there is not enough food to go around. The truth, writes Food First's Holly Poole-Kavana, is that "abundance, not scarcity, best describes the world's food supply. Enough wheat, rice and other grains are produced to provide every human being with 3,200 calories a day. That doesn't even count many other commonly eaten foods—vegetables, beans, nuts, root crops, fruits, grass-fed meats, and fish." The biggest cause of hunger, she argues, is simply poverty. In many parts of the world where hunger is widespread, ample food is indeed available. The hungry just cannot afford to buy it. Surplus food is exported from these countries for sale to people who can afford to import agricultural products.[5]

Many people also believe the myth that high birth rates cause hunger. The reality, Poole-Kavana writes, is far more complicated. "For every Bangladesh, a densely populated and hungry country, we find a Nigeria, Brazil or Bolivia, where abundant food resources coexist with hunger. Or we find a country like the Netherlands, where very little land per person has not prevented it from eliminating hunger and becoming a net exporter of food." Again, poverty itself is the cause, and not population growth.[6]

Myths about hunger abound. But what are its causes?

◆ The Poverty Cycle: Most hungry people are poor. In many countries, enough food is available, but many people cannot afford its costs. Food sits in silos and stores while millions go hungry. With poverty also comes a social cycle that can be difficult to break. Farmers cannot afford the seed for the crops that would feed their families. Skilled-trade workers cannot afford the tools for living-wage craft jobs. Many people living in poverty are landless and, therefore, cannot grow food for themselves. Hungry people can't think as well or work as hard. They contract more diseases and take longer to recover. The effect of poverty—hunger—itself becomes a cause of poverty, and the poverty cycle continues.[7]

◆ U.S. Agricultural Subsidies: Aid to U.S. farmers, once seen as a way of preserving family farming and stimulating the rural U.S. economy, now mainly benefits large agribusiness companies operating massive "factory farms." Subsidies of certain U.S. crops have caused farmers in LDCs to give up agricultural work, since the subsidized American crops cost less than those produced at home. For example, the U.S. government pays American farmers $434 million per year to grow rice. In Haiti, where rice farmers used to produce enough for the whole country, the nation now imports 80 percent of its rice, and rice farmers have left rural areas to seek employment in the capital, Port-au-Prince. Of his previous support for rice subsidies, former President Bill Clinton now says, "It may have been good for some of my farmers in Arkansas, but it has not worked. I have to live every day with the consequences of the lost capacity to produce a rice crop in Haiti to feed those people, because of what I did."[8]

◆ Climate Change: At one time, experts relegated the role of natural disasters to the "myth" column. Overall world food production continued to be great enough to compensate for the occasional drought or flood. Today, floods, tropical storms, and extended droughts are increasing in frequency due to climate change (see chapter 6), making food security in low-income countries an even greater challenge. Drought, for example, is now the single most common cause of food shortages in the world. The Horn of Africa and Central America have been especially hard hit.[9]

◆ War: Armed conflict displaces millions of people from their homes and livelihood. In the Darfur region of Sudan, good rains and crops typically produced strong harvests, until fighting displaced over a million people. Food can also be used as a weapon in wartime, as soldiers destroy food and livestock, wreck local markets, and contaminate wells.[10]

♦ Insufficient Agricultural Infrastructure: The world produces more food than its population needs, but locally, some food shortages are caused by a lack of adequate agricultural infrastructure such as enough roads, warehouses, and irrigation. This lack of infrastructure leads to high transportation costs, a lack of storage facilities, and scarcity of water for crops. Each of these factors limits the capacity of food production. And with populations worldwide migrating from the countryside to the cities, most developing nations are investing in urban areas, not farming.[11]

♦ Exploitation of the Environment: Poor stewardship practices like deforestation, along with overcropping and overgrazing, deplete the earth's resources and ultimately decrease its productive capacity.[12]

♦ Biofuels: The transformation of corn, sugarcane, soybeans, and other crops into fuels (biofuels) was long seen as a possible solution to global energy shortages. But the impact of biofuel expansion in the twenty-first century was disastrous for hungry people, doubling food prices from 2006 to 2008 and crowding out crops that could feed the hungry. The trade-off between food and fuel can be quantified. As Lester Brown of the Earth Policy Institute has stated, "The grain it takes to fill a 25-gallon tank with ethanol just once will feed one person for a whole year."[13]

♦ Growing Demand for Meat: The irony of the dramatic drops in poverty across parts of Asia is that it has produced hunger—as newly affluent peoples demand more meat and dairy products. It takes three to seven pounds of grain to produce a pound of meat, so an increase of meat means a decrease in grain supplies—one reason China has become, for the first time in history, an importer of soy. India is also seeing a growing demand for animal products—dairy in particular.

♦ Speculation: In 2008, when the triple factors of drought, biofuels, and rising oil prices doubled food prices, speculators flocked to futures markets, deserting riskier investments in housing and stocks, and instead betting on rice, wheat, corn, and soy. Prices rose further on this demand, attracting further speculation. This vicious cycle put food out of the reach of millions of previously food-secure people, who simply had to cut back on food they couldn't afford.[14]

Several of these causes of hunger have been with us for centuries, but globalization has produced new factors contributing to hunger (like climate change and speculation) while accentuating others (like the poverty cycle and exploitation of the environment). Some causes of hunger, like war, arise from combinations of the other factors listed. Armed conflict over food supplies may sound like ancient history, but new developments in the politics of food suggest the worst is yet to come.

Haiti: The Hypocrisy of "Free Trade"

Haiti is on the brink of famine.[15] One-half of the children under five are malnourished. Daily caloric intake is 460 calories less than the minimum established by the United Nations.[16] In the poorest areas, almost all mothers have lost children to malnutrition. Years after the earthquake of January 2010, despite billions promised by the international community, hunger has never been worse. Why can't Haiti feed itself?

In 1980, Haiti was highly self-sufficient in meeting its nutritional needs. Today Haiti is dependent on outside help. Neither the earthquake, climate change, wars, nor crop failures are the cause of hunger in Haiti. Hunger in Haiti is the result of policies imposed by the United States and the International Monetary Fund (IMF), policies which, as noted above, have promoted the importation of U.S. rice. With an extraordinary degree of hypocrisy, we have imposed free trade on the Haitians to eliminate tariffs while at the same time paying our own farmers to undermine their Haitian counterparts.

In 1986, under President Ronald Reagan, the IMF and the U.S. government required Haiti to lower its tariffs (taxes) on imported foods from approximately 150 percent to 3 percent, in the name of free trade. These free-trade policies continued in 1991, when Jean-Bertrand Aristide, the first democratically elected president of Haiti, was removed in a military coup, a coup Dr. Paul Farmer and other

Haiti experts say was engineered in part by the CIA.[17] As a condition for supporting his return, the United States, the IMF and the World Bank required Haiti to further reduce tariffs on rice.

At the same time, in violation of free-trade principles, we continued to subsidize our own farmers so they could sell rice in Haiti at a price well below what the Haitian farmers could charge. From 1995 to 2009, the U.S. government paid $12.5 billion to U.S. rice farmers.[18] This policy made it cheaper for Haitians to buy food from U.S. farmers than from Haitians. Haitian imports of rice then went from zero in 1980 to 200,000 tons by 1997. In 2008, Haiti became the third-largest importer of U.S. rice—240,000 metric tons.[19] Tens of thousands of farmers went out of business and moved to Port-au-Prince to live in shoddy houses on unstable terrain, in ravines and on steep mountainsides. Many of these farmers were among the 300,000 killed in the thirty-eight-second earthquake on January 12, 2010.

Currently, Haitian farmers are estimated to comprise 66 to 80 percent of all Haitians.[20] The question that should be asked is not why can't Haiti feed itself? Rather, we should ask why the richest nation on earth would destroy the most important industry in the poorest nation in their hemisphere.

Food Colonies: The New Face of Neocolonialism

When food prices doubled from 2006 to 2008, some food-exporting countries, like Vietnam and Argentina,[21] limited or prohibited the export of food to ensure an adequate domestic supply and to keep prices down locally. Some wealthier nations dependent on food imports panicked and began to look at novel methods to ensure a stable food supply for their citizens. Unlike the United States, blessed with enough arable land to feed its own population and still export food for profit, these countries cannot simply plant more food to meet their nutritional needs now or in the future. But they do have money from other sectors of the economy—like oil.

And they are using this affluence to purchase or lease land in poorer countries to grow food for themselves. Often, these deals force out small producers farming the land that is sold or leased, like those with whom Sr. Dorothy Stang ministered. The largest of these land acquisitions have been initiated by Saudi Arabia, South Korea, and China. Joining them in the hunt for further land acquisitions are Egypt, Libya, Bahrain, Qatar, and the United Arab Emirates.[22]

China has obtained the largest parcels of land, buying or leasing seven million acres in the Democratic Republic of the Congo to produce palm oil for food and fuel. The details of the agreement are not available—most of these deals are negotiated in secret, with binding confidentiality agreements. To illustrate the scale of the land deal, the Congolese utilize only three million acres to produce corn, their staple grain, for domestic food supplies. Other countries leasing or selling cropland to foreign countries include Sudan, Ethiopia, Mozambique, the Philippines, Brazil, Argentina, and Paraguay. Many of these countries also receive aid from the World Food Programme (WFP). For example, in January 2009, just as Saudi Arabia received the first shipment of rice from its lands in Ethiopia, the WFP distributed aid to 5 million Ethiopians.[23]

Land acquisition is also water acquisition, as many of the lands in question are rich in water resources. In Ethiopia, for example, the headwaters of the Nile might become part of a food deal, but then be diverted to irrigation projects benefiting the investing country and depleting the water supply of those downstream. Another environmental consequence is the clearing of rain forests. In Brazil, for example, expanding cropland often means shrinking the area of carbon-sequestering rain forests, raising greenhouse gas emissions (see chapter 6).[24]

Many Brazilian farmers and local political leaders view Chinese interest in their agricultural lands with suspicion, contradicting their government's stated policy of "strategic partnership" with China. Local officials in Urucu, Brazil, rebuffed Chinese overtures in 2011, under pressure from small- and medium-sized farmers. The Chinese who wanted land to grow soybeans needed to satisfy the increased demand for chicken and hog feed in China.

Negotiations led to a compromise: The Chinese would provide Brazilian farmers with access to credit to purchase seed, fertilizer, farming equipment, and so on. In return, the Chinese would obtain the right to purchase the soybeans at a fair price, an arrangement with far more benefits to Brazilians than simply selling or leasing the land. Brazil's Congress and courts have also taken action to limit the purchase of land by foreigners after growing uneasiness about the quantity of Brazilian land owned by people from outside Brazil. In Brazil's Sao Paulo state, foreigners own about 20 percent of the land.[25]

Such "push-back" agreements have not emerged in Africa, where populations are poorer, land is cheaper, and governments are more corrupt. An acre of land can be leased for a dollar a year in many parts of Africa, while the same land in Asia would cost $100/year to lease. Clearly, Africa will see more of these neocolonial arrangements, whereby affluent countries grow food in nations where hunger abounds. The violence of hunger will continue to ravage poor countries, but armed conflict is also expected. Lester Brown, director of the Earth Policy Institute, asks some tough questions on this subject: "If food prices are rising in the host country, will the investing country actually be able to remove the grain it has purchased on acquired land? Will the hungry people in these countries stand by and watch as grain is exported from land that was once theirs? Or will the investors have to hire security forces to ensure that the harvests can be shipped home?"[26] Imagine the "rice wars," "wheat wars," or "water wars" that would follow! Thus far, such arrangements have not produced this kind of violence. But as the practice becomes more widespread, it seems increasingly likely. Our world would experience an entirely new form of neocolonial conflict, a heretofore unseen dimension of the violence of globalization.

Our Fat, Malnourished Country

The experience of hunger, that is, not getting enough calories from food consumed, is one form of malnutrition. But in the United States, a new form of malnutrition has become widespread, characterized by the consumption of processed food with an excess of calories and an absence of nutrition. The same Americans are both obese and malnourished.

In response, Michael Pollan opens his best-selling book *In Defense of Food* with some simple advice. "Eat food. Not too much. Mostly plants."[27] Consider for a moment the first sentence: "Eat food." In many of the LDCs, the problem is the availability and the affordability of food. In the United States, health often eludes us because what we eat is not food ("edible nonfood substances"), or it is heavily processed, stripped of its nutrients, with all manner of chemicals added. Pollan explains:

> The chronic diseases that now kill us can be traced directly to the industrialization of our food: the rise of highly processed foods and refined grains; the use of chemicals to raise plants and animals in huge monocultures; the superabundance of cheap calories of sugar and fat produced by modern agriculture; and the narrowing of the biological diversity of the human diet to a tiny handful of staple crops, notably wheat, corn, and soy. These changes have given us the Western diet that we take for granted: lots of processed foods and meat, lots of added fat and sugar, lots of everything—except vegetables, fruits, and whole grains.[28]

It is those vegetables, fruits, and whole grains that satiate us, turning off the hunger pangs that make us overeat, and providing nutrients. On the other hand, processed grains and sugars have the opposite effect—they make us crave more while delivering less nutrition. Corn syrup–sweetened sodas and fruit "drinks" and "cocktails" do the same, efficiently delivering calories to our bodies while making us crave more.

The result of this abundance of calories and dearth of nutrients is a nationwide epidemic of obesity. Some concerned observers have called this epidemic "overnutrition."[29] Researchers at the Centers for Disease Control and Prevention conclude that about one-third (33.8 percent) of adults and 17 percent of children and adolescents in the United States are obese, meaning their "body mass index" (BMI), a measurement of body fat in relationship to height, is 30 or higher. A person who measures five feet nine inches and weighs 203 pounds would have a BMI of 30, the lower end of the definition.[30] Louisiana weighs in at 31 percent obese, a proportion that stood at 14 percent in 1990, before supersize fast-food portions and massive soda serving sizes appeared. Consequences of obesity include increased risk of coronary heart disease, type 2 diabetes, cancer, high blood pressure, stroke, liver disease, and arthritis.[31]

One of the most perverse trends of globalization is the phenomenon of large segments of people in LDCs rising up from poverty and then adopting the Western diet. Obesity and its associated health problems are always the result, with renewed pressure on world grain supplies. Is this what our antipoverty, antihunger efforts should lead to—an abundance of obese, malnourished people? Meanwhile, in our own country, federal subsidies of corn and soy produce cheap fatty meat and empty calories. Hungry people living in poverty reach for the most inexpensive foods and wind up purchasing low-nutrition, high-calorie foods. Some would like to purchase fresh produce but cannot find any locally. These areas are often called "food deserts." At day's end, the Western diet is but another form of malnutrition, a bitter irony of the politics of food.

WHAT THE CHURCH TEACHES

Church teaching on hunger is not simply a matter of what the church recommends or a question of increasing one's holiness—our very salvation depends on how we respond to hungry people. In Matthew's Gospel, Jesus describes the Last Judgment, "[w]hen the Son of Man comes into his glory, and all the angels with him" (Matt. 25:31). Christ sits on a "glorious throne," separating people into two groups—the righteous sheep, destined for heaven, and the accursed goats, thrown "into the eternal fire prepared for the devil and his angels." The test is how they treated the hungry, the thirsty, the stranger, the sick, and the imprisoned during life on earth, for "whatever you did for one of these least brothers of mine you did for me" (Matt. 25:31–46).

This dramatic teaching of Jesus is rooted in Hebrew traditions of care for the people living in poverty. For example, Proverbs 22:9 states, "The kindly man will be blessed, for he gives of his sustenance to the poor." Isaiah 58:10 teaches, "If you bestow your bread on the hungry and satisfy the afflicted; then light shall rise for you in the darkness, and the gloom shall become for you like midday." Lamentations 2:19 also exhorts, "Lift up your hands to him for the lives of your little ones who faint from hunger at the corner of every street." So, in the Gospels, when Jesus counsels care for those who are poor, he teaches as a rabbi. But when he states, "I was hungry and you gave me food," he takes the Hebrew teaching a step further, stressing that how one treats hungry people is how one treats God—and these actions have ramifications for salvation!

In Luke's Gospel, the parables of Jesus also demonstrate a commitment to hungry people. The "rich man who dressed in purple garments and fine linen and dined sumptuously each day" ignores the poor man lying at his door "who would have gladly eaten his fill" of the rich man's table scraps. When they both die, the rich man finds himself tormented in flames, and notices Lazarus at the side of Abraham, quite content and happy (Luke 16:19–31). The parable indicates where God's sympathies lie. When asked in Luke 3:10 about how to produce good fruits in one's life, Jesus replies, "Whoever has two cloaks should share with the person who has none. And whoever has food should do likewise."

The letter of James maintains Jesus' concern for the hungry in the life of the early church. James takes on those who would respond to hungry people with piety alone, stating, "If a brother or sister has nothing to wear and no food for the day and one of you says to them, 'Go in peace, keep warm, and eat well,' but you do not give them the necessities of the body, what good is it? So also faith of itself, if it does not have works, is dead" (James 2:14–17). Through the teachings of Jesus and James, we therefore move from the Hebrew notion of helping hungry people as an important part of God's law, to Christ's requirement for salvation, to James' assertion that responding to the hungry is essential for faith of any kind. In the fourth century, St. Basil the Great applied these teachings to his times, with words that still ring true today, "The bread that you store up belongs to the hungry; the coat that lies in your chest belongs to the naked; the gold you have hidden in the ground belongs to the poor."[32]

The *Catechism of the Catholic Church* affirms the requirement to give food to the hungry in its treatment of the profession of faith, quoting from the Last Judgment of Matthew 25.[33] The letter of James, and its insistence on works as the fruit of faith, is also addressed in the *Catechism*. In a section concerning "Love for the Poor," organized under the seventh commandment, "You shall not steal," paragraph

2447 elaborates on these works and identifies feeding the hungry as one of the "corporal works of mercy."[34]

The *Catechism* locates further discussion of hunger in its treatment of the fifth commandment, "You shall not kill," noting, "The acceptance by human society of murderous famines, without efforts to remedy them, is a scandalous injustice and a grave offense. Those whose usurious and avaricious dealings lead to the hunger and death of their brethren in the human family indirectly commit homicide, which is imputable to them."[35]

Finally, the *Catechism* takes response to hungry people out of the realm of individual volition, invoking the "grave moral responsibility" of rich nations toward poor countries, as "a duty in solidarity and charity . . . [and] an obligation in justice if the prosperity of the rich nations has come from resources that have not been paid for fairly."[36] Living up to these obligations may take the form of "direct aid" but must not end there. "International economic and financial institutions" must also be reformed "so that they will better promote equitable relationships with less advanced countries . . . especially in the area of agricultural labor."[37]

The *Compendium of the Social Doctrine of the Church*, like the *Catechism*, turns the focus back to Matthew 25,[38] but it also introduces a set of modern considerations such as the role of molecular biology and genetics in fighting hunger:

> [T]echnology could be a priceless tool in solving many serious problems, in the first place those of hunger and disease, though the production of more advanced and vigorous strains of plants and through the production of valuable medicines.

The *Compendium* is quick to point out that technology must always be subordinate to "moral principles and values," and scientists ought to "maintain an attitude of prudence and attentively sift out the nature, end, and means of the various forms of applied technology."[39] Simply put, the moral life cannot be set aside in pursuit of a noble end like eradicating hunger. Moreover, "*Entrepreneurs and directors of public agencies involved in the research, production, and selling of products derived from new biotechnologies must take into account not only legitimate profit, but also the common good"* [original italics].[40] Here the church cautions the inventors and patent owners of new seeds, fertilizers, and medicines that intellectual property laws and the right to make a profit only go so far—"the common patrimony of all" must also be kept in the foreground "as concerns the fight against hunger, especially in poorer countries."[41]

The Vatican has taken no position on the hot-button issue of genetically modified organisms (GMOs), but the Pontifical Academy of Sciences has offered a strong endorsement, on the grounds that GMOs will help to combat malnutrition in a hungry (and growing) world population. Many Catholics, including clergy involved in various environmental movements have, at the same time, strongly recommended official church positions against GMOs, because they believe these "Frankenfoods" (as GMOs are sometimes called) pose health risks to consumers and foster the dependency of small-scale farmers on multinational agribusiness corporations.[42]

Pope Benedict has affirmed Catholic teaching on hunger and other poverty issues in his two social encyclicals, *God Is Love* (*Deus Caritas Est*) and *Charity in Truth (Caritas in Veritate)*. He has specifically addressed hunger in several speeches and homilies, noting the persistence of global hunger and suggesting its root cause is simply greed. In a 2011 address to the Rome-based United Nations Food and Agriculture Organization, the pope decried the many victims of hunger, specifically the millions of children in the world who do not receive adequate nutrition. "Poverty, underdevelopment, and therefore, hunger, are often the result of selfish behaviors that, born in the human heart, manifest themselves in social life, economic exchange, in market conditions, and in the lack of access to food," he stated.

"How can we be silent about the fact that even food has become the object of speculation or is tied to the course of a financial market that, lacking definite rules and poor in moral principles, appears anchored to the sole objective of profit?" he asked.[43] At a previous visit to the U.N. division, the pope took on the "overpopulation myth," noting that the world's supply of food, in total, outstrips the needs of every man, woman, and child on the planet. In this speech, Benedict also underscored the importance of viewing "sufficient healthy and nutritious food" as a human right.[44]

SIGNS OF HOPE

Belief in the right to nutritious food fuels Catholic activity to promote food security for all people, whether through the local church and its Catholic Charities agencies, Catholic Relief Services, or ecumenical partnerships like Bread for the World. Despite almost a billion hungry people living in the world, many signs of hope have been inspired by church teachings on hunger. We now turn to these signs of hope, beginning with one of the most extraordinary antipoverty efforts in recent years—the Jubilee campaign to forgive the debts of the world's poorest countries.

From Jubilee to the Millennium Development Goals

The twenty parishioners seated in the basement of Holy Name of Mary Parish, Croton-on-Hudson, New York, were irritated. "You mean to tell me, after all that money we raised to help Honduras after Hurricane Mitch, they are still paying 40 percent of their budget on debt interest?" one man asked. Their pastor, Fr. Jerry Gentile, had asked leaders active in 1998 hurricane relief efforts to meet with their congresswoman, Rep. Sue Kelly (R-NY), to discuss debt relief for the world's poorest countries in the Jubilee year 2000. I[45] assisted Fr. Gentile at the meeting, along with my colleagues from the Archdiocese of New York Catholic Charities Department of Social and Community Development, George Horton and Tom Dobbins. Our role was to educate parishioners about the terms of the debt relief bill before Congress. We were encouraged by the attention Pope John Paul II's efforts received in the popular press and strengthened by the involvement of the rock star Bono and Christian leaders from across the political spectrum.

"Yes," I stated, "Honduras is one of forty of the world's poorest countries saddled with unpayable debt. Even if they continue to earmark 40 percent of their budget for debt service, they will never reduce the principal." The group looked stunned, then angry—angry enough to meet with their congresswoman.

The meeting took place at Rep. Sue Kelly's home district office, in a wealthy town in Westchester County. She sat at the head of the table, surrounded by twenty constituents from the parish. Fr. Gentile made a pitch for her support of the debt-relief bill. The bill provided for debt-relief funding for very poor countries committed to using their savings on debt servicing to expand education and health programs. These countries also promised financial transparency, making it clear to donors where the money would go. After Fr. Gentile spoke, a few parishioners chimed in, explaining why they supported the bill. "If we keep this up, they will always be poor," said one. "We're wasting the aid we do send them," added another.

Rep. Kelly listened politely to the presentation and then responded. "I understand your concern for poor people around the world," she said. "We do a lot of work with hungry people in my church. But we can't be forgiving the debts of countries like Mexico. They have a responsibility to pay back the money they borrowed!"

The room grew silent for a moment. Then a parishioner spoke, "I've got the bill right here, and Mexico is not on the list," he said. "What? Let me see that!" she shot back.

Rep. Kelly paged through the copy of the bill. "Let me talk to my legislative director and get back to you," she said. We didn't yet have an answer, but the parishioners felt empowered by the experience. They knew more about a bill than a member of Congress!

The answer came a week later: No.

But we weren't licked yet. Cardinal Edward Egan wrote a letter to Rep. Kelly urging passage of the bill, and Bread for the World arranged for other church delegations to weigh in, including Rep. Kelly's own Presbyterian Church (U.S.A.). We maintained regular communication with her legislative director until the final vote. The day before the vote, we learned that she would switch to a "yes" and support debt forgiveness for highly indebted poor countries. The proposed legislation passed by three votes.

The action shifted to the Senate, where Senator Phil Gramm of Texas, chair of the Senate banking committee, refused to take up the Jubilee bill. Without clearing the banking committee, it would never come up for a vote. One senator controlled its fate. A surprise ally stepped in. Evangelical televangelist Pat Robertson had been moved by a meeting on debt relief with key members of Congress, President Clinton, and religious leaders, including Bread for the World's Rev. David Beckmann. On camera, he urged viewers of his *700 Club* television show to call or write Senator Gramm to indicate their support for debt relief for the poorest countries. Senator Gramm responded to the flood of correspondence that followed, the bill advanced to the full Senate, and it passed.[46] An initially uninterested President Clinton signed the bill, and it remains one of the most important achievements of his presidency. Without people like the St. Mary's parishioners and their allies in Bread for the World and other Christian organizations, there is very little likelihood that the bill would have ever been considered by either chamber of Congress.

Today, thirty of the forty poorest countries in the world have received $78 billion worth of debt relief. Honduras and other countries are paying $3 billion less toward debt and more than that amount toward increases in funding for health and education programs. These funds are credited for the widespread increase in school enrollment across Africa.[47] But debt relief alone would not eradicate poverty. The next step came from a worldwide push to cut poverty in half by 2015: the Millennium Development Goals (MDGs).

Strongly endorsed by the Vatican and the USCCB, the MDGs were developed by the United Nations, the World Bank, the IMF, and the Organization for Economic Development and Cooperation. In 2001, all of the United Nations' 193 member states ratified the goals, which included halving extreme poverty and hunger; reducing infant mortality; fighting disease, especially HIV/AIDS; and promoting environmental sustainability and economic development. Aid from the most developed countries, including the United States, increased significantly, and more LDCs adopted transparency and anticorruption measures.

Ten years later, the results on hunger are mixed. The number of people living in extreme poverty dipped from 1.8 billion in 1990 to 1.4 billion in 2005. The worldwide extreme poverty rate dropped from 46 percent to 27 percent, an excellent start. But much of this progress occurred in China and India, with very little happening in sub-Saharan Africa, where the extreme poverty rate still stands at 51 percent. The global economic slowdown beginning in 2008 did not help matters, though progress is still being made.

Yet despite this decline in poverty rates, hunger remains. Even as strides were made in recent years against extreme poverty, the percentage of people living with hunger during the 1990–2005 period stayed steady at 16 percent. Researchers are still trying to understand how extreme poverty rates could decrease while hunger stayed level (before the sharp rise in food prices). The answers that emerge will, no doubt, influence future antipoverty efforts.

The Emergence of Evangelicals against Hunger

One of the most exciting developments of the Jubilee debt-forgiveness campaign was the role of the evangelical churches. Evangelicals were never monolithic, but some organizations and movement leaders left many Americans with the mistaken impression that evangelical Christians care only about abortion, homosexuality, and, at times, pornography. The Jubilee campaign and simultaneous efforts to raise awareness and funding to fight AIDS stirred the hearts of Bible-loving Christians who took Jesus' concern for lepers and the words "I was hungry and you gave me food" seriously. Their internal dialogue and actions in the public arena changed the wider public perception of evangelicals.

Religious Right leaders like Pat Robertson came to embrace Jubilee, but a new crop of evangelical leaders also began to emerge in the late 1990s. Christian leaders like Rev. Jim Wallis of the Sojourners community, Richard Cizik, president of the New Evangelical Partnership for the Common Good, Joel Hunter of Northland Church in Orlando, Florida, and Rev. Rick Warren, pastor of Saddleback Church in Orange County, California, have come to represent a new side to this corner of the Protestant tent—one that takes poverty, HIV/AIDS, and care of God's creation seriously. Organizations like the National Association of Evangelicals (NAE), representing 45,000 evangelical churches, began to trumpet the evangelical commitment to fighting poverty and working for justice in documents on Christians in the public square:

> Jesus summed up God's law by commanding us to love God with all that we are and to love our neighbors as ourselves (Matt. 22:35–40). By deed and parable, he taught us that anyone in need is our neighbor (Luke 10:29–37). Because all people are created in the image of God, we owe each other help in time of need. God identifies with the poor (Ps. 146:5–9), and says that those who "are kind to the poor lend

to the Lord" (Prov. 19:17), while those who oppress the poor "show contempt for their Maker" (Prov. 14:31). Jesus said that those who do not care for the needy and the imprisoned will depart eternally from the living God (Matt. 25:31–46). The vulnerable may include not only the poor, but women, children, the aged, persons with disabilities, immigrants, refugees, minorities, the persecuted, and prisoners. God measures societies by how they treat the people at the bottom. . . . Christians reach out to help others in various ways: through personal charity, effective faith-based ministries, and other nongovernmental associations, and by advocating for effective government programs and structural changes.[48]

The full text of *For the Health of the Nation: An Evangelical Call to Civic Responsibility* is available at www.nae.net.

The renewal of evangelical commitment to people living in poverty has been expressed through new forms of ecumenical cooperation. For example, in 2006, mainline Protestants, Catholics, and evangelical Christians founded a loose association called Christian Churches Together, whose first activities centered around fighting poverty and hunger. Early conversations indicated that despite their theological differences, members agreed "that conversion must lead to helping poor people, including advocacy."[49] Christian Churches Together has taken such steps by meeting with White House officials collectively, offering a consistent Christian voice on issues of poverty and hunger. Such is the vision of ecumenical cooperation held out in Catholic social teaching.

Science and Technology in Service to the Poor

Discussions about the politics of food can boil over when the subject of technology comes up. Some argue that the "green revolution" has not lived up to its promise, that its increased crop yields have left us dependent on fertilizers, pesticides, and giant factory farms owned by large corporations. On the other hand, some point to the hungry people fed by the green revolution and recent advances in the genetic engineering of foods and ask, "Why not feed a hungry world using these tools of science?"

The church position is a middle ground governed by prudence. In "What the Church Teaches," we looked at section 458 in the *Compendium of the Social Doctrine of the Church*, which hails the contributions of science to the common good but insists that the development of technology always adhere to the principles of the moral life. For this reason the church evaluates each technological development independently, testing each advance in the light of scripture and church teaching. The use of new technologies to fight hunger is not an all-or-nothing proposition. Factors like the economic, health, and environmental consequences of a particular technology must be factored in. The availability of the new technology and the role of profit are also important factors. This section will therefore identify new applications of technology that advance the dignity of the human person as they fight poverty and hunger: cell phones, the breeding of new drought and flood-resistant crop varieties, and the development of the orange sweet potato.

"Knowledge is power," some say. Low-income farmers living in remote areas of the world are now taking advantage of the cell-phone revolution to harvest knowledge, ensuring fair treatment by market middlemen. Previously, when buyers approached rural farmers at harvest, the farmers were at a disadvantage. Was the market price quoted to them by the buyers accurate? Were they being swindled? Today, before such visits, many rural farmers check commodity prices using cell phones they have purchased or obtained through sympathetic NGOs.

For example, in Ghana, farmers hundreds of miles from the capital of Accra are using text messages to determine corn and tomato prices before talking to buyers.[50] Cell phones save farmers travel costs as well. What once required a trip to the city can be accomplished through twenty minutes of texting. In Niger, researchers found that the cost of owning a mobile phone was about half the expense of traveling to market to research prices, and these inquiries could be accomplished far more often—hourly if necessary.[51] The use of cell phones by rural farmers has been found to increase their income by 29 percent,[52] which, in many cases, may be the difference between hunger and adequate nutrition. In some parts of the world, the green revolution works to eradicate hunger only when combined with the digital revolution.

A second area where technology holds great promise is in re sponse to climate change. Increased floods and drought, particularly, threaten to devastate future food supplies in Africa and Asia. But new developments in the science of agriculture have brought hope to farmers like Anand Kumar Singh in Samhauta, a flood-prone village in northeastern India.

Looking for ways to preserve his crops during natural disasters, Singh agreed to plant ten acres of a new strain of rice in early 2010. On August 23, a flood submerged his field for a week and a half. When the floodwaters receded, the rice rebounded and produced a normal harvest. "That was a miracle," he told the *New York Times*.[53]

Typically, a flood of this magnitude would have destroyed Singh's entire crop, but this new variety of rice, based on an old strain found in a small region of India, simply "sits and waits out the flood," according to agronomist Julia Bailey-Serres of the University of California, Riverside. The Bill and Melinda Gates Foundation has provided a $20 million grant to further develop and distribute the flood-resistant rice in India and other flood-prone countries. With India's climate change forecast calling for increased flooding, the new strain may be the best hope for Indian farmers hoping to elude famine.

Flood-induced famine is one way in which malnutrition threatens human dignity, but researchers point to a lack of micronutrients, noted earlier in this chapter, as the leading reason people die of malnutrition. A lack of zinc will turn a bout of diarrhea into a fatal illness. A shortage of iron will cause anemia in children and death during childbirth for women. Vitamin A deficiencies can cause blindness and death for small children.[54]

Consuming the orange sweet potatoes found in most American grocery stores would be an easy solution for vitamin A deficiencies, but the American variety does not grow well in Africa, where micronutrient deficiencies are most common. White sweet potatoes are a staple food in many parts of Africa, but they lack vitamin A. But scientists have been cross-breeding the two varieties, and recently a team developed an orange sweet potato that thrives in places like Uganda and Mozambique, where 170,000 families now grow the new variety.[55]

The stories of the orange sweet potato, flood-resistant rice, and the use of cell phones to obtain key information about commodity markets are all signs of hope. But technology alone will not solve the crisis of world hunger. Even a food-rich country like the United States has millions of hungry or malnourished citizens, many of them overweight. Overcoming the problems of hunger, malnutrition, and obesity requires crossing the food deserts of the United States.

St. Isidore's Garden Brings Fresh Produce to Food Bank

Maureen Jorgensen and ten other parishioners at St. John Vianney Church in Colonia, New Jersey, neared the end of their 2009–2010 JustFaith experience. JustFaith has become well known throughout the country as a transformational social justice reading and discussion group. The program's books and videos provoked conversations that yielded passionate conversion all around. By the end of the year, the group was ready for action. "Several of us were struck by hunger and obesity," Jorgensen said. "We realized that those who rely on food pantries eat mostly highly processed, nonperishable foods. They lacked access to more healthful foods."[56]

A direct service response to this widespread problem emerged after discussion with St. John Vianney's pastor, Msgr. Edward O'Neil. He designated a plot of parish land "St. Isidore's Garden": nine hundred square feet of tomatoes, peppers, green beans, lettuce, Swiss chard, spinach, collard greens, eggplant, cucumbers, squash, and even some herbs. Scores of parishioners joined in to cultivate the produce, which the parish donates to three food banks in nearby Woodbridge, New Jersey. Woodbridge itself is not a food desert, but many of its low-income residents lack transportation to its grocery stores or simply cannot afford fresh fruits and vegetables.

Volunteers at the food bank report that clients respond with delight to the vegetables. "It's just like going grocery shopping!" one woman exclaimed.[57] St. Isidore's Garden provides fresh vegetables and herbs to food banks for three seasons out of the year. During the winter, St. John Vianney Parish donates frozen containers of soup made with vegetables and herbs from the garden. Five neighboring churches and synagogues have founded their own gardens on the same model.

Readers may wonder how a direct-service effort like St. Isidore's Garden can even begin to alter the politics of food. On the one hand, the garden is simply an effort to build a better food bank, offering nutritious food to hungry people. On the other, St. Isidore's Garden is a frontal assault on our contemporary food system, offering an alternative model of community agriculture. Neighbors come together with neighbors to work the land, to plant many species, to see God's creation bud forth, and to reap a harvest of justice. This is a far cry from the monoculture cornfields of Iowa, where skeleton crews operate the machinery that farms the thousands of federally subsidized acres destined to become hamburgers or high-fructose corn sweetener.

Projects like St. Isidore's Garden are beginning to pop up throughout the United States, a response of communities of faith and others of goodwill to ensure that people living in poverty have at least some access to fresh food and to communicate alternative models of agriculture. In addition, many farmers markets now accept EBT (electronic benefit transfer) cards and food stamps, thanks to legislative campaigns to change state laws prohibiting such payments. These efforts, combined with the employment of technology to fight hunger, and with the church's successful legislative advocacy (with ecumenical partners like Bread for the World) on food issues, have truly altered the politics of hunger. Much still needs to be done (reforming the U.S. farm policies that encourage and subsidize giant factory farms, for example), but as we engage the politics of hunger, we build on these successes.

It has already been said that women and children number among the most common victims of hunger and malnutrition worldwide. Sadly, this could be stated about much of the violence of globalization discussed in this book. Those people with the least power—the unborn, children, and women—bear the brunt of these social problems, populations to which we now turn.

DISCUSSION QUESTIONS

1. Which of your beliefs about hunger was most challenged by what you read in this chapter?

2. What dimension of the politics of food most needs challenging? Why?

3. How might food and nutrition aid best be channeled?

GO MAKE A DIFFERENCE

1. Host an educational event at your parish, university, or school to discuss facts and myths about hunger. Invite a representative from Bread for the World to discuss how participants can make a difference on the issue of global hunger.

2. Go to the Bread for the World website and learn about this year's Offering of Letters. Consider leading an Offering of Letters in your parish, university, or school.

3. Research the presence of food deserts in your community. Visit a local food bank and ask what foods they most need. Meet with others in your parish, university, or school to discuss how to best meet the needs expressed.

8

Women and Children:
Double Victims

Samba Diara, aged fifteen years, lives in a plastic hut by himself, panning for gold in one of Mali's small artisanal gold mines. He traveled two hundred miles from home to work in the gold pits because his parents had no money to send him to school. He sends home as much of his earnings as he can to support his five younger siblings.

The high price of gold has created a boom in Mali's artisanal gold mines. In these primitive networks of pits and caves, children as young as six, far away from home, dig shafts with pickaxes, carry heavy bags of ore, and then pan the ore for gold using mercury. The work exposes children to hazards that would never be permitted in developed nations. Their pay comes in the form of a bag of dirt—which may or may not contain gold.[1] About 12 percent of the world's gold is produced under these conditions. Samba entered into mining willingly, but did he ever really have a choice? His is a common story of child labor—one of the special dimensions of institutionalized violence against women and children living in poverty, a violence that is so widespread that we can describe them as double victims of the violence of globalization—first because they are poor, and second because they are women or children. Like the widows and orphans of biblical times, women and children are still the most vulnerable among us.

SIGNS OF THE TIMES

The International Labour Organization (ILO) in Geneva estimates there are 215 million child laborers in the world today. The term refers to "work that deprives children of their childhood . . . and interferes with their schooling."[2] Of these child laborers, 53 percent of engage in "hazardous work."[3] This is defined by ILO convention no. 182 as "work which by its nature or the circumstances in which it is carried

155

out, is likely to harm the health, safety, or morals of children." The ILO's Worst Forms of Child Labour Recommendation, 1999 (no. 190) offers further detail, singling out work exposing children to dangerous machinery or tools, transporting heavy loads, ingesting hazardous substances, experiencing high temperatures, high noise levels or vibrations, working long hours, or facing the impossibility of returning home.[4]

Samba and many of his fellow child laborers will suffer brain damage from breathing mercury fumes[5] during the gold-separation process and will most likely get drawn into alcohol abuse, gambling, and prostitution (HIV/AIDS) in the saloon environment of mining towns. But gold mines contain just one set of risks for children engaged in hazardous work. Other child laborers breathe silica in quarries, wield exposed blades on tractors and other farm equipment, use toxic chemicals in tanneries, run around in traffic selling flowers, or are exposed to lead in smelters and automobile battery recycling centers, to name a few examples.

The ILO notes some progress in fighting child labor—overall numbers of child laborers declined 6 percent from 2004 to 2008, and the number of children aged five to fourteen doing hazardous work fell 31 percent during that same period. But hazardous work is increasing among older children like Samba. From 2004 to 2008, the hazardous child-labor rate for children aged fifteen to seventeen rose 20 percent, from 52 million to 62 million.[6]

Child labor is only one of the forms of violence disproportionately endured by women and children in the developing world, as their suffering persists at consistently higher rates than among men. This pervasive disparity shows up in many and varied ways.

Children

♦ The United Nations Children's Fund (UNICEF) estimates that each year 9.7 million children die from completely preventable causes like diarrhea and malaria. We know how to prevent these deaths through low-cost, highly effective interventions like vaccines, antibiotics, micronutrient supplements, bed nets, improved breast-feeding, and safe hygiene practices, but these preventable fatalities continue.[7]

◆ The under-five-years mortality rate for sub-Saharan Africa is 129 per 1,000 live births. In southern Asia it is 69. In developed regions of the world it is 7. Children in rural areas are at the greatest risk of dying. Having a mother with no formal education almost doubles the risk of death.[8]

◆ Bread for the World estimates that in 2008, three million children died before the age of five due to malnutrition (chapter 7 provides more details). Those who survived suffered poor physical growth (including a total of 178 million children under five with stunted growth), compromised immune functioning, and impaired cognitive abilities.[9]

◆ Nearly one in four children under the age of five in the developing world is underweight, an improvement over the nearly one in three of 1990, but still scandalous.[10] In southern Asia, according to Bread for the World, "there was no meaningful improvement [in health] among children in the poorest households" from 1995 to 2009.[11]

◆ At the end of 2009, there were 2.5 million children living with AIDS and 16.6 million AIDS orphans in the world.[12]

◆ UNICEF estimates that 2 million children are sexually exploited around the world each year. Over a million of these children are trafficked across borders (see chapter 4 for more details).[13]

Women

◆ The Nobel Prize–winning economist Amartya Sen uncovered a major conundrum in population studies in 1990, when he found surprisingly low populations of women in countries where women's status is unequal to men's. For example, China has 107 males for every female, India 108, and Pakistan 111. Although women tend to live longer than men, significant numbers of women in these nations have simply disappeared—victims of abortion or infanticide, sex trafficking, honor or witchcraft killings, famine or drought, or common domestic violence. Follow-up research has pegged the number of "missing" women in the world at 60–101 million, with about two million more added each year.[14]

- In developing countries, more girls than boys die in famines and droughts. Scarce food is mostly apportioned to boys, who are seen as more valuable to the family.[15]

- When determining whom to send to school, families favor boys over girls across the developing world. While developing nations have come a long way toward gender parity in education, much work still remains. Currently, 91 girls for every 100 boys are enrolled in the primary schools of the developing world. This proportion drops to 88 for secondary school, and 82 for tertiary education.[16] This educational disparity will naturally translate into income disparity as children begin their adult lives. Any person who would argue that men are simply better equipped for academic pursuits should look first to the United States, where, according to the American Council on Education, women have comprised 57 percent of college enrollments since 2000.[17]

- Women make up most of the workforce in the sweatshops of the export-processing zones of Latin America, Asia, and Jordan. As we learned in chapter 2, many of these women report inhumane working conditions, physical violence, emotional berating, and sexual harassment. Some, like the Hameem factory workers described in chapter 2, have paid with their lives because of management disregard for their safety.

- Women, especially immigrant workers, experience wage theft in the United States at a higher rate than men, as we learned in chapter 3. The percentage of women who, in 2009, said they were victims of wage theft in the past month was 47.4. The rate for men was 29.5 percent.

- Women in the United States earn 80 cents for every dollar that men earn, a chasm that, while narrowing, is still indefensible.[18] Internationally, women make, on average, 77.6 cents for every man's dollar of wages, including both developed nations and the LDCs.[19]

Underlying these indicators of misery is poverty—a poverty exacerbated by both the violence of globalization and traditional violence against women. Many of these heartbreaking statistics are improving slowly, due to application of Jubilee year debt relief, a massive increase in U.S. AIDS relief for the world's poorest countries in 2003, and increased funding for the Millennium Development Goals (MDG), but results in some parts of the world, like sub-Saharan Africa, are still well below the 2015 MDG targets.

Some international organizations funded by wealthy countries undermine the MDGs by promoting the structural adjustment programs (SAPs) explained in chapter 1. To review, these programs are the "strings attached" to loans from the World Bank and the IMF. SAPs are now called Poverty Reduction Strategy Papers (PRSPs), after international outcry forced modest reforms at the turn of the millennium. Structural adjustment programs open the door to massive World Bank and IMF loans by requiring cuts in social service, health, and education programs; focusing economic activity on exports and resource extraction; devaluing the local currency; lifting import and export restrictions, privatizing state-run businesses, and removing price controls or state subsidies of goods like food and fuel.

Terms like "shared sacrifice" are often used by those advocating structural adjustment programs, but it's usually women and children who pay the highest price. Cuts in government spending and currency devaluations lead women to increase their workloads to respond to the increased price of household goods and food. Mostly women feed the children, care for the sick, gather and prepare food, wash clothes, clean house, and carry water. The World Bank, in particular, has begun to address the needs of women living in poverty, through its Women in Development Unit, providing billions of dollars in grants and loans for women's education, health, and nutrition needs, but its SAPs remain, undercutting their own programs for women.

Violence against Women: A Brutal Tradition

The violence of globalization causes great suffering among women and children worldwide, but violence against women is an old story, even traditional. Just as disproportionately male political leaders in wealthy countries make decisions that harm women in developing countries, the same women are also victims of violence at the hands of the men in their lives. These forms of violence are perhaps the most pervasive human-rights violations today.

Some dimensions of globalization mitigate traditional violence against women, like increased communication among women's organizations and greater access to global travel and education opportunities among the middle classes in developing nations, not to mention increased awareness of women's status worldwide through the Internet. In addition, global organizations like the United Nations, its affiliated agencies (as well as unaffiliated NGOs) and most of its member nations have, in recent years, adopted the strongest standards against violence toward women the world has ever seen. Yet violence against women persists.

The World Health Organization (WHO) has identified violence against women as a "major health problem and a violation of women's human rights." A recent multicountry survey found that, for women aged fifteen to forty-nine, between 15 percent (Japan) and 70 percent (Ethiopia, Peru) reported physical or sexual violence at the hands of an intimate partner. The same survey found a range of 0.3–11.5 percent of women reporting sexual violence from a nonpartner. In addition, the WHO study discovered women reporting their first sexual experience as "forced" at rates as high as 24 percent in rural Peru, 28 percent in Tanzania, 30 percent in rural Bangladesh, and 40 percent in South Africa.[20] In the United States, the Centers for Disease Control and Prevention reports that 10.6 percent of American Women report experiencing forced sex at some point in their lives. And there are other specific forms of violence against women.

Female Genital Mutilation (FGM). FGM includes various traditional cutting operations performed on women and girls. It is sometimes explained as a way to ensure chastity, as these procedures remove the experience of pleasure from sexual activity. FGM occurs primarily in about twenty-five African nations, among some minority groups in Asia, and within some immigrant communities in the United States, Europe, Australia, and Canada. An estimated 100 to 140 million women and girls alive today have undergone FGM. In Africa alone, medical experts estimate 92 million girls ten years and older have undergone FGM.[21]

Dowry Deaths. A dowry death is the killing of a woman by her husband or in-laws or the suicide of a young woman after long harassment because her family is unable to pay for her dowry (or provide a larger one). Most dowry deaths take place in India, Pakistan, and Bangladesh, typically in kitchen fires designed to look like accidents. In 2008, 1,948 Indian men were convicted in dowry-death cases, and 3,876 acquitted, with 5,824 cases pending, and many were never even brought to justice.[22] In addition, in Bangladesh, 86 women were attacked with acid in 2010, and 12 percent of those attacks were related to disputes over dowries.[23] Acid attacks, while usually not lethal, are designed to maim or disfigure the victim, thus rendering victims unmarriageable and economically vulnerable.

Rape as a Weapon of War. Rape has been used as a weapon of war since prehistoric times, as men assert territory and redraw ethnic boundaries after war. In the past century, rape has been employed systematically by the Japanese, in its occupation of Nanking, China; by Pakistanis in the 1971 war for Bangladeshi independence; by Serbs in Bosnia during the 1990s; during and immediately after the Rwandan genocide of 1994; by Janjaweed militias in Darfur, Sudan, in 2004;[24] and in the past decade by rival gangs in Colombia. In 2006–2007, over 400,000 women were raped by combatants in what has been called "Africa's World War" in the Democratic Republic of the Congo. Rape as a weapon of war today also carries the risk of HIV/AIDS transmission.

Honor Killings. In many societies, rape victims, women suspected of engaging in premarital sex, and women accused of adultery have been murdered by their male relatives because the violation of the woman's chastity is viewed as an affront to the family's honor. Although the United Nations estimates the number of honor killings at five thousand per year, independent women's and human rights groups put the figure at closer to twenty thousand. Most troubling of all statistics is the Amnesty International finding that honor killings are increasing worldwide.[25] Honor killings are especially on the rise in the United States and Canada, as some immigrant groups bring such customs to North America. For example, Texas teenagers Amina and Sarah were shot dead, allegedly by Yaser Said, their father, on New Year's Day 2008. One of the daughters identified him with her dying words. Their mother later said that the Egyptian-born Said was upset with his daughters for dating non-Muslim boys. The family has called this murder an honor killing.[26]

Early Marriage. The practice of early marriage is prevalent in many areas of the world, especially in Africa and southern Asia. This is a form of sexual violence, since young girls are often forced into the marriage—and with it sexual relations—which may limit their chances of attending school and may result in fistulas and exposure to HIV/AIDS.

Fistulas. In many parts of the developing world and in Africa in particular, women face many health problems related to giving birth. In many rural areas in Ethiopia, for example, girls are given to husbands just after they experience their first menstrual flow—between nine and fifteen years of age. Many become pregnant before they develop enough pelvic width to give birth. Young girls may be in labor without medical help for five or six days. Eventually, the baby dies and passes. The prolonged pressure of the baby's head against the mother's pelvis cuts off the blood supply to the soft tissue surrounding her bladder, rectum, and vagina, leading to tissue necrosis. A fistula, or hole, is the result. If the hole is between her vagina and rectum, she loses control of her bowel movements. Most women who suffer fistulas are unaware that medical treatment is possible, and even for those who know this, treatment may not be available in their area, or they may not have the money to obtain it. Some simply cannot afford transportation to the hospital.

Can you imagine the anguish of a father or mother when their son-in-law returns a daughter with a fistula? Instead of beginning her new life as wife and mother, she will most likely be placed in a hut alongside the family house because the odor of the continually dripping urine and fecal material will be too strong for her to live with others. She will likely be ostracized from the community and suffer depression, shame, and self-loathing. Some fistula victims turn to commercial sex or are forced to beg. Women with untreated fistulas face slow, premature deaths from frequent infection and kidney failure. The WHO reports that over two million women are currently living with obstetric fistulas in Asia and sub-Saharan Africa, and that number grows by fifty to one hundred thousand each year.[27]

The medical literature shows that 80 to 90 percent of fistula cases can be successfully treated, and women can return to full, normal lives. Most fistulas can be repaired at a cost of between $100 and $400, but this sum is far beyond what most poor families can afford. Fistula repair centers also operate in only a few countries, most notably Ethiopia and Nigeria, and these centers cannot begin to meet the enormous need for fistula care. Obstetric fistula is an issue inextricably linked to the lower status accorded to women and girls—an issue of human rights.

HIV/AIDS: The Continuing Scourge

The HIV/AIDS pandemic may well become the greatest catastrophe to ever plague the human race. An estimated 25 million people worldwide have died of HIV-related causes since the beginning of the pandemic. In 2009, AIDS caused 1.8 million deaths, and close to 5,000 people die each day because of HIV, the virus that causes AIDS.[28]

Expanded prevention efforts and increased availability of antiretroviral drugs (due to efforts like the multi-billion dollar U.S. President's Emergency Program for AIDS Relief [PEPFAR]), have caused the rate of new HIV infections to drop 19 percent since 1999, and 5.2 million more people with HIV now have access to life-saving drugs than at the turn of the millennium,[29] but women in LDCs remain particularly vulnerable to HIV. According to UNAIDS, "power imbalances, harmful social gender norms, . . . low socioeconomic and political status, unequal access to education, and fear of violence add to the greater vulnerability of women and girls being infected with HIV." Whereas men make up most of the people with HIV in North America and Europe, 76 percent of all HIV-positive people living in sub-Saharan Africa are women.[30]

In the world's poorest countries, it is women who bear the brunt of this disease—the chaste spouse of an unfaithful husband, the young rape victim, the teenager seduced by a much-older man, the sex worker—double victims of poverty because of their status as women, and now triple victims because of their HIV status. We are beginning to see interventions focused on the unique needs of women in poverty beginning to make a difference, but these efforts are only starting to have an impact. For example, programs that reduce violence against women also reduce HIV infection. In addition, reducing the disproportionate stigmatization of HIV among women increases the number of women who get tested and then take responsibility for their health and possible transmission of the virus. While promising, these programs are often the last to be funded—women's health must move from the back of the line to the front if HIV/AIDS is to be prevented, managed, and eventually cured.

WHAT THE CHURCH TEACHES

The church's teaching on the special needs of women and children reaches back to the Hebrew scriptures and the code of law passed on by Moses. The "Covenant Code" of the book of Exodus first lays out the admonition "You shall not abuse any widow or orphan. If you do abuse them, when they cry out to me, I will surely heed their cry; my wrath will burn, and I will kill you with the sword, and your wives shall become widows and your children orphans" (Exod. 22:22–24).

From the time of Moses, God makes it clear that vulnerable women and children are under divine protection, elaborating further in Deuteronomy, "Every third year you shall bring out the full tithe of your produce for that year, and store it within your towns; . . . the orphans, and the widows in your towns, may come and eat their fill so that the Lord your God may bless you in all the work you undertake" (Deut. 14:28–29). The Deuteronomic Code offers further instructions to the Hebrews to include the widows and orphans in their feasts (Deut. 16:11–4), show compassion when collecting their debts, and make sure they receive fair treatment under the law (Deut. 24:17–21). The Lord even calls for a second harvest of crops to allow unripe or overlooked fruit in the fields to be picked by widows and orphans (Deut 24: 21).

The Book of Proverbs makes it clear that God sides with poor and vulnerable women and children in their disputes with the powerful, stating, "The Lord tears down the house of the proud, but maintains the widow's boundaries" (Prov. 15:25), and "Do not . . . encroach on the fields of orphans, for their redeemer is strong; he will plead their cause against you" (Prov. 23:10–11). This commitment carries into the New Testament, through Jesus' compassionate and healing responses to the widows and children he meets, the apostles' caring for widows in Acts 6:1–6, and James's definition of true faith: "Religion that is pure and undefiled before God the Father, is this: to care for orphans and widows in their distress, and to keep oneself unstained by the world" (James 1:27).

When we think of the implications of these admonitions for today, we should ask not where the widows and orphans in our community are, but instead ponder another question—who are the most at-risk women and children in our local area, nation, and world? In ancient times, widows and orphans were the most vulnerable human beings. Today, in the developing world, many married women and children with two parents suffer from the violence of globalization as well as traditional forms of violence. Recall the Signs of the Times section of this chapter. Would God take a special interest in these women and children?

The *Catechism of the Catholic Church* offers an unequivocal "Yes," affirming the fundamental equality of women and men as "created in the image and likeness of the personal God."[31] As equals, women share fully in all of the rights of the human person specified in Catholic social teaching, rights too often and disproportionately denied, as we saw earlier in this chapter. The *Catechism* also notes the importance of children to Christ himself,[32] and emphasizes the rights of children to solidarity, education, and respect for their personhood.[33]

The *Compendium of the Social Doctrine of the Church* specifies the rights of children that need the most attention: "the right to protection under the law,[34] the rights to health care, adequate food, basic education, and proper shelter and protection from sexual trafficking, child labor, becoming a child soldier, and becoming sexually exploited through prostitution or pornography."[35] The document laments the continued presence of child labor in the world, over a century after Pope Leo XIII decried such practices in the first major papal encyclical on Catholic social teaching, *Of New Things* (*Rerum Novarum*). "[I]n regard to children," the pope wrote, "great care should be taken not to place them in workshops and factories until their bodies are sufficiently developed. For, just as very rough weather destroys the buds of spring, so does too early an experience of life's hard toil blight the young promise of a child's faculties, and render any true education impossible." The *Compendium* goes on to characterize the continuing problem of child labor as an unacceptable form of violence against children.[36]

With regard to women, the *Compendium* again affirms the fundamental equality of all persons,[37] and specifies the rights that flow from that experience of full humanity. Here we should be most concerned with women's disproportionate experience of poverty, untreated health problems, and experiences of culturally sanctioned violence. Discrimination against women in the workplace is especially decried in the *Compendium*, in particular women becoming "relegated to the margins of society and even reduced to servitude."[38]

The church's special concern for women and children flows from its "option or preferential love"[39] for the poor. The USCCB has described this preferential option for the poor as follows: "A basic moral test is how our most vulnerable members are faring. In a society marred by deepening divisions between rich and poor, our tradition recalls the story of the Last Judgment (Matt. 25:31–46) and instructs us to put the needs of the poor and vulnerable first." As we read the Signs of the Times section in this chapter, we must ask ourselves, "Have we put the needs of poor and vulnerable women and children first?" The Signs of Hope presented in the next section begin to answer that painful question.

SIGNS OF HOPE

Children Free Children

Kim Plewes never planned on becoming an anti-child labor movement leader. A native of Oakville, Ontario, Canada, Kim was in sixth grade when, a few minutes before recess, her teacher offered a special presentation on child labor in several industries, including construction and garments. "We're not going to do anything, but I just wanted to open your eyes," the teacher said. That wasn't enough for Kim.[40]

At recess, she gathered two friends to compare clothing tags, determining what countries their clothing came from. "There was something tangible in what my teacher said," Kim remembered. "There was a boy named Ashique who worked in a brick kiln and said he could never see leaving. He was the same age as me. It could have been me if I had been born in another country." Kim's small group of friends started a petition drive to encourage the Canadian government to do more to stop child labor overseas. Later that year, Craig Kielburger, the fifteen-year old Canadian founder of the anti-child labor organization Free the Children, came to Oakville to speak. Craig had founded Free the Children three years earlier when he read of the assassination of twelve-year-old Iqbal Masih, a Pakistani former slave who crusaded against child labor in the last years of his life.[41] Craig was stunned. A boy his own age had been murdered, fighting an evil Craig did not know existed.

Fortified by outrage and encouraged by the example of older brother Marc, who had founded an environmental club at his school, Craig asked his teacher if he could speak to the class. After Craig's presentation, eleven students volunteered to form the first Free the Children chapter. Craig went on the road to share his concerns throughout Canada. His speeches inspired other children like Kim to set up Free the Children chapters throughout Canada.

Kim became an important leader in the movement, starting a Free the Children chapter in her high school and persuading her member of Parliament, David Kilgour, to address the House of Commons on the issue and work with the prime minister to find ways the Canadian government could stop child labor. During this time, Free the Children also shifted its focus, adding development activities. In its early years, Free the Children participated in raids overseas to simply "free the children." But to what kind of life did these children return? Destitute poverty and no schools. Parents simply sold their children back into slavery or child labor once the "rescued" returned. Free the Children's paradigm shifted to addressing the root causes of child labor as well as maintaining legal pressure through national and international organizations.

Photo by Laura Sheehan/CRS

Ms. Chuob Chhieng Eng has built up a business selling "Chinese cakes" (large steamed dumplings) through a CRS microfinance program in Cambodia. A forty-seven-year-old widow with six sons, she has been able to pay school fees and keep her children in school thanks to her dumpling business. She sells about five hundred of the dumplings every day.

Kim's high school chapter built a school in Nicaragua and joined a 1999 UNICEF campaign to promote adherence to the U.N. Convention on the Rights of the Child. Their activity took an odd twist when UNICEF asked children and teens to designate their "favorite right." Disgusted with the notion that children should "choose" rights, Kim and her Free the Children group responded with "All Rights for All Children" and convinced UNICEF to drop this distracting sidelight.

After her high school graduation, Kim worked four and a half years for Free the Children, helping young people like herself develop local chapters. She helped found Free the Children's new U.S. office, where she now works part time while finishing her studies at American University. Kim sees a lot to be hopeful for as she expands the organization's presence in the United States: the number of child laborers is decreasing, Free the Children has built (and continues to supply) over 650 free schools in developing countries, and its alter-native-income-generation programs are helping families and whole villages escape the trap of child labor through microenterprises like beekeeping, growing and drying ginger, and producing onions.[42] And just as important, Kim believes, she has helped young people in North America find their voice, making a difference in the "adult" world of public life, advocating for respect for children's rights while promoting economic and human development overseas. In a very real sense, FTC "frees" the children of North America from a false consciousness of apathy and self-centered attitudes and helps them move toward a commitment to solidarity among all children.[43]

Microfinance and the Empowerment of Women

When Muhammad Yunus received the 2006 Nobel Peace Prize for helping millions of poor people climb out of poverty through par-ticipation in microfinance programs, the Nobel Committee noted, "Micro-credit has proved to be an important liberating force in soci-eties where women in particular have to struggle against repressive social and economic conditions." When I[44] first read that citation, I assumed the committee meant that a number of women had received small loans, started small businesses, and lifted themselves out of poverty. That was only half the story. Some months later, trav-eling with CRS in India, I learned the full effects of microfinance self-help groups on women's lives—fostering empowerment, education, and participation in public life, while liberating many from domestic violence.

Until relatively recently, low-income people in developing countries like India did not have access to financial services such as savings accounts and loans, except for loans obtained through unscrupulous moneylenders, local loan sharks charging usurious interest rates (as high as 380 percent). In India, CRS works with local partners to provide microfinance services to clusters of twenty women in rural villages.[45]

CRS's focus on women derives first from the reality that women tend to be poorer than men but second because they default on microfinance loans at a lower rate. Globally, 95 percent of women in self-help groups pay back the loans, while 50 percent of men do so.

CRS-India and its local partners offer training and technical assistance to self-help groups developing small businesses (microenterprises), provide literacy,[46] health, and disaster-preparedness training to interested group members, and recruit promoters of new groups. In April 2006, I became acquainted with more than twenty such groups, scattered throughout a dozen rural villages near Calcutta.

Wherever we went, we heard similar stories of thrift, human development, and entrepreneurship. In the village of Ghagighi, we met Chabbi Ghosh, a member of a self-help group called Freedom. Chabbi identified herself as living in two kinds of poverty before joining the group: a material poverty, in which needs for food, medical care, and housing often went unmet, and a poverty of mind and spirit. "I used to sit at home and just ponder and do nothing," she recalled. "Now I am open to new ideas."

Chabbi gained a taste for education by learning how to sign her own name and gaining the right to manage her own documents in the process. That experience raised her commitment to educating her three children. Much of the profits from her growing dairy business now cover educational expenses for the children. She buys milk wholesale, one hundred liters at a time, and converts it to cottage cheese, which she sells to shops in Calcutta. She has successfully grown the family's income to the point that their basic needs are met *and* she saves seventy rupees (about $1.50) per month.

One of Chabbi's family's greatest needs was housing. "Before, we did not have a proper house," she said. "Now we have a proper house." Curious, I asked her what a proper house was. It seemed a term open to interpretation. "One with a roof," she replied.

Currently, Chabbi has saved over 13,000 rupees. With a future loan, she hopes to expand the business to process an additional hundred liters of milk. Her increased prosperity has caught the attention of relatives, who now approach her when they have financial problems. Chabbi does not see this as a burden, but rather enjoys taking a leadership role within her extended family. "Actually," she confided, "the most common thing they want to do after seeing my success is join a group of their own."

Freedom members are most proud of the group's name. Chabbi offered this explanation, "The group has taught us to experience freedom: freedom from superstition and ignorance, economic free-dom, physical freedom, and mental freedom." Those freedoms have been earned through the tight discipline of weekly savings and loan payments and the growing social bonds within the group.

Chabbi and the other Freedom members outlined a typical meeting. They begin each week on the same spot of common ground at the center of the village, seated in a circle so they can see each other's faces. They start with prayers, one each from the Hindu, Muslim, and Christian traditions, reflecting the religious diversity of the group. They sing an inspirational song. Everyone signs in, and they elect a leader for the meeting. The group then discusses any issues relating to repayment of loans and any social problems experienced by group members. They collect both savings and loan payments, recording each transaction carefully. Sometimes this group also takes part in local Catholic Charities programs on health, particularly those dealing with the issue of neighbors defecating outdoors, a serious public health problem in this area.

They produce records: meeting notes in Bengali, one of the written languages of India, and ledgers indicating deposits and intra-group loan payments. These records are critically important for gaining bankers' confidence. Loans of up to ten times the group's savings depend on clear, standardized records indicating consistent deposits and timely repayment of loans.

The keys to self-help group success are discipline and imagination: discipline to keep timely attendance records and collect savings and loan payments, imagination to create successful businesses. The development of financial skills like thrift tends to release other human resources: business acumen, social networks, leadership. A woman who never dreamed of working as anything other than an agricultural laborer might discover that she is an expert saleswoman, for example. One group adopted the name Hidden Skills after observing this phenomenon at work among its members.

When I asked Chabbi and hundreds of other self-help group members, "How is your life different now because of your participation in the groups?" they did not respond, "I was hungry, and now I am satisfied." They replied, "My husband has stopped beating me. He is no longer drunk all of the time. The men in this village now treat the women as partners." I pressed them, "Surely, you have food and medical care that you once lacked!" and they responded, without exception, "Oh yes, we have those things, but what has changed most is how the men treat the women in this village."

These changes did not come easily. In the late 1990s and the first years of the new century, CRS self-help-group pioneers encountered obstacles in every small village. Group founders encountered extreme opposition from men in the villages early on, particularly the husbands of group members, regardless of whether the village was Hindu, Muslim, Christian, traditional Santali religion, or a blend of faiths.

The men's views began to evolve as the women in the groups learned teamwork and business acumen. Husbands began to take notice of these results, especially as new income flowed into the family. As families reaped the benefits of increased income and food productivity, the men's opposition melted. Some husbands, like Chabbi's, became employees in their wives' business.

The idea that saving handfuls of rupees would lead to a revolution in gender relations caught me by surprise. But nothing prepared me for learning that over seven thousand women in CRS self-help groups ran for local political offices during the previous three years— and 61 percent (4,334) won election. Many of these women did not, until recently, even know that they had the right to vote. Several are the first women elected to any office in their village.

Most self-help-group candidates who run for office vie for a seat on the Panchayat Raj Institution (PRI). The PRI is a local governmental structure, founded by Mahatma Gandhi, based on what Catholics would call subsidiarity: the principle that the smallest possible social unit should take responsibility for social life. The PRI ensures a local voice in determining where roads, bridges, wells, schools, and health centers will be built. U.S. readers might understand the PRI as analogous to a U.S. city council that determines how federal block grants are spent.

Participation of women in local governance is guided by the seventy-third amendment to the Constitution of India, passed in 1993, which reserves one-third of all PRI seats for women. Self-help groups provide an unanticipated entry-level platform for women to enter public life. Some self-help-group members serving in the PRI have gone on to higher office, winning election to the Lok Sabha (House of the People) in India's Parliament, bringing women's wisdom, leadership styles, and distaste for corruption to political institutions that have traditionally been the sole province of men. In some developing countries, like Liberia, we are beginning to see the emergence of women leaders all the way up to the presidency.

New Wave of Women Leaders Sparks Hope

Goal 3 of the MDGs calls for the empowerment of women, with one of the measures of gender equality being the number of women represented in political office. The aim of having women in elective offices comes not only from a sense of fairness, but also research demonstrating that women in LDCs make spending decisions with the good of family and community in mind, more so than men do. For example, the women of East Asia who have moved to cities to take up factory jobs have financed the education of younger relatives and still saved enough money to increase national savings rates.[47] Further studies have shown that when married women control at least some family income, these funds are more likely to be spent on nutrition, health, education, housing expenses, and starting small businesses. The result is greater child health and educational achievement.[48] On the other hand, as Nicholas Kristof and Sheryl WuDunn observe, when men control the purse strings, on average 20 percent of family income is spent "on a combination of alcohol, prostitutes, candy, sugary drinks, and lavish feasts" (at weddings and festivals).[49] This sum is ten times the typical outlay for children's education. In short, when women control family income, priorities shift from instant gratification to human development.

It's not a great jump in logic to suggest that an increase in women political leaders would result in more emphasis on education, health, and economic development in national budgets, and less on individual enrichment and corruption, military conquests, and settling political scores. Liberia's president, the Nobel Peace Prize–winning Ellen Johnson Sirleaf, is representative of this new wave of female leadership, but the world has not yet experienced widespread women's leadership at this level. Most female leaders of developing countries, like Indira Gandhi, Corazón Aquino, Benazir Bhutto, and Gloria Macapagal-Arroyo, have been the wives or daughters of successful male politicians, and grew up in elite families—hardly the story of the self-help-group leaders now serving in the PRI. It may well be too early to judge the difference women leaders make until we see more of these grass-roots leaders achieve positions of higher responsibility.

But early research has supported the idea that female political leaders outperform their male counterparts in promoting human development. For example, in India, beginning in 1993, the state allocated one-third of village chief positions for women. Social scientists who compared the male-led villages to the female-led villages found that more water pumps and taps were installed in female-led villages, all public services were judged as good or better, and residents reported they were less likely to have to pay a bribe to a public official.[50]

The MDGs have emphasized the encouragement of women to become involved in public life, and empowerment and protection of women has become a condition of nations receiving U.S. Millennium Challenge Corporation funding. For example, when the southern African nation Lesotho requested Millennium Challenge grants, the United States insisted on a revision of law to allow women to buy land or borrow money without their husbands' permission, an obstacle to microenterprise development and female participation in family finances. Lesotho changed the law, and has now received over $350 million in funding from the U.S. Millennium Challenge Corporation, which distributes targeted aid to 39 LDCs.

The United Nations has noted progress on the inclusion of women in national parliaments—one of the MDGs—but lamented the still-low percentage. The good news is that the representation of women in the world's parliaments is at an all-time high. Most regions of the world have shown progress in this area. For example, in sub-Saharan Africa, the share of women parliamentarians has grown from 13 percent to 20 percent since 1990. In Latin America and the Caribbean, the percentage rose from 15 percent to 23 percent. Some countries, like Rwanda, have even achieved parity, with 56.3-percent-female parliamentarians. But the overall worldwide percentage of female parliamentarians is still only 19 percent. The report also noted that nine countries, including Belize, Qatar, Saudi Arabia, and the Solomon Islands, have not a single woman parliamentarian.[51]

Even with more work to be done, progress is being made, thanks to the efforts of people of faith and others of goodwill who advocated for Jubilee debt forgiveness, the MDGs, and funding for the Millennium Development Corporation. The multinational MDGs, coordinated through the United Nations, show what can happen when the nations of the world approach the challenge of global poverty through the lens of solidarity and subsidiarity, with accountability and transparency.

U.S. Church Leaders Bring Needed Attention to HIV/AIDS

Along with the adoption of the MDGs, one of the most important achievements for women and children in the first decade of the twenty-first century was the passage of the President's Emergency Plan for AIDS Relief, or PEPFAR, in 2003. People of faith and others who had grown tired of what the first edition of this book termed "mass murder by complacency" roused the conscience of a nation to pass the largest global health bills in U.S. history. PEPFAR included $15 billion in funding for U.S-manufactured antiretroviral medicines, nutrition supplements, women's empowerment activities, AIDS-orphans programs, and HIV/AIDS-prevention education. PEPFAR was reauthorized in 2008 as a $48 billion, five-year program.

As was the case with the Jubilee campaign, Congress passed the bill only after churchgoers wrote letters and met personally with almost every member of Congress. Catholics in key congressional districts played an essential role, like Sr. Sheila Kinsey, a Franciscan nun from Wheaton, Illinois. Sr. Sheila had been a leader in the Jubilee movement. Like many others, she became convinced that without addressing the HIV/AIDS pandemic, the impact of debt forgiveness in Africa would be minimal. She arranged for Assumption Sister of Nairobi Florence Mulia to travel to the United States to speak about the HIV/AIDS pandemic in Africa. The first stop on her tour was the office of hometown congressman Rep. Henry Hyde (R-IL), then chair of the powerful House International Relations Committee. Rep. Hyde responded positively to Sr. Sheila and Sr. Florence's message:

find a way to increase dramatically spending for the treatment and prevention of HIV/AIDS.

Conversations among the USCCB, CRS, and allied groups with the executive branch paid off when President Bush announced, in his 2003 State of the Union address, a proposal to increase spending to combat HIV/AIDS by $15 billion over five years. Expenditures would be concentrated on the hardest-hit areas of Africa and the Caribbean. The initiative would be called The President's Emergency Plan for AIDS Relief, or PEPFAR.

Responding to continued urging from Catholics in the Diocese of Joliet and evangelical Christians at Wheaton College (stirred by a timely visit from Bono, one of the most effective individual advocates for PEPFAR), Rep. Hyde introduced H.R. 1298,[52] the United States Leadership sgainst HIV/AIDS, Tuberculosis, and Malaria Act of 2003. The USCCB and CRS considered Rep. Hyde, as a committee chair and a senior member of Congress, to be an ideal chief sponsor for the PEPFAR legislation.

With Rep. Hyde's leadership, the bill passed the House International Relations Committee by a vote of 37 to 8. In the full House, an amendment passed to ensure that organizations like CRS would not be discriminated against on the basis of religious or moral convictions. The House also affirmed an amendment requiring the expenditure of at least 33 percent of HIV/AIDS prevention funds for abstinence-until-marriage programs. On May 1, 2003, the House of Representatives passed H.R. 1298 by a vote of 375 to 41, a rare expression of bipartisanship in an otherwise polarized Congress.

The action then shifted to the Senate, as CRS, the USCCB, and colleague organizations like Bread for the World urged local legislative networks to lobby senators to pass a PEPFAR bill similar to H.R. 1298. The Senate added one amendment, to provide deeper debt relief to highly indebted poor countries, especially those with high rates of HIV/AIDS. The bill passed by voice vote.[53] On May 19, 2003, the Senate sent the bill as amended back to the House for another vote. The House passed the amended bill on May 23, and President Bush signed PEPFAR into law four days later.

Laws like PEPFAR are indeed signs of hope. But simply sparing the lives of women or interrupting their beatings will not reverse the violence of globalization. Here, the kinds of cultural and structural changes we observed occurring alongside the development of the self-help groups in India are needed. Such efforts, including micro-enterprise development, literacy, health education, and encouragement toward public service, are necessary to unfetter the creative leadership of women in LDCs and create a world in which the "widows and orphans" have a seat at the table where the decisions governing their lives are made.

DISCUSSION QUESTIONS

1. Research the U.N. Convention on the Rights of the Child. Develop a report card for each right.

2. In what ways does globalization promote violence against women? In what ways does it mitigate violence against women? What evidence do you cite for either position?

3. How do CRS self-help groups address violence against women?

GO MAKE A DIFFERENCE

1. Invite a speaker from Free the Children to your parish or school to discuss child labor and what you can do about it.

2. Set up a meeting with your member of Congress or senator to discuss PEPFAR and its continued funding.

3. Raise money in your parish or school to support microfinance self-help groups in developing countries. Contact your diocesan CRS director to discuss possibilities of following the progress of beneficiaries.

9

A New Pentecost

Teach us, good Lord, to serve the need of others,
Help us to give and not to count the cost.
Unite us all, for we are born as brothers [and sisters];
Defeat our Babel with your Pentecost.

—Fred Kaan

In St. Matthew's treatment of the Last Judgment (see chapter 7), Jesus identifies with poor and vulnerable people in a way never before seen in human history. Prior to Christ, it would be difficult to identify a world religion that did not teach care for the poor, but, describing the sorting of the righteous sheep and the wicked goats in the afterlife, Jesus declares, "I was hungry and you gave me food. I was thirsty and you gave me something to drink, I was a stranger and you welcomed me, was naked and you gave me clothing, I was sick and you took care of me. I was in prison and you visited me" (Matt. 25:35–36). In so doing, Christ identifies, quite literally, with the poor and marginalized. For the first time, God says, "I *am* the poor." How one responds to the hungry, the sick, the prisoner, and other people in need therefore becomes essential to salvation.

This teaching is at the heart of Catholic doctrine on the "preferential option for the poor," a concept adapted from liberation theologies and embraced by then Cardinal Ratzinger in his 1984 "Instruction on Certain Aspects of the 'Theology of Liberation.'" In this document, the future Pope Benedict XVI praised some aspects of liberation theology, like the preferential option for the poor, while condemning other, Marxist, notions, like the inevitability of class struggle.[1]

The preferential option for the poor is the Catholic belief that God has a special—but not exclusive—love of the poor. All liberation theologies, be they Latin American, African, Asian, Black, feminist, disabled, or emanating from some other marginalized group, begin with this favored love of God for the poor and marginalized, the *anawim* of the Bible. It's a good place to root any response to the violence of globalization.

Perhaps, as you read each chapter, you began to consider your own response to institutionalized violence. But where to start? Each of us makes a few hundred choices a day and thousands of decisions each year that support the violence of globalization. Like death by a thousand cuts—or a hundred piranhas—we make social sin possible through our choices: to buy this product, to dispose of waste that way, to ignore those signs of injustice. When we, like Pilate, wash our hands of responsibility, the blood of our brothers and sisters cries out—like Abel's blood from the soil and Christ's from the cross. Our faith, through the teachings of scripture and the *Catechism*, calls us to make different choices, choices rooted in solidarity, practiced with subsidiarity, and considered in light of the preferential option for the poor.

OVERCOMING BARRIERS TO SOLIDARITY

We all encounter barriers to solidarity, even when we seek it. Cultural norms, our own hurts and fears, guilt, and a lack of imagination can serve as barriers to the experience of connection to other human beings. We begin to overcome these obstructions when we name and understand them.

One barrier is what we might call "the American dream of success." In the United States, success is measured primarily in dollars and fame. We have been socialized since birth in many subtle ways to seek this consumerist vision. Some believe that after they fulfill the American dream and have all they need, they will then have the time, energy, and money to devote to service to the world beyond their immediate families. So they put off the call to live the authentic life of the disciple of Jesus Christ.

Our own wounds can also be a barrier. Many of us have done shameful things. We have all hurt others and been hurt by others. Our wounds can cause us to disconnect from people who are hurting, wrapped up in our own pain or guilt over what we have done.

Some people also trip over the barrier of their own self-righteousness. Perhaps they pray for the poor, give generously to the church, worship often, perform meaningful work, and serve a day or two each month at a soup kitchen or nursing home. But they may still think of the poor as uneducated, unsophisticated, and with little to offer the rest of the world. So they give money, food, and clothing out of pity, without humility. They see no connection between themselves and the *anawim*. They have no relationship with those whom they serve—solidarity eludes them.

Some people are unable to live in solidarity with poor and vulnerable people because they are lazy, comfortable, or simply afraid of confrontation. It takes courage to do things that your friends don't do, to be a stranger, to enter a new culture, to be unsure of what you will say and of what you will do. Some just want to play it safe and not face those kinds of risks. They want what is familiar and secure.

It's also hard for some Americans to imagine alternatives to the life they expect to lead. They see themselves as little people, cogs in the wheel, without power, without voice, and without great compassion, love, or integrity. When the opportunity to respond, to speak out, to act with great courage and integrity presents itself, they let the moment pass because they just never expected, hoped, or dreamed that they could do such a thing. We become the person whom we expect to become, and we surrender our power as much as it is taken from us. When we imagine, believe, and let the Holy Spirit move within us, we set in motion something new and mysterious within and outside of ourselves. As the Scottish mountaineer W. H. Murray put it,

> Until one is committed there is hesitancy, the chance to draw back, always ineffectiveness. Concerning all acts of initiative (and creation), there is one elementary truth, the ignorance of which kills countless ideas and splendid plans: That the moment one definitely commits oneself, then Providence moves too. All sorts of things occur to help one that would otherwise never have occurred. . . . I have learned a deep respect for one of Goethe's couplets: "Whatever you can do, or dream you can—begin it. Boldness has genius, power, and magic in it."[2]

SOLIDARITY OF PLACE AND TIME

With boldness we enter into solidarity. Typically, we understand solidarity as a notion of place—the worker in Bangladesh has as much claim on us as the hungry child in our hometown. But, as Pope Benedict has pointed out,[3] solidarity must also include the dimension of time. We are connected, through the communion of saints, back in time to St. Vincent de Paul and St. Louise de Marillac, to Dorothy Day, Servant of God, to Blessed John XXIII, and to Blessed Mother Teresa. We are also linked *forward* in time to the Ghanaian child poisoned by exposure to e-waste from the computer we use today, to the Tuvalu citizen staring at the rising tide of climate change, and to the Chinese baby who will be aborted simply because she is a girl.

The subsidiarity we speak of is grounded in respect for poor and vulnerable people and committed to seating them at the table where decisions are made, respecting their reservations about, for example, the siting of a landfill or the effects of World Bank and IMF structural adjustment programs on community health. It is a solidarity that reaches out to women in the developing world, inviting them to run for office and take their rightful place at this table of public life, recognizing the role of workers in policing the sweatshop economy. Enacting this solidarity of place and of time, fused with subsidiarity, begins with taking responsibility for our choices.

The signs of hope we highlight in this book point to individuals and groups owning their role in the violence of globalization and acting in community to reverse its effects: the college student who demands that apparel bearing her school's name comply with an independent code of conduct; the commuter who insists on drinking Fair Trade coffee on his way to work; the citizen outraged that a local branch of a national hotel chain is a haven for sex slavery; the Catholic school principal who responds to a call to environmental stewardship through the "green" design of a new student athletic center; the North American child moved to fight child labor on other continents. All are signs of hope, unraveling the violence of globalization to build relationships of solidarity, charity, and justice.

In David Beckmann's book *Exodus from Hunger,* the president of Bread for the World writes of God moving through history, freeing the Israelites from the yoke of slavery under Pharaoh, sending Jesus

Christ to redeem all humanity, and breathing on the apostles at Pentecost with the Holy Spirit. Beckmann suggests that, with an end to hunger and extreme poverty within our grasp, we stand at an exodus moment of "God's saving presence in world history."[4] Our Creator invites us to embrace our own role in this "exodus from hunger," by responding with both direct services and social action.

Beckmann compares this deliverance of humanity from hunger and extreme poverty to the deliverance of the Jews from slavery in Egypt. He reminds us that God's action in human history has not ended. We might begin to understand our efforts to unravel the institutionalized violence of globalization similarly, as a "new pentecost."

At Pentecost, the Jewish celebration of the Law of Moses, the Holy Spirit descended upon the apostles and the other disciples like "tongues . . . of fire" (Acts 2:3). They began to converse, and "each one heard them speaking in the native language of each" (Acts 2:6). It was as if God had reversed the scattering of the people at Babel, reunifying humanity and facilitating the spread of the Gospel—an act of globalization.

Today, God moves into human history by countering the violence of globalization with the signs of hope profiled in these pages, a new Pentecost fostering what John Paul II, called "a globalization without marginalization,"[5] the antidote to the violence of globalization and a fruit of the Holy Spirit. As disciples of Jesus Christ, we are called to build upon these signs of hope with movements of solidarity that unravel the institutionalized violence of globalization. Otherwise, the true cost of low prices is nothing short of our souls.

Epilogue

If Only You Knew

When I was hungry, I know you would have fed me, if you knew where I was. But you didn't know me. How could you know me? You never held and fed a baby like me before. You never held a baby too hungry to cry.

When I was lonely, you didn't know where I was. I lived in a dangerous place. I know you are afraid to go where I live. It's not safe where I live.

When I was sick, you thought the doctors and hospitals wouldn't turn me away. How could you know?

When I was homeless, you gave me some money, and I felt your prayers. But you couldn't have known the terror in that shelter and why I stayed on the street. You didn't know that I was sick—that I saw demons but they were real. How could you know? We never talked.

When I lost my little girl because we had no money for medicine, you didn't know what I needed. You didn't know where we were. We lived so far from you. They call it the Third World.

When I sent my boy to sell lottery tickets, you didn't know us. You didn't know I wanted him to go to school but I needed his earnings for food. We were so far away from you. We spoke in a foreign tongue. How could you know us?

You didn't know why my boy didn't come home that night. We knew. His father took his money and bought alcohol and beat him so many times. He stayed in the streets and never came back to me. How could you have known he didn't come home?

You didn't know how the kids live on the street—and what the older ones and the men do to the little ones. And you didn't know about the drugs. How could you? You didn't know that I am with those boys too, and they do it to me. But how could you know?

When I pleaded for fair wages, they tortured me. We made your clothes. But you didn't know who we were. You didn't know what they did to those of us who spoke for fair wages and safe conditions. How could you know how far they'd go?

When I gathered your food and got sick from the chemicals, you couldn't know. You didn't know what the chemicals did to our children. You didn't know of the nightmares they caused. How could you know? You never gathered foods from the fields. You never touched or smelled the chemicals.

Did you know that my children work in the garbage? They collect paper and bottles and cans. And they sell them so we can eat. It's so dangerous there. Surely you don't know of the dangers—of the gas explosions and fires, of the chemicals and disease. But what can I do? I have no other way to feed my children. But you didn't know.

When we spoke for our land, our ancestors' land, they slaughtered us. They mutilated and tortured me so many times in so many ways. They smashed my children against the rocks. They raped and killed my wife and daughters. They did it for the land owners who sell you your food. They did it to me. But how could you know what they did? It wasn't on the news. None of your friends could tell you. We live so far from you.

You were so busy. You had your children. You rocked them and sang to them and helped them with their homework and read them stories and tucked them in and taught them to pray. You took them to soccer practice and baseball games, to dance classes and music lessons. You were so busy.

You worshipped me often. You met with your friends and talked of your love for me. I heard your love songs. And I heard your praise and thanks. You thought I was in heaven. That's what they told you. You just didn't know.

You worked so hard. I know it wasn't easy. They'd fire you so quickly. So you had to work hard to provide for your family. I know you were afraid.

But you shouldn't have feared. I sent you food from the fields so you wouldn't go hungry. I sent you your clothes and I sent you my love. Even when you didn't know it or believe it. I loved you always.

When you smashed my baby against the rocks, you didn't know it was me. You were so afraid of the sergeant. You didn't know what to do. You didn't want to kill me. He said he'd kill you if you didn't do it. You were so afraid.

When you took my money for alcohol and you beat me, you didn't know that I'd go to the streets and never come home. You didn't know what they'd do to me. I know you loved me. You just didn't know how much I loved you.

And when I needed money for my daughter's medicine, I know you would have bought it for her, if only you knew where we were.

I loved you when I was hungry and you had extra food. I know you would have fed me if you could—if you saw me, if you held me. I'm sure you wouldn't have left me to starve, if you knew who I was.

If only you knew. I come to you through the children. I come a million times a day. But look what is done to me. I'm hungry and sick, beaten and abandoned. I'm tortured and mutilated, abused and battered.

I'm waiting in the children. Can you hear me? Listen. I'm in your heart—your Sacred Heart. And you are always in my heart.

Come to me. Come to the children. Don't be afraid. I'll mend your heart.

Can you hear me? I love you. I love you. I love you. If only you knew.

—Vincent Gallagher

Notes

1. The Violence of Globalization

1. John Paul II, *Reconciliation and Penance (Reconciliato et Paenitentia)* (Vatican City: Libreria Editrice Vaticana, 1984), no. 16, www.vatican.va.

2. Charles C. Mann, *1493: Uncovering the New World Columbus Created* (New York: Knopf, 2011), xii–xix.

3. Vince Gallagher.

4. Eric Klinenberg, *Fighting for Air: The Battle to Control America's Media* (New York: Holt Paperbacks, 2008), 31–32.

5. "Interlocking Directorates," Fairness and Accuracy in Reporting (FAIR), www.fair.org.

6. "Issue Area: Narrow Range of Debate," Fairness and Accuracy in Reporting (FAIR), www.fair.org.

7. Jeffry Korgen.

8. Benedict XVI, *Charity in Truth (Caritas in Veritate)* (Vatican City: Libreria Editrice Vaticana, 2009), no. 21.

9. Ibid., 37–38.

10. Ibid., 25.

11. Ibid., 27.

12. Ibid., 28.

13. Ibid., 29.

14. Ibid., 35.

15. Ibid., 37.

16. Pontifical Council for Justice and Peace, *Compendium of the Social Doctrine of the Church* (Vatican City: Libreria Editrice Vaticana, 2004), no. 363.

17. Ben Somberg, "The World's Most Generous Misers," Fairness and Accuracy in Reporting, www.fair.org.

18. *Catechism of the Catholic Church*, 2nd ed. (Washington, D.C.: United States Catholic Conference, 1997), no. 1939.

2. The Search for the Most Desperate Workers

1. Tania Munsura is a composite based on several workers with similar background information. Interviews with survivors have suggested the thoughts she expresses in these paragraphs.

2. Charles Kernaghan, *Triangle Returns: Young Women Continue to Die in Locked Sweatshops* (Pittsburgh: Institute for Global Labour and Human Rights, 2011), 1–11.

3. Ibid.

4. David Von Drehlem, *Triangle: The Fire That Changed America* (New York: Grove Press, 2003), 194–218.

5. Kernaghan, *Triangle Returns*, 6.

6. Author interview with Charles Kernaghan, Executive Director, Institute for Global Labour and Human Rights, July 7, 2011.

7. Chrystia Freeland, "The Rise of the New Global Elite," *Atlantic*, January/February 2011, 44–54.

8. The World Bank, *Changes in Country Classifications*, July 1, 2011; data.worldbank.org.

9. Glenn Firebaugh, *The New Geography of Global Income Equality* (Cambridge, Mass.: Harvard University Press, 2003).

10. "The World's Billionaires," *Forbes*, www.forbes.com.

11. Shaohua Chen and Martin Ravallion, Development Research Group, The World Bank, *China Is Poorer Than We Thought, but No Less Successful in the Fight against Poverty*, 14.

12. Ibid.

13. David Barboza, "Bridge Comes to California with Made in China Label," *New York Times*, June 26, 2001, A1.

14. Author interview with Charles Kernaghan, Executive Director, Institute for Global Labour and Human Rights, July 7, 2011.

15. Associated Press, "Mattel Issues New Massive China Toy Recall," August 14, 2007, www.msnbc.msn.com.

16. Jeffrey Sachs, *The End of Poverty* (New York: Penguin Books, 2005), 11.

17. Ambar Narayan, Nobuo Yoshida, and Hassan Zaman, *Trends and Patterns of Poverty in Bangladesh in Recent Years* (World Bank, South Asia Region, 2007), 2.

18. Sachs, *The End of Poverty*, 12.

19. Charles Kernaghan, *Toys of Misery Made in Abusive Chinese Sweatshops* (Pittsburgh: Institute for Global Labour and Human Rights, December 11, 2008), 1–25.

20. Charles Kernaghan, *Chinese Guest Workers Flee Living Hell in Jordan* (Pittsburgh: Institute for Global Labour and Human Rights, June 13, 2011).

21. Dexter Roberts et al., "Secrets, Lies, and Sweatshops," *Businessweek*, November 27, 2006 (cover story), www.businessweek.com.

22. Jeffry Korgen.

23. Charles Kernaghan, *Dirty Parts/Where Lost Fingers Come Cheap: Ford in China* (Pittsburgh: Institute for Global Labour and Human Rights, March 2011), 1–26.

24. Ibid., i.

25. Charles Kernaghan, *Women Paid Just Eight Cents for Each $25 NFL Shirt They Sew at Ocean Sky Sweatshop in El Salvador* (Pittsburgh: Institute for Global Labour and Human Rights, January 24, 2011), 1–43.

26. Charles Kernaghan, *China's Youth Meet Microsoft* (Pittsburgh: Institute for Global Labour and Human Rights, April 2010), 1–31.

27. Charles Duhigg and Steven Greenhouse, "Electronic Giant Vowing Reforms in China Plants," *New York Times*, March 30, 2012, www.nytimes.com.

28. Jeffry Korgen.

29. *Brockton Enterprise*, "Creedon Squashes Religious Legislation" February 11, 1997, 1.

30. Learn more at www.vatican.va.

31. John Paul II, *On Social Concerns*, 36.

32. *Catechism of the Catholic Church*, 2nd ed. (Washington, D.C.: United States Catholic Conference, 1997), no. 2427.

33. Ibid., no. 2428.

34. Ibid.

35. Ibid., no. 1941.

36. Ibid., no. 2433.

37. Ibid., no. 2428.

38. Ibid., no. 2434.

39. Ibid., no. 2435.

40. Ibid., nos. 2429, 2432, 2452.

41. Ibid., no. 2432.

42. Ibid., no. 2436.

43. Pontifical Council for Justice and Peace, *Compendium of the Social Doctrine of the Church* (Vatican City: Libreria Editrice Vaticana, 2004), nos. 301–4.

44. Ibid., no. 301.

45. Ibid., no. 79.

46. Ibid., 80.

47. Pontifical Council for Justice and Peace, *Vocation of the Business Leader* (Vatican City: Libreria Editrice Vaticana, 2012), no. 1.

48. Ibid., 8, no 18.

49. Ibid., 13, no 40.

50. *Faithful Citizenship* (Washington, D.C.: United States Conference of Catholic Bishops, 2007), 15.

51. Benedict XVI, *Charity in Truth (Caritas in Veritate)* (Vatican City: Liberia Editrice Vaticana, 2009), no. 21.

52. Ibid., no. 22.

53. Ibid., no. 25.

54. Ibid., no. 36.

55. Ibid., no. 37.

56. "Factory Defies Sweatshop Label, but Can It Thrive?" *New York Times*, July 18, 2010, BU1.

57. William Bole, "Ban on Sweatshop Products Becomes Rule at Local Level," *Village Life News*, December 4, 1997.

58. Jaqueline DeCarlo, *Fair Trade* (Oxford, England: OneWorld, 2007), 39.

59. Verité, "New Online Toolkit for Multinational Brands to Rid Their Supply Chains of Labor Abuses," www.verite.org.

60. Susan Ferriss, "Schwarzenegger Signs Two Anti-Human Trafficking Bills," *Sacramento Bee*, September 20, 2010, blogs.sacbee.com.

61. Interfaith Center on Corporate Responsibility, www.iccr.org.

62. Amalgamated Bank, Christian Brothers Investment Services, Connecticut Pension and Retirement System, Interfaith Center on Corporate Responsibility, New York City Employees Retirement System, "Sourcing Standards: Concerns for Investors," September 2004.

63. Jeffry Odell Korgen, interview with Rev. David Schilling, Interfaith Center on Corporate Responsibility, July 28, 2011.

64. Ibid.

65. Project Kaleidoscope Working Group, *Project Kaleidoscope*, March 2008, 1.

66. Ibid., 2.

67. Korgen, Interview with Rev. David Schilling, July 28, 2011.

3. Immigrant Workers

1. John Cote, "Wage Theft a Scourge for Low-income Workers," *San Francisco Chronicle*, July 18, 2011.

2. Ibid.

3. Rick Relinger, "NAFTA and U.S. Corn Subsidies: Explaining the Displacement of Mexico's Corn Farmers," *Prospect: Journal of International Affairs* (April 2010): 1, prospectjournal.ucsd.edu.

4. You can watch Stephen Colbert's farm worker experience at www.ufw.org. You can read more about the "Take Our Jobs" campaign at www.ufw.org.

5. Annette Bernhardt, Ruth Milkman, Nik Theodore, et al., *Broken Laws, Unprotected Workers: Violations of Employment and Labor Laws in America's Cities* (Chicago: Center for Urban Economic Development, 2009), 13.

6. Ibid., 15.

7. Ibid., 31.

8. Ibid., 42–43.

9. Ibid., 44–45.

10. Ibid., 46.

11. Ibid., 42–46.

12. Ibid., 5.

13. Ibid., 23.

14. Ibid., 3.

15. Kim Bobo, *Wage Theft in America: Why Millions of Working Americans Are Not Getting Paid—And What We Can Do about It* (New York: The New Press, 2009), 7.

16. Ibid.

17. Government Accountability Office, *Wage and Hour Division's Complaint Intake and Investigative Processes Leave Low Wage Workers Vulnerable to Wage Theft* (Washington, D.C.: Government Accountability Office, 2009), 2, 4, 11.

18. Ibid., 5–7, 9–10.

19. Ibid, 10.

20. Ibid., 15–16.

21. Ibid.

22. Ibid., 23.

23. Ibid., 22.

24. Department of Labor, "Statement of U.S. Secretary of Labor Hilda L. Solis on GAO Investigation Regarding Past Wage and Hour Division Enforcement," *Release No. 09–0324–NAT*, March 25, 2009.

25. Abel Valenzuela Jr., Nik Theodore, Edwin Melendez, and Anna Cruz Gonzalez, "On the Corner: Day Labor in the United States," Center for Urban Economic Development, University of Illinois at Chicago (January 2006).

26. Justin Pritchard and Julie Reed, "A Mexican Worker Dies Each Day, AP Finds," *Safer Times* (Philadelphia), no. 103 (Spring 2004)

27. Ibid., 4.

28.Cierpich Styles, "Work-Related Injury Deaths among Hispanics—United States, 1992–2006," *Morbidity and Mortality Weekly Report* 57, no. 22 (June 6, 2008), www.cdc.gov.

29. Author (Vince Gallagher) experience. This is particularly true for Spanish-speaking workers. It is very rare indeed that a Spanish-speaking worker from Latin America who works on roofs has received the OSHA fall protection training in Spanish. In fact, I've never come across it.

30. Ibid.

31. Bernhardt et al., *Broken Laws, Unprotected Workers*, 25.

32. Ibid., 26.

33. Occupational Safety and Health Administration, "Frequently Asked Questions," United States Department of Labor, www.osha.gov.

34. Bureau of Labor Statistics, "Occupational Employment and Wages," Bureau of Labor Statistics, www.bls.gov.

35. Author (Vince Gallagher) experience.

36. Author (Vince Gallagher) experience.

37. Massachusetts Committee on Occupational Safety, "Recycling Jobs: Not Green Unless They Are Safe," in *Dying for Work in Massachusetts: Loss of Life and Limb in Massachusetts Workplaces* (Boston: Massachusetts Committee on Occupational Safety, 2009), 4.

38. *Catechism of the Catholic Church: Revised in Accordance with the Official Latin Text Promulgated by Pope John Paul II*, 2nd ed. (Washington, D.C.: Libreria Editrice Vaticana, 2000), no. 2434.

39. Ibid. 541 (2241).

40. Ibid.

41. John Paul II, *Ecclesia in America* (*The Church in America*) (January 22, 1999) (Washington, D.C.: USCCB, 1999), no. 65.

42. *Compendium of the Social Doctrine of the Church* (Washington, D.C.: Libreria Editrice Vaticana, 2004), no. 298.

43. *Strangers No Longer: Together on the Journey of Hope* (Washington, D.C.: United States Catholic Conference, 2003), nos. 33–37.

44. Marnie Eisenstadt, "State Fair Vendor Abused Workers from Mexico," *Syracuse Post-Standard*, April 7, 2011, www.syracuse.com.

45. Ibid.

46. Special Agent Thomas Kirwin, *Complaint M-10-1041, 18 U.s.c. Ss 1351 and 1589* (n.p.: United States District court, Eastern District of New York, 2010), 5.

47. Rebecca Fuentes, interview with Jeffry Odell Korgen, August 13, 2011.

48. Eisenstadt, "State Fair Vendor Abused Workers from Mexico."

49. Fuentes, interview.

50. Cynthia Hernandez, *Wage Theft in Florida: A Real Problem with Real Solutions* (Miami: Research Institute on Social and Economic Policy, Center for Labor Research and Studies, Florida International University, 2010), 3–8.

51. Jose Rodriguez, "Lawmakers Would Encourage Wage Theft," *Miami Herald*, April 14, 2011.www.miamiherald.com.

52. Hernandez, *Wage Theft in Florida*, 3–8.

53. Evelyn Nieves, "Accord with Tomato Pickers Ends Boycott of Taco Bell," *Washington Post*, March 9, 2005, A6.

54. Kari Lydersen, "After McDonald's Victory, Labor Activists Target Burger King," *New Standard*, April 19, 2007, newstandardnews.net.

55. Andrew Martin, "Burger King Grants Raise to Pickers," *New York Times*, May 24, 2008, www.nytimes.com.

56. Steven Greenhouse, "Tomato Pickers' Wages Fight Faces Obstacles," *New York Times*, December 24, 2007, www.nytimes.com.

57. See "Frequently Asked Questions," Global Exchange, www.globalexchange.org.

58. Ibid.

59. Benedict XVI, *Caritas in Veritate* (*Charity in Truth*), no. 38.

60. Ibid.

61. Bobo, *Wage Theft in America*, 208.
62. Ibid., 210–13.

4. Modern-Day Slavery

1. Only first names are used in this story of debt bondage documented by David Batstone in David Batstone, *Not for Sale: The Return of the Global Slave Trade—And How We Can Fight It*, 1st rev. ed. (New York: HarperOne, 2010), 52–77.

2. Ibid.

3. Each of the examples of slavery cited in three paragraphs above is found in the U.S. State Department's 2011 *Trafficking in Persons Report*. Country reports are listed alphabetically and rated according to a tier system. United States Department of State, *Trafficking in Persons Report: June 2011* (Washington, D.C.: U.S. Department of State, 2011), 62–346.

4. Kevin Bales, *Ending Slavery: How We Free Today's Slaves* (Berkeley: University of California Press, 2008), 11.

5. Jesse Sage and Liora Kasten, eds., *Enslaved: True Stories of Modern Day Slavery* (New York: Palgrave Macmillan, 2008), 2–3.

6. Ibid., 3.

7. Ibid., 3–4.

8. Ibid., 4.

9. E. Benjamin Skinner, *A Crime So Monstrous: Face-to-Face with Modern-Day Slavery* (New York: Free Press, 2009), 112. Also see Batstone, *Not for Sale*, 6.

10. Bales, *Ending Slavery*, 15.

11. Ibid., 18.

12. Ibid., 13.

13. Ibid.

14. Sage and Kasten, *Enslaved*, 5.

15. Ibid.

16. Bales, *Ending Slavery*, 184.

17. Ibid., 178–98.

18. Ibid., photo gallery at 60–61.

19. Ibid., 178.

20. U. Roberto Romano and Miki Mistrati, *The Dark Side of Chocolate* (Copenhagen: Bastard Film and TV, 2010).

21. For additional links and further information on the film *The Dark Side of Chocolate* see www.thedarksideofchocolate.org.

22. Bales, *Ending Slavery*, 189.

23. Carol Off, *Bitter Chocolate: The Dark Side of the World's Most Seductive Sweet* (New York: New Press, 2008), 143.

24. Ibid., 189.

25. Ibid., 192.

26. International Labour Organization, "Africa: Child Labor in Cocoa Fields/ Harkin-Engel Protocol," *International Labour Organization Website*, July 8, 2011,www.ilo.org.

27. Associated Press, "U.N.: 2.4 Million Human Trafficking Victims," *New York Times*, April 3, 2012, www.nytimes.com.

28. Skinner, *A Crime So Monstrous*, 127–32.

29. Batstone, *Not for Sale*, 138.

30. Ibid., 143–45.

31. Ibid., 159.

32. Bales, *Ending Slavery*, 189.

33. Pseudonym for a Mexican worker held as a slave in the orange groves of Florida. The unedited transcript of Miguel's interview is available at www.freetheslaves.net.

34. Peggy Callahan, "In Their Own Words: Miguel," *Free the Slaves* (website), February 13, 2005, www.freetheslaves.net.

35. Anita McSorley, "The St. Patrick You Never Knew," *St. Anthony Messenger*, March 1997, www.americancatholic.org.

36. John Francis Maxwell, *Slavery and the Catholic Church: The History of Catholic Teaching Concerning the Moral Legitimacy of the Institution of Slavery* (Chichester: Rose [for] the Anti-Slavery Society for the Protection of Human Rights, 1975), 83–84.

37. Ibid., 75.

38. Ibid., 108.

39. Paul Finkelman, *Encyclopedia of African-American History, 1619–1895: From the Colonial Period to the Age of Frederick Douglass*, vol. 2 (New York: Oxford University Press, 2006), 243.

40. Joel S. Panzer. *The Popes and Slavery* (New York: Alba House, 1996), 44–48.

41. *Gaudium et Spes*, no. 27.

42. John Paul II, *Veritatis Splendor*, no. 80.

43. Ibid.

44. Richard Owen, "Pope Calls for Action to Stop Human Trafficking," *Times* (London), April 5, 2009, www.timesonline.co.uk.

45. *Catechism of the Catholic Church*, 2nd ed. (Washington, D.C.: United States Catholic Conference, 1997), no. 2414.

46. Pontifical Council for Justice and Peace, *Compendium of the Social Doctrine of the Church* (Vatican City: Libreria Editrice Vaticana, 2004), no. 158.

47. *On Human Trafficking* (Washington, D.C.: USCCB, 2007).

48. Ibid.

49. Ibid.

50. Jeffry Odell Korgen, interview with Mary deLorey, Catholic Relief Services, September 6, 2011.

51. Batstone, *Not for Sale*, 86.

52. Ibid., 87.

53. Ibid., 68.

54. Alex Renton, "Chocolate Gives Sierra Leone's Villages New Hope," *Guardian* (UK), September 19, 2010, www.guardian.uk.

55. Off, *Bitter Chocolate*, 282–83.

56. Jacqueline DeCaralo, *Fair Trade: A Beginner's Guide* (Oxford: Oneworld, 2007), 26–30.

57. Renton, "Chocolate Gives Sierra Leone's Villages New Hope."

58. The Hershey Company, "Hershey Expands Responsible Cocoa Community Programs in West Africa," January 30, 2012, see also online www.hersheycocoasustainability.com.

59. Jim T. Ryan, "Hershey to Use 100 Percent Fair-Trade Cocoa by 2020," *Central Penn Business Journal*, October 3, 2012, www. centralpennbusiness. com.

60. Sr. Pat Daly, OP, interview with Jeffry Odell Korgen, September 13, 2011.

61. Ibid.

62. Michael Martinez, "Hotel Chain Boosting Staff Training to Fight Child Prostitution," CNN, July 29, 2011, www.cnn.com.

63. "Hilton Worldwide Signs Tourism Code of Conduct," *Code of Conduct for the Protection of Children from Sexual Exploitation in Travel and Tourism* 1, no. 28 (April–June 2011), 6.

64. "The Six Criteria," The Code, www.thecode.org.

65. Pat Gillespie, "Sixth Immokalee Slavery Case Suspect Arrested," *Fort Myers News-Press*, January 18, 2008, ciw-online.org.

66. Colin Moynihan, "Rolling Museum Casts Light on Current-Day Forced Labor," *New York Times*, August 4, 2010,www.nytimes.com.

67. John Bowe, "Nobodies," *New Yorker*, April 21, 2003, www.newyorker. com.

68. www.ciw-online.org.

69.www.thedarksideofchocolate.org.

70. vision.ucsd.edu.

71. www.serrv.org.

5. Torture and Assassination

1. Binka Le Breton, *The Greatest Gift: The Courageous Life and Death of Sister Dorothy Stang* (New York: Doubleday Religion, 2008), 220–23. Many details of the killing are now known because of Rayfran's detailed confession (including a reenactment based on his testimony broadcast on CNN) and the testimony of an eyewitness, a farmer hidden in the bushes.

2. Roseanne Murphy, *Martyr of the Amazon: The Life of Sister Dorothy Stang* (Maryknoll, N.Y.: Orbis Books, 2007), 142.

3. Small, local church groups that gather to discuss the relevance of the Gospel to everyday life.

4. Le Breton, *The Greatest Gift*, 88–89.

5. Murphy, *Martyr of the Amazon*, 68.

6. Le Breton, *The Greatest Gift*, 106.

7. Ibid., 67–76.

8. Murphy, *Martyr of the Amazon*, 131.

9. Ibid., 158.

10. Associated Press, "Brazil: Ruling in Nun's Killing," *New York Times*, September 6, 2011, www.nytimes.com. See also Times Topics: Sr. Dorothy Stang at topics.nytimes.com.

11. Le Breton, *The Greatest Gift*, 228.

12. Alfred W. McCoy, *A Question of Torture: CIA Interrogation, from the Cold War to the War on Terror* (New York: Metropolitan Books, 2006), 105.

13. Ibid., 25.

14. Ibid., 31.

15. Ibid., 51–53.

16. Ibid., 64–71.

17. Ibid., 89.

18. James LeMoyne, "Testifying to Torture," *New York Times*, June 5, 1988, www.nytimes.com.

19. James Hodge and Linda Cooper, *Disturbing the Peace: The Story of Roy Bourgeois and the Movement to Close the School of the Americas* (Maryknoll, N.Y.: Orbis Books, 2004), 170.

20. Ibid., 59.

21. Ibid., 147.

22. Ibid.

23. Ibid., 91–92.

24. Ibid., 147.

25. Ibid., 131–32.

26. Ibid., 144.

27. Ibid., 180–81.

28. Ibid., 181.

29. Ibid., 173.

30. Ibid., 179.

31. Ibid., 157.

32. Ibid., 185.

33. Jack Nelson-Pallmeyer, *School of Assassins: Guns, Greed, and Globalization*, rev. exp. ed. (Maryknoll, N.Y.: Orbis Books, 2001), 119.

34. Thomas Fox, "Madison's Morlino Noted for Othodoxy, Controversy," *National Catholic Reporter*, March 18, 2009, www.ncronline.org.

35. Jeffry Odell Korgen, interview with Thomas Quigley, October 6, 2011.

36. Kim Severson, "Fort Benning Protest Dwindles, If Not Its Passion," *New York Times*, November 21, 2010, www.nytimes.com.

37. Associated Press, "Victims of Colombian Conflicts Sue Chiquita Brands," *New York Times*, November 15, 2007, www.nytimes.com.

38. Carmen Gentile, "Families Sue Chiquita in Deaths of 5 Men," *New York Times*, March 17, 2008, www.nytimes.com.

39. Ibid.

40. Curt Anderson, "Lawsuit: Chiquita Banana Company Backed Terrorists," *Miami Herald-Tribune*, May 30, 2011, www.heraldtribune.com.

41. Judge Kenneth Marra, "Case No. 08–01916–MD-MARRA" (United States District Court, Southern District of Florida, West Palm Beach, Florida, June 3, 2011), www.courthousenews.com/2011/07/29/Chiquita.pdf.

42. Hannah Aronowitz, "Chiquita Faces Mass Lawsuit over 4,000 Killings in Colombia," *Colombia Reports*, March 24, 2011, www.colombiareports.com.

43. Edward Peters, *Torture*, exp. ed. (Philadelphia: University of Pennsylvania Press, 1996), 236.

44. *Catechism of the Catholic Church*, 2nd ed. (Washington, D.C.: United States Catholic Conference, 1997), no. 2297.

45. Ibid., no. 2298.

46. Pontifical Council for Justice and Peace, *Compendium of the Social Doctrine of the Church* (Vatican City: Libreria Editrice Vaticana, 2004), no. 404.

47. *Catechism of the Catholic Church*, 2309.

48. Ibid., nos. 2313, 2314.

49. "National Religious Campaign against Torture 2011 Agenda," National Religious Campaign against Torture, www.nrcat.org.

50. Ibid.

51. Available at www.usccb.org.

52. Jeffry Odell Korgen, "End of a Partnership," *America*, June 23, 2008, www.americamagazine.org.

53. *Catechism of the Catholic Church*, no. 2271.

54. Korgen, "End of a Partnership."

55. Ibid.

56. For more information, see www.tassc.org.

57. Scott Wright, *In the Steps of the Crucified: Torture Is Never Justified* (Louisville: JustFaith Ministries, 2010), 1–5.

58. "Providing for New and Enhanced Laws against Terrorism Created within the Existing Law Enforcement Paradigm," Duke Law, www.law.duke.edu.

59. Curt Anderson, "Lawsuit: Chiquita Banana Company Backed Terrorists," *Miami Herald-Tribune*, May 30, 2011, www.heraldtribune.com.

6. Violence against God's Creation

1. Sharon LaFraniere, "Lead Poisoning in China: The Hidden Scourge," *New York Times*, June 15, 2011, www.nytimes.com.

2. Joseph Kahn, "As China Roars, Pollution Reaches Deadly Extremes," *New York Times*, August 26, 2007.

3. Kevin Holden Platt, "Chinese Air Pollution Deadliest in World, Report Says," *National Geographic News*, July 9, 2007, www.nationalgeographic/news.

4. Kahn, "As China Roars."

5. *The Economist*, "Raising a Stink: Efforts to Improve China's Environment Are Having Far Too Little Effect," August 5, 2010, www.economist.com.

6. Kahn, "As China Roars."

7. The U.S. Centers for Disease Control and Prevention defines lead poisoning as any blood concentration over 10 micrograms per deciliter of blood, whereas the World Health Organization believes any presence of lead in the blood to be harmful.

8. Human Rights Watch, *My Children Have Been Poisoned: A Public Health Crisis in Four Chinese Provinces* (New York: Human Rights Watch, 2011), 28.

9. Ibid., 32–36.

10. Ibid., 23.

11. Jeffry Korgen.

12. Alexis Madrigal, "The Hardware Scavengers of Ghana," *Atlantic*, September 14, 2011, www.theatlantic.com.

13. Lauren Ornelas, "Mike Anane Interview," Silicon Valley Toxics Coalition, September 2011, www.svtc.org.

14. Ibid.

15. Basel Action Network and Silicon Valley Toxics Coalition, *Exporting Harm: The High-Tech Trashing of Asia* (Seattle, Washington, and San Jose, California, February 25, 2002).

16. United States Government Accountability Office, *Electronic Waste EPA Needs to Better Control Harmful U.S. Exports through Stronger Enforcement and More Comprehensive Regulation* (Washington, D.C.: United States Government Accountability Office, 2008), 5–10.

17. Elizabeth Rosenthal, "Lead from Old U.S. Batteries Sent to Mexico Raises Risks," *New York Times*, December 8, 2011, www.nytimes.com.

18. John Jalsevac, "Is Environmentalism Infiltrating the Pro-Life Movement?" *Life Site News*, June 8, 2011, www.lifesitenews.com.

19. *Basel Action Network*, 178 Countries Agree to Allow the Ban on Exports of Toxic Wastes to Developing Countries to Become Law, October 21, 2011, www.ban.org.

20. U.S. GAO, 10.

21. John Colapinto, "Message in a Bottle," *New Yorker*, April 6, 2009, www.newyorker.com.

22. Sylvia Earle, *The World Is Blue: How Our Fate and the Ocean's Are One* (Washington, D.C.: National Geographic, 2010), 102.

23. Ibid., 105.

24. Richard Grant, "Drowning in Plastic: The Great Pacific Garbage Patch Is Twice the Size of France," *Telegraph* (London), April 24, 2009, www.telegraph.co.uk.

25. Ibid.

26. Earle, *The World Is Blue*, 111.

27. Veronique Greenwood, "Plastic and Humankind: An Unhealthy Relationship," *Atlantic*, April 19, 2011, www.theatlantic.com.

28. Lindsey Hoshaw, "Afloat in the Ocean, Expanding Islands of Trash," *New York Times*, November 9, 2009, www.nytimes.com.

29. Jeffry Korgen.

30. United States Conference of Catholic Bishops, *Global Climate Change: A Plea for Dialogue, Prudence, and the Common Good* (Washington, D.C.: United States Conference of Catholic Bishops, 2001), www.usccb.org.

31. Intergovernmental Panel on Climate Change, *Climate Change 2007: Synthesis Report* (Valencia, Spain: Intergovernmental Panel on Climate Change, 2007), 30.

32. Ibid.

33. Ibid.

34. Ibid., 38.

35. Ibid., 30.

36. Ibid., 36.

37. Ibid., 37.

38. Ibid.

39. Elizabeth Rosenthal and Andrew Lehren, "Relief in Every Window, but Global Worry Too," *New York Times,* June 20, 2012, www.nytimes.com.

40. Ibid., 44.

41. Ibid., 45.

42. Ibid., 46.

43. Thomas Friedman, "Going Cheney on Climate," *New York Times,* December 8, 2009, www.nytimes.com.

44. Benedict XVI, *Charity in Truth (Caritas in Veritate)* (Vatican City: Libreria Editrice Vaticana, 2009), no. 48.

45. Actus-Fioretti 16, Omnibus translation, as quoted in Robert D. Sorrell, *St. Francis of Assisi and Nature* (New York: Oxford University Press, 1988).

46. *Catechism,* 354.

47. Ibid., no. 355.

48. Ibid., no. 2415.

49. Ibid., no. 2417.

50. *Compendium,* no. 106, 466.

51. Ibid., no. 461.

52. Ibid., no. 465.

53. Ibid., no. 180.

54. Ibid., no. 299.

55. Ibid., no. 319.

56. Ibid., no. 470.

57. Ibid., nos. 340, 345.

58. Ibid., no. 359

59. Ibid., no. 360.

60. Ibid., no. 486.

61. Ibid., no. 462.

62. Ibid., no. 468.

63. Ibid., no. 484.

64. Ibid., no. 463.

65. Ibid., no. 464.

66. *Charity in Truth,* no. 49.

67. Ibid., no. 51.

68. Ibid.

69. Benedict XVI, 2010 World Day of Peace Message, www.vatican.va.

70. Visit the Washington State Catholic Conference at www.thewscc.org to obtain a copy.

71. Visit the USCCB at www.usccb.org to obtain a copy.

72. Marty Ostrow. "Going Green," *Renewal*. DVD. Directed by Marty Ostrow (Cambridge, Mass.: Fine Cut Productions, LLC, 2007).

73. Jeffry Odell Korgen, interviews with Dennis Foley and Fr. Robert Stag, November 17, 2011.

74. Jeffry Odell Korgen, interview with Sr. Mary Schmuck, RSM, November 3, 2011

75. Most Rev. Joseph Kurtz, "Discipleship Includes Feeding the Hungry and Caring for the Earth," *Record*, November 8, 2011, 4.

76. Korgen, interview with Sr. Mary Schmuck.

77. Marnie McAllister, "Pledge Calls the Church to Care for Creation," *Record* (Archdiocese of Louisville), October 6, 2011,www.archlou.org.

78. Julie Schmit, "New Program Makes Sure E-Waste Is Recycled Right," *USA Today*, April 16, 2010, www.usatoday.com.

79. Electronics TakeBack Coalition, " 'R2' Is not the Answer," Electronics TakeBack Coalition, www.electronicstakeback.com.

80. Woodeene Koenig-Bricker, *Ten Commandments for the Environment: Pope Benedict XVI Speaks Out for Creation and Justice* (Notre Dame, Ind.: Ave Maria Press, 2009), 8–10.

81. Pontifical Academy of Sciences, *Fate of Mountain Glaciers in the Anthropocene* (Vatican City: Pontifical Academy of Sciences, 2011), 3.

82. Ibid., 8.

7. The Politics of Food

1. "925 Million in Chronic Hunger Worldwide," Food and Agriculture Organization of the United Nations, www.fao.org.

2. "Horn of Africa Food Crisis: Millions Face Starvation," World Vision, www.worldvision.org.

3. Data: Poverty," The World Bank: Working for a World Free of Poverty, www.worldbank.org.

4. David Beckmann, *Exodus from Hunger: We Are Called to Change the Politics of Hunger* (Louisville: Westminster John Knox Press, 2010), 21.

5. Holly Poole-Kavana, "12 Myths about Hunger," *Food First Institute for Food and Development Policy Backgrounder*, Summer 2006, 1.

6. Ibid.

7. Ibid.

8. Mark Doyle, "U.S. Urged to Stop Haiti Rice Subsidies," *BBC Mobile*, October 4, 2010, www.bbc.co.uk.

9. "What Causes Hunger," World Food Programme, www.wfp.org.

10. Ibid.

11. Ibid.

12. Ibid.

13. Eric Holt-Giménez and Raj Patel, *Food Rebellions! Crisis and the Hunger for Justice*, ed. Eric Holt-Giménez (Cape Town: Food First Books, 2009), 68–72.

14. Ibid., 16.

15. Gary Mathies, National Coordination for Food Security as reported in *Haiti Libre*, August 13, 2011.

16. *Time* World, "Food Crisis Renews Haiti's Agony," Kathie Klarreich, April 9, 2008.

17. Paul Farmer, *The Uses of Haiti* (Monroe, ME: Common Courage Press, 1994), 219.

18. Environmental Working Group Farm Subsidies Database, available at www.ewg.org.

19. "The U.S. Role in Haiti's Food Riots," Bill Quigley, Partners in Health, April 7, 2008, www.pih.org.

20. The CIA claims 66 percent (CIA Factbook, 2010, www.cia.gov., while Haitian peasant farmer organizations typically use a figure of 80 percent, www.otherworldsarepossible.org.

21. Lester R. Brown, *World on the Edge: How to Prevent Environmental and Economic Collapse* (New York: W. W. Norton & Company, 2011), 63.

22. Ibid., 64.

23. Ibid., 64–65.

24. Ibid., 66.

25. Alexei Barrionuevo, "China's Interest in Farmland Makes Brazil Uneasy," *New York Times*, May 26, 2011, www.nytimes.com.

26. Brown, *World on the Edge*, 67–68.

27. Michael Pollan, *In Defense of Food: An Eater's Manifesto* (New York: Penguin, 2009), 1.

28. Ibid., 10.

29. Ibid., 7.

30. "Overweight and Obesity Data and Statistics," CDC 24/7: Saving Lives, Protecting People, Saving Money through Prevention, www.cdc.gov.

31. Ibid.

32. www.americancatholic.org.

33. *Catechism*, no. 1039.

34. Ibid., 2447.

35. Ibid., no. 2269.

36. Ibid., no. 2439.

37. Ibid., no. 2440.

38. *Compendium*, no. 57.

39. Ibid., no. 458.

40. Ibid., no. 478.

41. Ibid.

42. John Allen, "Vatican Study Endorses GMOs for Food Security," *National Catholic Reporter*, May 26, 2009, www.ncronline.org.

43. John Thavis, "Pope Says Selfish Economic Models at Root of World Hunger," *Catholic News Service*, July 1, 2011, www.catholicnews.com.

44. On World Hunger: Pope Decries Indifference, *ZENIT The World Seen From Rome*, November 16, 2009, www.zenit.org.

45. Jeffry Korgen.

46. Beckmann, *Exodus from Hunger*, 98–99.

47. Ibid., 99.

48. *For the Health of the Nation: An Evangelical Call to Civic Responsibility* (Washington, D.C.: National Association of Evangelicals, 2004), 8–9, www.nae.net.

49. Beckmann, *Exodus from Hunger*, 126.

50. Jenny Aker and Isaac Mbiti, "Mobile Phones and Economic Development in Africa," *Journal of Economic Perspectives* 24 (Summer 2010): 207–32.

51. Ibid., 9.

52. Ibid., 13.

53. Justin Gillis, "A Warming Planet Struggles to Feed Itself," *New York Times*, June 4, 2011, www.nytimes.com.

54. Nicholas Kristof, "Bless the Orange Sweet Potato," *New York Times*, November 24, 2010, www.nytimes.com.

55. Ibid.

56. Jeffry Odell Korgen, interview with Maureen Jorgensen, December 9, 2011.

57. Ibid.

8. Women and Children: Double Victims

1. Jessica Hopper, "Digging for Gold, Children Work in Harsh Conditions, Paid with Bags of Dirt," *Rock Center with Brian Williams*, December 5, 2011, www.msnbc.msn.com.

2. "About Child Labour," International Labour Organization: Protecting People, Promoting Jobs, www.ilo.org.

3. International Labor Office, *Children in Hazardous Work: A Review of Knowledge and Policy Changes* (Geneva: International Labor Office, 2011), xii.

4. Ibid., 3–4.

5. "Mercury: Health Effects," U.S. Environmental Protection Agency, www.epa.gov.

6. ILO, *Children in Hazardous Work*, xiii.

7. "Young Child Survival and Development," UNICEF, www: unicef.org.

8. Department of Economic and Social Affairs of the United Nations Secretariat, *The Millennium Development Goals Report 2011* (New York: United Nations, 2011), 26.

9. "Hunger and Poverty Facts," Bread for the World: Have Faith, End Hunger, www.bread.org.

10. *The Millennium Development Goals Report 2011*, 13.

11. Ibid.

12. Joint United Nations Programme on HIV/AIDS (UNAIDS), *Global Report: UNAIDS Report on the Global Aids Epidemic 2010* (New York: Joint United Nations Programme on HIV/AIDS (UNAIDS), 2010), 20, 24.

13. "Factsheet on Commercial Sexual Exploitation and Trafficking of Children," UNICEF, www.unicef.org.

14. Nicholas D. Kristof and Sheryl WuDunn, *Half the Sky: Turning Oppression into Opportunity for Women Worldwide*, reprint ed. (New York: Vintage, 2010), xiv–xv.

15. Ibid., 192.

16. *The Millennium Development Goals Report 2011*, 20.

17. Alex Williams, "The New Math on Campus," *New York Times*, February 5, 2010, www.nytimes.com.

18. Catherine Rampell, "Women Earn Less Than Men, Especially at the Top," *New York Times*, November 16, 2009, www.nytimes.com.

19. Incomes Data Services, *Gender (in)equality in the Labour Market: An Overview of Global Trends and Developments* (Brussels: International Trade Union Confederation, 2009), 9.

20. World Health Organization, "Violence against Women: Intimate Partner and Sexual Violence against Women, Fact Sheet No. 239," World Health Organization Media Centre, www.who.int.

21. World Health Organization, "Female Genital Mutilation, Fact Sheet No. 241," World Health Organization Media Centre, www.who.int.

22. "Disposal of IPC Cases by Courts During 2008," National Crime Records Bureau, Ministry of Home Affairs, ncrb.nic.in.

23. "Acid Attacks Statistics," Acid Survivor's Foundation, www.acidsurvivors.org.

24. Laura Smith-Spark, "How Did Rape Become a Weapon of War?" *BBC News*, January 2005, news.bbc.co.uk.

25. Robert Fisk, "The Crimewave That Shames the World," *Independent* (London), September 7, 2010, www.independent.co.uk.

26. Danielle Cangelosi, " 'Honor Killing' Dad Secretly Taped Girls," Fox News.com.

27. World Health Organization, "10 Facts on Obstetric Fistula," World Health Organization, March 2010, www.who.int.

28. "HIV/AIDS," USAID: From the American People, March 1, 2011, www.usaid.gov.

29. UNAIDS, *Global Report: UNAIDS Report on the Global AIDS Epidemic 2010* (Joint United Nations Programme On HIV/AIDS (UNAIDS)), pap/chrt ed. (Geneva: World Health Organization, 2011), 7.

30. Ibid., no. 130.

31. *Catechism*, no. 2334.

32. Ibid., no. 1244.

33. Ibid., nos. 2221–22.

34. *Compendium*, no. 244.

35. Ibid., no. 245.

36. Ibid., no. 296.

37. Ibid., no. 145.

38. Ibid., no. 295.

39. Ibid., no. 449.

40. Jeffry Odell Korgen, interview with Kim Plewes, December 30, 2011.

41. Craig Kielburger and Marc Kielburger, *Me to We: Finding Meaning in a Material World* (Mississauga, Ontario: John Wiley & Sons Canada, Limited, 2007), 2.

42. Jeffry Odell Korgen, interview with Kim Plewes, December 30, 2011.

43. Kielburger and Kielburger, *Me to We*, 74.

44. Jeffry Korgen.

45. The self-help group stories presented in this chapter also appear in altered form in Jeffrey Odell Korgen, *Solidarity Will Transform the World: Stories of Hope from Catholic Relief Services* (Maryknoll, N.Y.: Orbis Books, 2007).

46. Research in developing countries indicates that when women's literacy rises, so do economic, social, and health indicators.

47. Kristoff and WuDunn, *Half the Sky*, xix.

48. Ibid., 192–94.

49. Ibid., 192.

50. Ibid., 197.

51. *The Millennium Development Goals Report 2011*, 22–23.

52. Bills in the House of Representatives and the Senate are numbered when introduced. House bills always begin with H.R., Senate bills with S.

53. To save time when lopsided votes are expected, the leadership of the House and the Senate may call for a voice vote. Members shout "Aye" and "No" just as they might at a local civic meeting.

9. A New Pentecost

1. Cardinal Joseph Ratzinger, "Instruction on Certain Aspects of 'Theology of Liberation,'" www.vatican.va.

2. W. N. Murray, *The Scottish Himalayan Expedition* (London: J. M. Dent and Sons, 1951), 6.

3. Benedict XVI, "If You Want to Cultivate Peace, Protect Creation: Message of His Holiness Pope Benedict XVI for the Celebration of the 2010 World Day of Peace," 9, www.vatican.va.

4. David Beckmann, *Exodus from Hunger: We Are Called to Change the Politics of Hunger* (Louisville: Westminster John Knox Press, 2010), 9, 65–80.

5. Pontifical Council for Justice and Peace, *Compendium of the Social Doctrine of the Church* (Vatican City: Libreria Editrice Vaticana, 2004), no. 363.

For Further Reading

On Catholic Social Doctrine

Benedict XVI. *Charity in Truth* (*Caritas in Veritate.*) Vatican City: Libreria Editrice Vaticana, 2008.

Benedict XVI. *God Is Love (Deus Caritas Est)* San Francisco: Ignatius Press, 2006.

Groody, Daniel G. *Globalization, Spirituality, and Justice: Navigating the Path to Peace.* Theology in Global Perspective Series. Maryknoll, N.Y.: Orbis Books, 2007.

Mich, Marvin L. Krier. *The Challenge and Spirituality of Catholic Social Teaching.* Rev. ed. Maryknoll, N.Y.: Orbis Books, 2011.

Pontifical Council for Justice and Peace. *Compendium of the Social Doctrine of the Church.* Vatican City: Libreria Editrice Vaticana, 2004.

On Child Labor

International Labor Office. *Children in Hazardous Work: A Review of Knowledge and Policy Changes.* Geneva: International Labor Office, 2011.

Kielburger, Craig, and Kevin Major. *Free the Children: A Young Man Fights against Child Labor and Proves That Children Can Change the World.* New York: Harper Perennial, 1999.

Kielburger Craig, and Marc Kielburger. *Me to We: Finding Meaning in a Material World.* Mississauga, Ontario: John Wiley & Sons Canada, Limited, 2007.

Parker, David L. *Before Their Time: The World of Child Labor.* New York: Quantuck Lane Press, 2007.

Schmitz, Cathryne L., Elizabeth K. Collardey, and Deborah Larson, eds. *Child Labor: A Global View.* Westport, Conn.: Greenwood, 2004.

On the Environment

Earle, Sylvia. *The World Is Blue: How Our Fate and the Ocean's Are One.* Washington, D.C.: National Geographic, 2010.

Greenwood, Veronique. "Plastic and Humankind: An Unhealthy Relationship." *Atlantic*, April 19, 2011. www.theatlantic.com.

Intergovernmental Panel on Climate Change. *Climate Change 2007: Synthesis Report.* Valencia, Spain: Intergovernmental Panel on Climate Change, 2007.

Koenig-Bricker, Woodeene. *Ten Commandments for the Environment: Pope Benedict XVI Speaks Out for Creation and Justice*. Notre Dame, Ind.: Ave Maria Press, 2009.

United States Conference of Catholic Bishops. *Global Climate Change: A Plea for Dialogue, Prudence, and the Common Good*. Washington, D.C.: United States Conference of Catholic Bishops, 2001.

On Hunger and Poverty

Beckmann, David. *Exodus from Hunger: We Are Called to Change the Politics of Hunger*. Louisville: Westminster John Knox Press, 2010.

Brown, Lester R. *World on the Edge: How to Prevent Environmental and Economic Collapse*. New York: W. W. Norton & Company, 2011.

Department of Economic and Social Affairs of the United Nations Secretariat. *The Millennium Development Goals Report 2011*. New York: United Nations, 2011.

Firebaugh, Glenn. *The New Geography of Global Income Equality*. Cambridge, Mass.: Harvard University Press, 2003.

Sachs, Jeffrey. *The End of Poverty*. New York: Penguin Books, 2005.

On Slavery

Bales, Kevin. *Ending Slavery: How We Free Today's Slaves*. Berkeley: University of California Press, 2008.

Batstone, David. *Not for Sale: The Return of the Global Slave Trade—And How We Can Fight It*. 1st rev. ed. New York: HarperOne, 2010.

Off, Carol. *Bitter Chocolate: The Dark Side of the World's Most Seductive Sweet*. New York: The New Press, 2008.

Sage, Jesse, and Liora Kasten, eds. *Enslaved: True Stories of Modern Day Slavery*. New York: Palgrave Macmillan, 2008.

Skinner, E. Benjamin. *A Crime So Monstrous: Face-to-Face with Modern-Day Slavery*. New York: Free Press, 2009.

On Torture and Assassination

Hodge, James, and Linda Cooper. *Disturbing the Peace: The Story of Roy Bourgeois and the Movement to Close the School of the Americas*. Maryknoll, N.Y.: Orbis Books, 2004.

Le Breton, Binka. *The Greatest Gift: The Courageous Life and Death of Sister Dorothy Stang*. New York: Doubleday Religion, 2008.

Murphy, Roseanne. *Martyr of the Amazon: The Life of Sister Dorothy Stang*. Maryknoll, N.Y.: Orbis Books, 2007.

McCoy, Alfred W. *A Question of Torture: CIA Interrogation, from the Cold War to the War on Terror*. New York: Metropolitan Books, 2006.

Peters, Edward. *Torture*. Expanded ed. Philadelphia: University of Pennsylvania Press, 1996.

On Women's Issues

Incomes Data Services. *Gender (In)equality in the Labour Market: An Overview of Global Trends and Developments*. Brussels: International Trade Union Confederation, 2009.

Korgen, Jeffry Odell. *Solidarity Will Transform the World: Stories of Hope from Catholic Relief Services*. Maryknoll, N.Y.: Orbis Books, 2007.

Kristof, Nicholas D.,and Sheryl WuDunn. *Half the Sky: Turning Oppression into Opportunity for Women Worldwide*. Reprint ed. New York: Vintage, 2010.

Skaine, Rosemarie. *Female Genital Mutilation: Legal, Cultural, and Medical Issues*. Jefferson, N.C.: McFarland & Company, 2005.

UNAIDS, *Global Report: UNAIDS Report on the Global AIDS Epidemic 2010* (Joint United Nations Programme On HIV/AIDS [UNAIDS]). Geneva: World Health Organization, 2011.

On Worker Justice

Bernhardt, Annette, Ruth Milkman, Nik Theodore, et al. *Broken Laws, Unprotected Workers: Violations of Employment and Labor Laws in America's Cities*. Chicago: Center for Urban Economic Development, 2009.

Bobo, Kim. *Wage Theft in America: Why Millions of Working Americans Are Not Getting Paid—And What We Can Do about It*. New York: The New Press, 2009.

DeCarlo, Jaqueline. *Fair Trade*. Oxford, England: OneWorld, 2007.

Pontifical Council for Justice and Peace. *Vocation of the Business Leader*. Vatican City: Libreria Editrice Vaticana, 2012.

Von Drehlem, David. *Triangle: The Fire That Changed America*. New York: Grove Press, 2003.

Index

Numbers in *italics* indicate images.

211